BERLITZ®

PORTUGUESE
for travellers

By the staff of Berlitz Guides

How best to use this phrase book

● We suggest that you start with the **Guide to pronunciation** (pp. 6–10), then go on to **Some basic expressions** (pp. 11–16). This gives you not only a minimum vocabulary, but also helps you get used to pronouncing the language.

● Consult the **Contents** pages (3–5) for the section you need. In each chapter you'll find travel facts, hints and useful information. Simple phrases are followed by a list of words applicable to the situation.

● Separate, detailed contents lists are included at the beginning of the extensive **Eating out** and **Shopping guide** sections (Menus, p. 39, Shops and services, p. 97).

● If you want to find out how to say something in Portuguese, your fastest look-up is via the **Dictionary** section (pp. 164–189). This not only gives you the word, but is also cross-referenced to its use in a phrase on a specific page.

● If you wish to learn more about constructing sentences, check the **Basic grammar** (pp. 159–163).

● Note the **colour margins** are indexed in Portuguese and English to help both listener and speaker. And, in addition, there is also an **index in Portuguese** for the use of your listener.

● Throughout the book, this symbol ☞ suggests phrases your listener can use to answer you. If you still can't understand, hand this phrase book to the Portuguese-speaker to encourage pointing to an appropriate answer.

● Sometimes you will find alternatives for words given in brackets [ ]. These are the expressions used in Brazil.

Second revised edition – 3rd printing 1988   Printed in Hungary

Contents

Travelling around 65

Sightseeing 80

Relaxing 86

Making friends 92

Shopping guide 97

Acknowledgments
We are particularly grateful to Amélia Jeandrevin for her help in the preparation of this book, and to Dr. T.J.A. Bennett who devised the phonetic transcription.

Guide to pronunciation

The imitated pronunciation used in this book should be read as if it were English except for any special rules set out below. It is based on Standard British pronunciation, though we have tried to take account of General American pronunciation also. Of course, the sounds of any two languages are never exactly the same; but if you follow carefully the indications supplied here, you'll have no difficulty in reading our transcriptions in such a way as to make yourself understood. Letters written in **bold** should be read with more stress (louder) than the others.

Brazilian Portuguese differs from the Portuguese spoken in Portugal in several important respects. Brazilian speech is slower and the words are less linked together than in Portugal. Unstressed vowels sound clearer when spoken by Brazilians, while in Portugal they're rapidly slurred over; s and z at the end of a syllable tend to be pronounced like s in sit and z in razor (rather than like sh in shut or s in pleasure). Vowel groups or diphthongs are often simplified.

Consonants

Letter	Approximate pronunciation	Symbol	Example	
f, l, p, p, t, v	as in English			
b	as in English, but often less decisive, especially between vowels	b	**boca**	**bo**aker
c	1) before **a, o, u,** or a consonant, like **k** in kill	k	**casa**	**kah**zer
	2) before **e** and **i**, like **s** in sit	s	**cedo**	**say**doo
ç	like **s** in sit	s	**começar**	koomer**ssahr**
ch	like **sh** in shut	sh	**chamar**	sher**mahr**

d	as in English, but often less decisive, especially between vowels	d	**dia**	deeer
g	1) before **a**, **o** and **u** or a consonant, like **g** in go, but often less decisive, especially between vowels	g/gh	**garfo** **guia**	gahrfoo gheeer
	2) before **e** and **i**, like **s** in pleasure	zh	**gelo**	zhayloo
h	always silent		**homem**	ommahng^y
j	like **s** in pleasure	zh	**já**	zhah
lh	like **lli** in million	ly	**olho**	oalyoo
m	1) when initial or between vowels, like **m** in met	m	**mais**	mighsh
	2) between a vowel and a consonant, or if the last letter of a word, it indicates that the vowel is nasalized, but the **m** is then generally silent*	ng ng^y	**tempo** **tem**	tayngpoo tayng^y
n	1) when initial or between vowels, like **n** in no	n ng	**novo** **branco**	noavoo brahngkoo
	2) in a consonant group and in plural endings it nasalizes the preceeding vowel, but the **n** is then generally silent*	ng^y	**homens**	ommahng^ysh
nh	like **ni** in onion	ny	**vinho**	veenyoo
q	like **k** in kill	k	**querer**	kerrayr
r	strongly trilled as in Scottish speech	r	**rua**	rooer
s	1) when initial, after a consonant or written **ss**, like **s** in sit	s/ss	**saber**	serbayr
	2) between vowels (not necessarily in the same word), like **z** in razor	z	**casa**	kahzer
	3) when final, or before **c**, **f**, **p**, **q**, **t**, like **sh** in shut	sh	**país**	pereesh
	4) elsewhere, like **s** in pleasure	zh	**cisne**	seezhner

---

* See "Nasal vowels" and "Semi-nasalized diphthongs".

x	1) generally like **sh** in sh**ut**	sh	bai**x**o	**bighsh**oo
	2) in **ex-** before a vowel, like **z** in ra**z**or	z	e**x**acto	i**zz**ahtoo
	3) sometimes like **x** in e**x**it	ks	tá**x**i	tah**ksi**
z	1) when initial or between vowels like **z** in ra**z**or	z	**z**ero	**z**ehroo
	2) when final or before **c, f, p, q, s** or **t**, like **sh** in sh**ut**	sh	feli**z**	ferlee**sh**
	3) elsewhere like **s** in plea**s**ure	zh	lu**z** da	loo**zh** der

Vowels

a	1) like a mixture of **u** in c**u**t and **ar** in p**ar**ty	ah	n**a**do	n**ah**doo
	2) when unstressed or before **m, n** or **nh**, but not in the same syllable, like **a** in **a**bout	er*	port**a**	port**er**
e	1) when stressed generally like **e** in g**e**t	eh	p**e**rto	p**eh**rtoo
	2) when stressed sometimes like **a** in l**a**te**	ay	cab**e**lo	kerb**ay**loo
	3) when unstressed, like **er** in oth**er**	er*	p**e**sado	p**er**zahdoo
	4) at the beginning of a word and in certain other cases, like **i** in h**i**t	i	**e**xacto antes	**i**zzahtoo ahngt**i**sh
é	like **e** in g**e**t	eh	caf**é**	kerf**eh**
ê	like **a** in l**a**te**	ay	m**ê**s	m**ay**sh
i	1) when stressed like **ee** in s**ee**d	ee	r**i**so	r**ee**zoo
	2) when unstressed, like **i** in com**i**ng	i	f**i**nal	f**i**nnahl
o	1) when stressed, like **o** in r**o**d	o	f**o**ra	f**o**rrer
	2) sometimes when stressed or unstressed, like **o** in n**o**te** (most common **o**-sound)	oa	v**o**ltar Lisb**o**a	v**oa**ltahr lizhb**oa**er
	3) when unstressed, usually like **oo** in f**oo**t	oo	cas**o**	kah**zoo**

---

* The **r** should not be pronounced when reading this transcription.
** But a pure vowel, not a diphthong.

ô, ou	like o in note, but a pure vowel, not a diphthong	oa	pôs	poash
u	1) generally like oo in soon 2) silent in gu and qu before e or i	oo	número querer	noomerroo kerrayr

Diphthongs

A diphthong is two vowels pronounced as a single vowel sound, e.g., in English boy there is a diphthong consisting of o plus a weak i sound. In Portuguese diphthongs, a, e and o are strong vowels and i and u are weak vowels. In diphthongs the strong vowels are pronounced with more emphasis than the weak ones, e.g., ai is pronounced like igh in sigh, and au like ow in how. Sometimes the weak vowels can combine to make a diphthong. In the word muito, the diphthong ui is pronounced nasally (oong^y). This is the only example in the language of a semi-nasalized diphthong. Apart from these generalizations the exact pronunciation of Portuguese diphthongs is not easy to predict.

Nasal vowels

These are pronounced through the mouth and through the nose at the same time, just as in the French nasal vowels (e.g., in the French bon) and quite similar to the nasal twang heard in some areas of America and Britain.

ã, am, an	something like ung in lung, or like an in French dans	ahng	maçã	merssahng
em, en	something like ing in sing, but recalling also the a in late	ayng	cento	sayngtoo
im, in	a nasalized version of the ee in feet	eeng	cinco	seengkoo
om, on	like orn in corncob or like on in French bon	awng	bom	bawng
um, un	a nasalized version of the oo in foot	oong	um	oong

Semi-nasalized diphthongs

In these, the first element is nasalized and combined with a weak **i** (pronounced like **y** in yet) or **u** (pronounced like **w** in was).

ãe, ãi, êm, final en(s), usually final **em**	pronounced as **ã** followed by **y** in yet	ahng^y	**mãe**	mahng^y
			sem	sahng^y
ão, final unstressed **am**	pronounced as **ã** followed by **w** in was	ahng^w	**mão**	mahng^w
õe	pronounced as **orn** in corn-cob or as **on** in French bon, followed by **y** in yet	awng^y	**põe**	pawng^y

Stress

1) If a word ends with **a**, **e** or **o**, the stress falls on the next to the last syllable, e.g., **rosa** (pronounced **ro**zzer). Plural endings **m** and **s** are generally disregarded.

2) All other words are stressed on the last syllable, e.g., **animal** (pronounced ernimmahl).

3) Words not stressed in accordance with these rules have an accent (´ or `) over the vowel of the stressed syllable.

Pronunciation of the Portuguese alphabet

A	ah	**G**	zhay	**N**	ehn	**T**	tay
B	bay	**H**	ergah	**O**	oa	**U**	oo
C	say	**I**	ee	**P**	pay	**V**	vay
D	day	**J**	zhotter	**Q**	kay	**X**	sheesh
E	eh	**L**	ehl	**R**	ehr	**Z**	zay
F	ehf	**M**	ehm	**S**	ehss		

The letters **k**, **w**, **y** occur only in foreign names and their derivatives, as well as in certain abbreviations.

Some basic expressions

Yes.	Sim.	seeng
No.	Não.	nahng^w
Please.	Por favor/Se faz favor.	poor fervoar/ser fahsh fervoar
Thank you.	Obrigado(a)*.	oabriggahdoo(er)
Thank you very much.	Muito obrigado(a)*.	moong^too oabriggahdoo(er)
You're welcome.	De nada.	der nahder
That's all right. (Don't mention it.)	Não tem de quê.	nahng^w tahng^y der kay

Greetings *Saudações*

Good morning.	Bom dia.	bawng deeer
Good afternoon.	Boa tarde.	boaer tahrder
Good evening.	Boa noite.	boaer noyter
Good night.	Boa noite.	boaer noyter
Good-bye.	Adeus.	erdehoosh
See you later.	Até logo.	erteh loggoo
This is Mr. ...	Apresento-lhe o Senhor ...	erprerzayngtoo lyer oo sinnyoar
This is Mrs./Miss ...	Apresento-lhe a Senhora/Menina [Senhorita] ...	erprerzayngtoo lyer er sinnyoarer/merneener [sinnyoareetah]
How do you do? (Pleased to meet you.)	Muito prazer em conhecê-lo(la).	moong^too prerzayr ahng^y koonyerssay loo(ler)
How are you?	Como está?	koamoo ishtah
Very well, thanks. And you?	Muito bem, obrigado(a). E você?	moong^too bahng^y oabriggadoo(er). ee vossay

---

*In the case where there are masculine and feminine forms of a word, we give the masculine first, with the feminine in parentheses afterwards; in this example, a woman would say **obrigada**.

SOME BASIC EXPRESSIONS

How's life?	**Como vai isso?**	koamoo vigh eessoo
Fine.	**Bem.**	bahng^y
I beg your pardon?	**Como disse?**	koamoo deesser
Excuse me. (May I get past?)	**Com licença.**	kawng lissayngser
Sorry!	**Desculpe!/Perdão!**	dishkoolper/perrdahng^w

Questions *Perguntas*

Where?	**Onde?**	awngder
How?	**Como?**	koamoo
When?	**Quando?**	kwahngdoo
What?	**O quê?**	oo kay
Why?	**Porquê?**	poorkay
Who?	**Quem?**	kahng^y
Which?	**Qual?**	kwahl
Where is ...?	**Onde é/fica ...?**	awngder eh/feeker
Where are ...?	**Onde são/ficam ...?**	awngder sahng^w/feekahng^w
Where can I find/get ...?	**Onde posso encontrar/arranjar ...?**	awngder possoo ayngkawngtrahr/errahngzhahr
How far?	**A que distância?**	er ker dishtahngsyer
How long?	**Quanto tempo?**	kwahngtoo tayngpoo
How much?	**Quanto?**	kwahngtoo
How many?	**Quantos*?**	kwahngtoosh
How much does this cost?	**Quanto custa isto?**	kwahngtoo kooshter eeshtoo
When does ... open/close?	**Quando abre/fecha ...?**	kwahngdoo ahbrer/faysher
What do you call this/that in Portuguese?	**Como se chama isto/aquilo em português?**	koamoo ser shermer eeshtoo/erkeeloo ahng^y poortoogaysh
What does this/that mean?	**O que quer dizer isto/aquilo?**	oo ker kehr dizzayr eeshtoo/erkeeloo

*For feminine and plural forms, see grammar section page 160 (adjectives).

Do you speak ...? *Fala ...?*

Do you speak English?	**Fala inglês?**	fahler eengglaysh
Does anyone here speak English?	**Há aqui alguém que fale inglês?**	ah erkee ahlgahng^y ker fahler eengglaysh
I don't speak (much) Portuguese.	**Não falo (bem) português.**	nahng^w fahloo (bahng^y) poortoogaysh
Could you speak more slowly, please?	**Pode falar mais devagar, por favor?**	podder ferlahr mighsh dervergahr poor fervoar
Could you repeat that?	**Pode repetir?**	podder rerperteer
Could you spell it?	**Pode soletrar?**	podder soolertrahr
Please write it down.	**Escreva, por favor.**	ishkrayver poor fervoar
Can you translate this for me?	**Pode traduzir-me isto?**	podder trerdoozeer mer eeshtoo
Please point to the ... in the book.	**Por favor, mostre- -me ... no livro.**	poor fervoar moshtrer mer ... noo leevroo
word	**a palavra**	er perlahvrer
phrase	**a expressão**	er ishprerssahng^w
sentence	**a frase**	er frahzer
I understand.	**Compreendo*.**	kawngpryayngdoo
I don't understand.	**Não compreendo*.**	nahng^w kawngpryayngdoo
Do you understand?	**Compreende?***	kawngpryayngder

Can/May ...? *Pode ...?*

Can I have ...?	**Pode dar-me ...?**	podder dahr mer
Can we have ...?	**Pode dar-nos ...?**	podder dahr noosh
Can you show me ...?	**Pode mostrar-me ...?**	podder mooshtrahr mer
I can't.	**Não posso.**	nahng^w possoo
Can you tell me ...?	**Pode dizer-me ...?**	podder dizzayr mer
Can you help me?	**Pode ajudar-me?**	podder erzhoodahr mer

* In Brazil: **Entendo/Não entendo/Entende** (ayng**tayng**doa/nawng^w ayng**tayng**doa/ ayng**tayng**di).

| Can I help you? | **Posso ajudá-lo(la)?** | possoo erzhoodah loo(ler) |
| Can you direct me to ...? | **Pode indicar-me a direcção para ...?** | podder eengdikkahr mer er dirrehssahng perrer |

Wanting ... *Desejos* ...

I'd like ...	**Queria ...**	kerreeer
We'd like ...	**Queríamos ...**	kerreeermoosh
What do you want?	**O que deseja?**	oo ker derzayzher
Give me ...	**Dê-me ...**	day mer
Give it to me.	**Dê-mo.**	day moo
Bring me ...	**Traga-me ...**	trahger mer
Bring it to me.	**Traga-mo.**	trahger moo
Show me ...	**Mostre-me ...**	moshtrer mer
Show it to me.	**Mostre-mo.**	moshtrer moo
I'm looking for ...	**Estou à procura de ...**	ishtoa ah prokkoorer der
I'm hungry.	**Tenho fome.**	taynyoo fommer
I'm thirsty.	**Tenho sede.**	taynyoo sayder
I'm tired.	**Estou cansado(a).**	ishtoa kahngsahdoo(er)
I'm lost.	**Perdi-me.**	perrdee mer
It's important.	**É importante.**	eh eengpoortahngter
It's urgent.	**É urgente.**	eh oorzhayngter

It is/There is ... *É/Está/Há* ...

It is ...	**É/Está* ...**	eh/ishtah
Is it ...?	**É/Está ...?**	eh/ishtah
It isn't ...	**Não é/Não está ...**	nahng^w eh/nahng^w ishtah
Here it is.	**Aqui está.**	erkee ishtah
Here they are.	**Aqui estão.**	erkee ishtahng^w
There it is.	**Aí está.**	eree ishtah
There they are.	**Aí estão.**	eree ishtahng^w

---

* See grammar section page 162 (verbs).

There is/are ...	**Há ...**	ah
Is/Are there ...?	**Há ...?**	ah
There isn't/aren't ...	**Não há ...**	nahng^w ah
There isn't any.	**Não há nenhum (nenhuma).**	nahng^w ah ninnyoong (ninnyoomer)
There aren't any.	**Não há nenhuns (nenhumas).**	nahng^w ah ninnyoongsh (ninnyoomersh)

It's ... *É/Está ...*

big/small	**grande/pequeno***	grahngder/perkaynoo
long/short	**comprido/curto**	kawngpreedoo/koortoo
quick/slow	**rápido/lento**	rahpiddoo/layngtoo
hot/cold	**quente/frio**	kayngter/freeoo
full/empty	**cheio/vazio**	shayoo/verzeeoo
easy/difficult	**fácil/difícil**	fahssil/diffeessil
heavy/light	**pesado/leve**	perzahdoo/lehver
open/shut	**aberto/fechado**	erbehrtoo/fishahdoo
right/wrong	**certo/errado**	sehrtoo/irrahdoo
old/new	**velho/novo**	vehlyoo/noavoo
old/young	**idoso/jovem**	iddoazoo/zhovvahng^y
next/last	**próximo/último**	prossimmoo/ooltimmoo
beautiful/ugly	**lindo/feio**	leengdoo/fayoo
free (vacant)/ occupied	**livre/ocupado**	leevrer/okkoopahdoo
good/bad	**bom/mau**	bawng/mow
better/worse	**melhor/pior**	millyor/pyor
early/late	**cedo/tarde**	saydoo/tahrder
cheap/expensive	**barato/caro**	berrahtoo/kahroo
near/far	**perto/longe**	pehrtoo/lawngzher
here/there	**aqui/aí**	erkee/eree

Quantities *Quantidades*

a little/a lot	**um pouco/muito**	oong poakoo/moong^{y}too
few/a few	**poucos/alguns (algumas)**	poakoosh/ahlgoongsh (ahlgoomersh)
much/many	**muito/muitos**	moong^{y}too/moong^{y}toosh
more/less	**mais/menos**	mighsh/maynoosh
more than/less than	**mais que/menos que**	mighsh ker/maynoosh ker
enough/too	**bastante/demasiado**	bershtahngter/dermerzyahdoo

* For feminine and plural forms, see grammar section page 160 (adjectives).

A few more useful words   *Outras palavras úteis*

at	**a, em**	er, ahng^y
on	**sobre**	soabrer
in	**em**	ahng^y
to	**a**	er
after	**depois (de)**	derpo^ysh (der)
before (time)	**antes (de)**	ahngtish (der)
before (place)	**em frente (de)**	ahng^y frayngter (der)
for	**por, para**	poor, perrer
from	**de**	der
with	**com**	kawng^y
without	**sem**	sahng^y
through	**através (de)**	ertrervehsh (der)
towards	**para, cerca de**	perrer, sayrker der
until	**até**	erteh
during	**durante**	doorahngter
next to	**ao lado de**	ow lahdoo der
near	**perto de**	pehrtoo der
behind	**atrás (de)**	ertrahsh (der)
between	**entre**	ayngtrer
since	**desde**	dayzhder
above	**acima (de)**	ersseemer (der)
below	**abaixo (de)**	erbighshoo (der)
under	**debaixo (de)**	derbighshoo (der)
inside	**dentro**	dayngtroo
outside	**fora**	forrer
up	**para cima**	perrer seemer
upstairs	**em cima**	ahng^y seemer
down	**para baixo**	perrer bighshoo
downstairs	**em baixo**	ahng^y bighshoo
and	**e**	ee
or	**ou**	oa
but	**mas**	mersh
not	**não**	nahng^w
never	**nunca**	noongker
nothing	**nada**	nahder
none	**nenhum, nenhuma**	ninnyoong, ninnyoomer
very	**muito**	moong^ytoo
too (also)	**também**	tahngbahng^y
yet	**ainda**	ereengder
only	**só**	saw
soon	**em breve**	ahng^y brehver
now	**agora**	ergorrer
then	**então**	ayngtahng^w
perhaps	**talvez**	tahlvaysh

Arrival

Passport control *Controle de passaportes*

Here's my passport.	**Aqui está o meu passaporte.**	erkee ishtah oo mehoo persserporrter
I'll be staying ...	**Fico ...**	feekoo
a few days	**alguns dias**	ahlgoongsh deeersh
a week	**uma semana**	oomer sermerner
a month	**um mês**	oong maysh
I don't know yet.	**Ainda não sei.**	ereengder nahng{w} say
I'm here on holiday.	**Estou aqui de férias.**	ishtoa erkee der fehryersh
I'm here on business.	**Estou aqui em [a] negócios.**	ishtoa erkee ahng{y} [ah] nergossyoosh
I'm just passing through.	**Estou de passagem.**	ishtoa der perssahzhahng{y}

> **ALFÂNDEGA**
> CUSTOMS

After collecting your baggage at the airport (*o aeroporto*— ow erehro**ppoar**too) you have a choice: use the green exit if you have nothing to declare. Or leave via the red exit if you have items to declare (in excess of those allowed).

> **artigos a declarar**
> goods to declare

> **nada a declarar**
> nothing to declare

I've nothing to declare.	**Não tenho nada a declarar.**	nahng{w} taynyoo nahder er derklerrahr
I've ...	**Tenho ...**	taynyoo
a carton of cigarettes	**um pacote de cigarros**	oong perkotter der siggahrroosh
a bottle of ...	**uma garrafa de ...**	oomer gherrahfer der
It's for my personal use.	**É para uso pessoal.**	eh perrer oozoo persswahl

O seu passaporte, por favor.	Your passport, please.
Tem alguma coisa a declarar?	Do you have anything to declare?
É favor abrir este saco.	Please open this bag.
Tem de pagar direitos por isto.	You'll have to pay duty on this.
Tem mais bagagem?	Do you have any more luggage?

Baggage—Porter *Bagagem—Carregador*

Porter!	**Carregador!**	kerrerger**doar**
Please take this luggage.	**Por favor, leve esta bagagem.**	poor fer**voar** lehver ehshter bergahzhahng^y
That's mine.	**Essa é a minha.**	ehsser eh er meenyer
That's my bag/ suitcase.	**Esse é o meu saco/ Essa é a minha mala.**	aysser eh oo mehoo sahkoo/ ehsser eh er meenyer mahler
One piece is missing.	**Falta um volume.**	fahlter oong vooloomer
Please take this/my luggage to the ...	**Por favor, leve esta/ a minha bagagem até ...**	poor fer**voar** lehver ehshter/er meenyer bergahzhahng^y erteh
bus	**ao autocarro [ônibus]**	ow owtokkahrroo [oanibbooss]
taxi	**ao táxi**	ow tahksi
Where are the luggage trolleys (carts)?	**Onde estão os carrinhos da bagagem?**	awngder ishtahng^w oosh kerreenyoosh der bergahzhahng^y

Changing money *Câmbio*

Where's the currency exchange office?	**Onde fica a agência de câmbio?**	awngder feeker er erzhayngsyer der kahngbyoo
Can you change these traveller's cheques (checks)?	**Pode trocar estes cheques de viagem?**	podder trookahr ayshtersh shehkersh der vyahzhahng^y
I want to change some dollars/pounds.	**Quero trocar dólares/libras.**	kehroo trookahr dollersh/leebrersh

BANK—CURRENCY, see page 129

| Can you change this into escudos/cruzados? | **Pode trocar isto em escudos/cruzados?** | podder trookahr eeshtoo ahng^y ishkoodoosh/ kroozahdoass |
| What's the exchange rate? | **Qual é o câmbio?** | kwahl eh oo **kahng**byoo |

Where is ...? *Onde é ...?*

Where is the ...?	**Onde é ...?**	awngder eh
booking office	**a marcação de lugares**	er merrkerssahng^w der loogahrersh
duty-free shop	**a free shop**	er "free shop"
newsstand	**o quiosque [a banca] de jornais**	oo kyoshker [ah bahngkah] der zhoornighsh
restaurant	**o restaurante**	oo rishtowrahngter
How do I get to ...?	**Como posso ir para ...?**	koamoo possoo eer perrer
Is there a bus into town?	**Há um autocarro [ônibus] para o centro da cidade?**	ah oong owtokkahrroo [oanibbooss] perrer oo sayngtroo der siddahder
Where can I get a taxi?	**Onde posso apanhar [pegar] um táxi?**	awngder possoo erpernyahr [paygahr] oong tahksi
Where can I hire a car?	**Onde posso alugar um automóvel?**	awngder possoo erloogahr oong owtoomovvehl

Hotel reservation *Reserva de hotel*

Do you have a hotel guide?	**Tem um guia de hotéis?**	tahng^y oong gheeer der ottehish
Could you reserve a room for me at a hotel?	**Podia reservar-me um quarto num hotel?**	poodeeer rerzerrvahr mer oong kwahrtoo noong ottehl
in the centre	**no centro**	noo sayngtroo
by the sea	**à beira-mar**	ah bayrer mahr
a double/single room	**um quarto duplo/ individual**	oong kwahrtoo dooploo/ eengdivviddwahl
not too expensive	**não muito caro**	nahng^w moong^ytoo kahroo
Where is the hotel?	**Onde é o hotel?**	awngder eh oo ottehl
Do you have a street map?	**Tem uma planta da cidade?**	tahng^y oomer plahngter der siddahder

HOTEL/ACCOMMODATION, see page 22

Car hire (rental) *Aluguer de automóveis*

To hire a car you must produce a valid driving licence (held for at least one year). Some firms set the minimum age at 23, others at 25. Holders of major credit cards are normally exempt from deposit payments, otherwise you must leave a substantial (refundable) deposit for a car. Third-party insurance is usually automatically included.

I'd like to hire (rent) a ... car.	Queria alugar um automóvel ...	kerreeer erloogahr oong owtoomovvehl
small	pequeno	perkaynoo
medium-sized	de tamanho médio	der termernyoo mehdyoo
large	grande	grahngder
automatic	automático	owtoomahtikkoo
I'd like it for a day/ a week.	Queria-o por um dia/uma semana.	kerreeer oo poor oong deeer/oomer sermerner
I want to leave it in ...	Quero deixá-lo em ...	kehroo dayshah loo ahng^y
Are there any week-end arrangements?	Há condições especiais de fim-de--semana?	ah kawngdissawng^ysh ishperssyighsh der feeng der sermerner
Do you have any special rates?	Há tarifas especiais?	ah terreefersh ishperssyighsh
What's the charge per day/week?	Qual é o preço por dia/semana?	kwahl eh oo prayssoo poor deeer/sermerner
Is mileage included?	A quilometragem está incluída?	er killoomertrahzhahng^y ishtah eengklweeder
What's the charge per kilometre?	Qual é o preço por quilómetro?	kwahl eh oo prayssoo poor killommertroo
I want full insurance.	Quero um seguro contra todos os riscos.	kehroo oong sergooroo kawngtrer toadoosh oosh reeshkoosh
How much is the deposit?	De quanto é o sinal?	der kwahngtoo eh oo sinnahl
I've a credit card.	Tenho um cartão de crédito.	taynyoo oong kerrtahng^w der krehdittoo
Here's my driving licence.	Aqui está a minha carta de condução [carteira de motorista].	erkee ishtah er meenyer kahrter de kawng-doossahng^w [kahrtayrah di moatoareestah]

CAR, see page 75

Taxi *Táxi*

In Portugal, taxis are usually found at taxi ranks. Rural taxis, marked "A" for *aluguer,* are not normally metered, but follow a standard-fare table based on mileage. All Brazilian taxis have meters.

Where can I get a taxi?	**Onde posso apanhar [pegar] um táxi?**	awngder possoo erpernyahr [paygahr] oong tahksi
Please get me a taxi.	**Chame-me um táxi, por favor.**	shermer mer oong tahksi poor fervoar
What's the fare to ...?	**Qual é o preço do percurso [da corrida] para ...?**	kwahl eh oo prayssoo doo perrkoorsoo [dah koarree-dah] perrer
How far is it to ...?	**A que distância fica ...?**	er ker dishtahngsyer feeker
Take me to ...	**Leve-me ...**	lehver mer
this address	**a este endereço**	er ayshter ayngderrayssoo
the airport	**ao aeroporto**	ow erehroppoartoo
the town centre	**ao centro da cidade**	ow sayngtroo der siddahder
the ... Hotel	**ao Hotel ...**	ow ottehl
the railway station	**à estação dos caminhos de ferro [estação ferroviária]**	ah ishterssahng^w doosh kermeenyoosh der fehrroo [istahssahng^w fehrrovvyahryah]
Turn left/right at the next corner.	**Vire à esquerda/ à direita na próxima esquina.**	veerer ah ishkayrder/ ah dirrayter ner prossimmer ishkeener
Go straight ahead.	**Vá sempre em frente.**	vah sayngprer ahng^y fraynyter
Please stop here.	**Páre aqui, por favor.**	pahrer erkee poor fervoar
I'm in a hurry.	**Estou com pressa.**	ishtoa kawng prehsser
Could you drive more slowly?	**Pode conduzir mais devagar?**	podder kawngdoozeer mighsh dervergahr
Could you help me carry my luggage?	**Pode ajudar-me a levar a bagagem?**	podder erzhoodahr mer er lervahr er bergahzhahng^y
Could you wait for me?	**Pode esperar por mim?**	podder ishperrahr poor meeng
I'll be back in 10 minutes.	**Volto daqui a 10 minutos.**	volltoo derkee er 10 minnootoosh

TIPPING, see inside back-cover

Hotel — Other accommodation

Early reservation and confirmation are essential in major tourist centres during the high season. But if you're stuck without a room, go to the tourist information office (*turismo*—too**reezh**moo). You'll find one in most towns.

Hotel (ot**tehl**)	In addition to the family-run "hotel rurais", hotels in Portugal are graded from 2-star to 5-star-deluxe; in Brazil there are five official categories. You may, however, still find price variations within the same category, depending on the location and the facilities offered.
Pousada (poa**zahd**her)	A state-owned inn (Portugal) in the regional style, located near places of interest to tourists. It's comfortable and serves good food. You're allowed to stay for only 5 days during high season.
Estalagem (ershter**lahzh**ayng)	Similar to the pousada, but more expensive; a privately-owned inn.
Motel (mot**tehl**)	Increasingly found, especially in Brazil.
Pensão (payng**sahng**ᵂ)	Corresponds to a boarding house. Usually divided into four categories.
Pousada de juventude (poa**zahd**er der zhoo**vayng**toodher)	Youth hostel (Portugal). You'll find Y.M.C.A. *(Associações Cristãs de Moços)* accommodation in Lisbon, and a few youth hostels on the coast.

Furnished flats (apartments) or bungalows are available through specialized estate agents.

Can you recommend a hotel/a boarding house?	**Pode recomendar-me um hotel/uma pensão?**	podder rerkoomayng**dahr** mer oong ot**tehl**/**oo**mer payng**sahng**ᵂ
Are there any flats (apartments)/villas vacant?	**Tem apartamentos/ casas para alugar?**	tahngʸ erperrter**mayng**toosh/**kah**zersh perrer erloo**gahr**

Checking in—Reception *Recepção*

My name is ...	O meu nome é...	oo mehoo noamer eh
I've a reservation.	Mandei reservar.	mahngday rerzerrvahr
We've reserved two rooms.	Reservámos dois quartos.	rerzerrvahmoosh doysh kwahrtoosh
Here's the confirmation.	Aqui está a confirmação.	erkee ishtah er kawngfirrmerssahng^w
Do you have any vacancies?	Tem quartos vagos?	tahng^y kwahrtoosh vahgoosh
I'd like a ... room ...	Queria um quarto ...	kerreeer oong kwahrtoo
single	individual	eengdivvidwahl
double	duplo	dooploo
with twin beds	com duas camas	kawng dooersh kermersh
with a double bed	de casal	der kerzahl
with a bath	com banho	kawng bernyoo
with a shower	com duche	kawng doosher
with a balcony	com varanda	kawng verrahngder
with a view	com vista	kawng veeshter
We'd like a room ...	Queríamos um quarto ...	kerreeermoosh oong kwahrtoo
in the front	para a frente	perrer er frayngter
at the back	para as traseiras [nos fundos]	perrer ersh trerzayrersh [noass foongdoass]
overlooking the sea	com vista para o mar	kawng veeshter perrer oo mahr
It must be quiet.	Tem de ser tranquilo.	tahng^y der sayr trahngkweeloo
Is there ...?	Há ...?	ah
air conditioning	ar condicionado	ahr kawngdissyoonahdoo
heating	aquecimento	erkehssimmayngtoo
a radio/television in the room	rádio/televisão no quarto	rahdyoo/terlervizzahng^w noo kwahrtoo
a laundry service	serviço de lavandaria	serrveessoo der lervahngderreeer
room service	serviço de quartos	serrveessoo der kwahrtoosh
hot water	água quente	ahgwer kayngter
running water	água corrente	ahgwer koorrayngter
a private toilet	casa de banho [banheiro] particular	kahzer der bernyoo [bahnyayroa] perrtikkoolahr

CHECKING OUT, see page 31

Could you put ...	Podia pôr ...	poodeeer poar ...
in the room?	no quarto?	noo kwahrtoo
a cot	uma cama de bebé [nenê]	oomer kermer der behbeh [naynay]
an extra bed	mais uma cama	mighsh oomer kermer

How much? *Quanto?*

What's the price ...?	Qual é o preço?	kwahl eh oo prayssoo
per night/week	por noite/semana	poor noyter/sermerner
for bed and breakfast	da dormida e pequeno almoço*	der doormeeder ee perkaynoo ahlmoassoo
excluding meals	sem refeições	sahng rerfayssahng wsh
for full board (A.P.)	da pensão completa	der payngsahng kawng-plehter
for half board (M.A.P.)	da meia-pensão	der mayer payngsahng w
Does it include ...?	O preço inclui ...?	oo prayssoo eengklooy
breakfast	o pequeno almoço [café da manhã]	oo perkaynoo ahlmoassoo [kahfeh dah mahnyahng]
service	o serviço	oo serveessoo
value-added tax (VAT)	o IVA	oo eever
Is there any reduction for children?	Há desconto para crianças?	ah dishkawngtoo perrer kryahngsersh
Do you charge for the baby?	O bebé [nenê] paga?	oo behbeh [naynay] pahger
That's too expensive.	É caro demais.	eh kahroo dermighsh
Haven't you anything cheaper?	Não tem nada mais barato?	nahng w tahng y nahder mighsh berrahtoo

How long? *Quanto tempo?*

We'll be staying ...	Ficamos ...	fikkermoosh
overnight only	só esta noite	saw ehshter noyter
a few days	alguns dias	ahlgoongsh deeersh
a week (at least)	uma semana (pelo menos)	oomer sermerner (payloo maynoosh)
I don't know yet.	Ainda não sei.	ereengder nahng w say

---

* In Brazil: **pernoite e café da manhã** (pehrnoyti ee kahfeh dah mahnyahng).

NUMBERS, see page 147

Decision *Decisão*

May I see the room?	**Posso ver o quarto?**	possoo vayr oo **kwahr**too
That's fine. I'll take it.	**Está bem. Fico com ele.**	ishtah bahng^y. **fee**koo kawng **ay**ler
No. I don't like it.	**Não, não gosto dele.**	nahng^w nahng^w **gosh**too **day**ler
It's too ...	**É muito ...**	eh **moong**^ytoo
cold/hot	**frio/quente**	**free**oo/**kayng**ter
dark/small	**escuro/pequeno**	ish**koo**roo/per**kay**noo
noisy	**barulhento**	berroo**lyayng**too
I asked for a room with a bath.	**Pedi um quarto com banho.**	per**dee** oong **kwahr**too kawng **ber**nyoo
Do you have anything ...?	**Tem alguma coisa ...?**	tahng^y ahl**goo**mer **koy**zer
better	**melhor**	mi**llyor**
bigger	**maior**	ma**yor**
cheaper	**mais barata**	mighsh ber**rah**ter
quieter	**mais sossegada**	mighsh soosser**gah**der
Do you have a room with a better view?	**Tem um quarto com uma vista melhor?**	tahng^y oong **kwahr**too kawng **oo**mer **veesh**ter mi**llyor**

Registration *Registo*

Upon arrival at a hotel or boarding house you'll be asked to fill in a registration form (*uma ficha*—**oo**mer **fee**sher).

Apelido/Nomes próprios*	Name/First name(s)
Morada/Rua/Nº	Home address/Street/Number
Nacionalidade/Profissão	Nationality/Profession
Data/Lugar de nascimento	Date/Place of birth
Origem/Destino	Coming from .../Going to ...
Número do passaporte	Passport number
Lugar/Data	Place/Date
Assinatura	Signature

* In Brazil: Sobrenome/Nomes.

What does this mean?	**O que quer dizer isto?**	oo ker kehr di**zzayr eesh**too

Posso ver o seu passaporte?	May I see your passport?
Queira preencher esta ficha, se faz favor.	Would you mind filling in this registration form?
Assine aqui, por favor.	Please sign here.
Quanto tempo vai ficar?	How long will you be staying?

What's my room number?	**Qual é o número do meu quarto?**	kwahl eh oo noomerroo doo mehoo kwahrtoo
Will you have our luggage sent up?	**Pode mandar subir a nossa bagagem?**	podder mahngdahr soobeer er nosser bergahzhahngᵞ
Where can I park my car?	**Onde posso estacionar o carro?**	awngder possoo ishterssyoonahr oo kahrroo
Does the hotel have a garage?	**O hotel tem garagem?**	oo ottehl tahngᵞ gerrahzhahngᵞ
I'd like to leave this in your safe.	**Gostava de deixar isto no cofre do hotel.**	gooshtahver der dayshahr eeshtoo noo koffrer doo ottehl

Hotel staff *Pessoal do hotel*

hall porter	**o porteiro**	oo poortayroo
maid	**a criada de quarto [arrumadeira]**	er kryahder der kwahrtoo [ahrroomahdayrah]
manager	**o gerente**	oo zherrayngter
page (bellboy)	**o paquete/groom [boy de hotel]**	oo perkayter/groom [boy di ottehl]
porter	**o bagageiro**	oo bergerzhayroo
receptionist	**o recepcionista**	oo rerssehssyooneeshter
switchboard operator	**a telefonista**	er terlerfooneeshter
waiter	**o criado de mesa [garçom]**	oo kryahdoo der mayzer [gahrsawng]
waitress	**a criada de mesa [garçonete]**	er kryahder der mayzer [gahrsonnehti]

Call the members of the staff *senhor* (si**nny**oar), *senhora* (si**nny**oarer) or *menina [senhorita]* (mer**nee**ner [sinnyoa**ree**-tah]).

TELLING THE TIME, see page 153

General requirements *Perguntas gerais*

The key to room ..., please.	A chave do quarto ..., por favor.	er shahver doo kwahrtoo ... poor fervoar
Will you wake me at ..., please?	Pode acordar-me às ...?	podder erkoordahr mer ahsh
Is there a bathroom on this floor?	Há uma casa de banho [um banheiro] neste andar?	ah oomer kahzer der bernyoo [oong bahnyay-roa] nayshter ahngdahr
What's the voltage?	Qual é a voltagem?	kwahl eh er volltahzhahng^y
Where's the socket (outlet) for the shaver?	Onde está a tomada para a máquina de barbear [o barbeador]?	awngder ishtah er too-mahder perrer er mahkinner der berrbyahr [oa bahrbyahdoar]
Can you find me a ...?	Pode arranjar-me [arrumar-me]?	podder errahngzhahr mer [ahrroomahr mi]
baby-sitter	uma babysitter	oomer "babysitter"
secretary	uma secretária	oomer serkrertahryer
typewriter	uma máquina de escrever	oomer mahkinner der ishkrervayr
May I have a/an/ some ...?	Pode dar-me ...?	podder dahr mer
ashtray	um cinzeiro	oong seengzayroo
bath towel	uma toalha de banho	oomer twahlyer der bernyoo
(extra) blanket	(mais) um cobertor	(mighsh) oong kooberrtoar
envelopes	uns envelopes	oongsh ayngverloppish
(more) hangers	(mais) cabides	(mighsh) kerbeedish
hot-water bottle	um saco de água quente	oong sahkoo der ahgwer kayngter
ice cubes	cubos de gelo	kooboosh der zhayloo
needle and thread	uma agulha e linha	oomer ergoolyer ee leenyer
(extra) pillow	(mais) uma almofada [um travesseiro]	(mighsh) oomer ahlmoofah-der [oong trahvayssayroa]
reading lamp	um candeeiro [abajur]	oong kahngdyayroo [ahbahzhoor]
soap	um sabonete	oong serboonayter
writing paper	papel de carta	perpehl der kahrter
Where's the ...?	Onde é ...?	awngder eh
dining room	a sala de jantar	er sahler der zhahngtahr
emergency exit	a saída de emergência	er sereeder der immerr-zhayngsyer
hairdresser's	o cabeleireiro	oo kerberlayrayroo
lift (elevator)	o elevador	oo illerverdoar

BREAKFAST, see page 38

Telephone—Post (mail)   *Telefone—Correio*

Can you get me Lisbon 12 34 56?	**Pode ligar-me para o 12 34 56 em Lisboa?**	podder liggahr mer perrer oo 12 34 56 ahng[y] lizhboaer
Do you have stamps?	**Tem selos?**	tahng[y] **sayloosh**
Would you post (mail) this for me, please?	**Pode pôr-me isto no correio, por favor?**	podder poar mer **eesh**too noo koorrayoo poor fervoar
Is there any post (mail) for me?	**Há correio para mim?**	ah koorrayoo perrer meeng
Are there any messages for me?	**Há algum recado para mim?**	ah ahlgoong rerkahdoo perrer meeng
How much is my telephone bill?	**Quanto devo pelas chamadas telefónicas?**	**kwahng**too dayvoo paylersh shermahdersh terlerfonnikkersh

Difficulties   *Dificuldades*

The ... doesn't work.	**... não funciona.**	nahng[w] foong**syon**ner
air conditioner	**o ar condicionado**	oo ahr kawngdissyoonahdoo
fan	**a ventoinha**	er vayngt**ween**yer
heating	**o aquecimento**	oo erkehssimmayngtoo
light	**a luz**	er loosh
radio	**o rádio**	oo rahdyoo
television	**a televisão**	er terlervizzahng[w]
The tap (faucet) is dripping.	**A torneira da água verte.**	er toornayrer der ahgwer vehrter
There's no hot water.	**Não há água quente.**	nahng[w] ah ahgwer kayngter
The washbasin is blocked.	**O lavatório está entupido [A pia está entupida].**	oo lervertorryoo ishtah ayngtoopeedoo [ah peer istah ayngtoopeedah]
The window/door is jammed.	**A janela/porta está empenada.**	er zhernehler/porrter ishtah ayngpernahder
The curtains are stuck.	**Os cortinados estão perros.**	oosh koortinnahdoosh ishtahng[w] payrroosh
The bulb is burned out.	**A lâmpada está fundida.**	er lahngperder ishtah foongdeeder
My room has not been made up.	**O meu quarto não foi arrumado.**	oo mehoo kwahrtoo nahng[w] foy erroomahdoo

POST OFFICE AND TELEPHONE, see page 132

The ... is broken.	... está partido(a) [quebrado(a)].	ishtah perrteedoo(er) [kaybrahdoa(er)]
blind	o estore	oo ishtorrer
lamp	o candeeiro [abajur]	oo kahngdyayroo [ahbahzhoor]
plug	a ficha	er feesher
shutter	a janela de madeira	er zhernehler der merdayrer
switch	o interruptor	oo eengterrooptoar
Can you get it repaired?	Pode mandar consertar?	podder mahngdahr kawngserrtahr

Laundry—Dry cleaner's *Lavandaria—Lavandaria a seco*

I want these clothes ...	Quero que esta roupa seja ...	kehroo ker ehshter roaper sayzher
cleaned	limpa	leengper
ironed/pressed	passada a ferro	perssahder er fehrroo
washed	lavada	lervahder
When will they be ready?	Quando estará pronta?	kwahngdoo ishterrah prawngter
I need them ...	Preciso dela ...	prersseezoo dehler
today	hoje	oazher
tomorrow	amanhã	ahmernyahng
before Saturday	antes de sábado	ahngtish der sahberdoo
Can you ... this?	Pode ... isto?	podder ... eeshtoo
mend	arranjar [consertar]	errahngzahr [kawngsayrtahr]
patch	remendar	rermayngdahr
stitch	coser [costurar]	koozayr [koastoorahr]
Can you sew on this button?	Pode pregar este botão?	podder prergahr ayshter bootahng^w
Can you get this stain out?	Pode tirar esta nódoa [mancha]?	podder tirrahr ehshter noddwer [mahngshah]
Is my laundry ready?	A minha roupa está pronta?	er meenyer roaper ishtah prawngter
This isn't mine.	Isto não é meu.	eeshtoo nahng^w eh mehoo
There's something missing.	Falta qualquer coisa.	fahlter kwahlkehr koyzer
There's a hole in this.	Isto tem um buraco.	eeshtoo tahng^y oong boorahkoo

Hairdresser — Barber *Cabeleireiro — Barbeiro*

Is there a hairdresser/ beauty salon in the hotel?	Há um cabeleireiro/ instituto de beleza no hotel?	ah oong kerberlayrayroo/ eengshtittootoo der berlayzer noo ottehl
Can I make an appointment for Thursday?	Posso fazer uma marcação para quinta-feira?	posso ferzayr oomer merrkerssahng^w perrer keengter fayrer
I'd like it cut and shaped.	Quero cortar e fazer mise.	kehroo koortahr ee ferzayr meezer
I want a haircut, please.	Quero cortar o cabelo, por favor.	kehroo koortahr oo kerbayloo poor fervoar
bleach	uma descoloração	oomer dishkooloorerssahng^w
blow-dry	um brushing	oong "brushing"
colour rinse	uma rinsage	oomer rahngsahzher
dye	uma pintura do cabelo	oomer peengtoorer doo kerbayloo
face pack	uma máscara de beleza	oomer mahshkerrer der berlayzer
manicure	uma manicura	oomer mernikkoorer
permanent wave	uma permanente	oomer perrmernayngter
setting lotion	um fixador	oong fikserdoar
shampoo and set	lavar e fazer mise	lervahr ee ferzayr meezer
with a fringe (bangs)	com franja	kawng frahngzher
I'd like a shampoo for ... hair.	Queria um shampoo [xampu] para cabelo ...	kerreeer oong shahngpoa [shahngpoo] perrer kerbayloo
normal/dry/ greasy (oily)	normal/seco/ oleoso	norrmahl/saykoo/ ollyoazoo
Do you have a colour chart?	Tem um mostruário de cores?	tahng^y oong mooshtrwah- ryoo der koarersh
Don't cut it too short.	Não corte muito curto.	nahng^w korrter moong^{y}too koortoo
A little more off the ...	Corte um pouco mais ...	korrter oong poakoo mighsh
back	atrás	ertrahsh
neck	na nuca	ner nooker
sides	dos lados	doosh lahdoosh
top	em cima	ahng^y seemer
I don't want any hairspray.	Não quero laca [laquê].	nahng^w kehroo lahker [lahkay]

DAYS OF THE WEEK, see page 151

I'd like a shave.	**Queria fazer a barba.**	kerreeer ferzayr er bahrber
Would you trim my ..., please?	**Pode aparar-me ...?**	podder erperrahr mer
beard	**a barba**	er bahrber
moustache	**o bigode**	oo biggodder
sideboards (sideburns)	**as suíças** [costeletas]	ersh sweessersh [coasterlaytahss]

Checking out *Partida*

May I have my bill, please?	**Pode dar-me a conta, por favor?**	podder dahr mer er kawngter poor fervoar
I'm leaving early in the morning. Please have my bill ready.	**Parto amanhã de manhã cedo. Por favor, prepare-me a conta.**	pahrtoo ahmernyahng der mernyahng saydoo. poor fervoar prerpahrer mer er kawngter
We'll be checking out around noon.	**Partiremos por volta do meio-dia.**	perrtirraymoosh poor vollter doo mayoo deeer
I must leave at once.	**Tenho de partir já.**	taynyoo der perrteer zhah
Is everything included?	**Está tudo incluído?**	ishtah toodoo eengklweedoo
Can I pay by credit card?	**Posso pagar com cartão de crédito?**	possoo pergahr kawng kerrtahng^w der krehdittoo
I think there's a mistake in the bill.	**Creio que se enganou na conta.**	krayoo ker ser aynggernoa ner kawngter
Can you get us a taxi?	**Pode chamar-nos um táxi?**	podder shermahr noosh oong tahksi
Would you send someone to bring down our luggage?	**Pode mandar trazer para baixo a nossa bagagem?**	podder mahngdahr trerzayr perrer bighshoo er nosser bergahzhahng^y
Here's the forwarding address.	**Aqui está o meu próximo endereço.**	erkee ishtah oo mehoo prossimmoo ayngderrayssoo
You have my home address.	**Já têm a minha morada.**	zhah tahng^{y}ahng^y er meenyer moorahder
It's been a very enjoyable stay.	**Tivemos uma estadia muito agradável.**	tivvehmoosh oomer ishterdeeer moong^{y}too ergrerdahvehl

TIPPING, see inside back-cover

Camping *Campismo*

Most Portuguese camp sites are within easy reach of a beach. They range from basic grounds to vast recreational centres with all amenities. You must register with your passport, certain sites require membership of a national or international camping association. In Brazil camping outside official sites is not recommended.

Is there a camp site near here?	**Há um parque de campismo aqui perto?**	ah oong **pah**rker der kahng-peezhmoo erkee pehrtoo
Can we camp here?	**Podemos acampar aqui?**	poodaymoosh erkahng**pah**r erkee
Have you room for a tent/caravan (trailer)?	**Tem lugar para uma tenda/rulote?**	tahng^y loogahr perrer oomer tayng**d**er/roolotter
What's the charge ...?	**Qual é o preço ...?**	kwahl eh oo **prays**soo
per day/person	**por dia/pessoa**	poor **dee**er/persoaer
for a car	**por automóvel**	poor owtoomovvehl
for a tent	**por tenda**	poor tayng**d**er
for a caravan (trailer)	**por rulote**	poor roolotter
Is the tourist tax included?	**A taxa de turismo está incluída?**	er **tah**sher der tooreezhmoo ishtah eengklweeder
Is there/Are there (a) ...?	**Há ...?**	ah
drinking water	**água potável**	ah**g**wer pootahvehl
electricity	**electricidade**	illehtrissiddahder
playground	**um campo de jogos**	oong **kahng**poo der **zhog**goosh
restaurant	**um restaurante**	oong rishtow**rahng**ter
shopping facilities	**lojas**	lozhersh
swimming pool	**uma piscina**	oomer pishseener
Where are the showers/toilets?	**Onde são os duches/ as casas de banho [os banheiros]?**	awngder sahng^w oosh **doo**shersh/ersh kah**z**ersh der bernyoo [oass bahnyayroass]
Where can I get butane gas?	**Onde posso arranjar [arrumar] gás butano?**	awngder possoo errahng**zhah**r [ahrroomahr] gahsh booternoo
Is there a youth hostel near here?	**Há uma pousada de juventude aqui perto?**	ah oomer poazahder der zhoovayng**too**der erkee **pehr**too

CAMPING EQUIPMENT, see page 106

Eating out

From snack bars to luxury restaurants, eating out can be one of the most interesting experiences of your trip. Here are some of the types of eating and drinking places you'll come across. In Portugal the most distinctive are the *pousadas* and the *casas de fados* or *adegas típicas*, the little restaurants where you eat or drink to the sound of the *fado*, the national folk song.

In Brazil, don't miss the *churrascarias*, restaurants specializing in excellent barbecues.

Café (kerfeh)	Coffee shop and bar, where hot and cold drinks are served; you should be able to get a snack there.
Casa de fados (kahzer der fahdoosh)	A typical Portuguese restaurant, where you can listen to the famous *fado* songs, accompanied by guitars.
Cervejaria (serrverzherreeer)	A large *café* where you can drink beer and eat seafood snacks.
Churrasqueira (shoorrershkayrer)	Restaurant; specializes in chicken.
Churrascaria (shoorrahskahreeah)	Restaurant; specializing in barbecue, a *churrascaria* offers a great variety of grilled meat, generally served with fried potatoes and a hot sauce of onions, tomatoes and green peppers (Brazil).
Confeitaria (kawngfayterreeer)	A cake shop, also serving coffee, tea and other drinks.
Estalagem (ishterlahzhayng^y)	Privately-owned inn, serving regional specialities.
Lanchonete (lahngshoanehti)	Snack-bar (Brazil).
Pastelaria (pershterlerreeer)	The same as a *confeitaria*.
Pousada (poazahder)	State-owned inn, specializing in local dishes; located near places of interest to tourists.

Restaurante (rishtow**rahng**ter)	According to the cuisine and standard of service: *de luxo* (luxury), *de primeira, de segunda* or *de terceira classe* (first, second or third class).
Salão de chá (serlahng^w der shah)	A smart tearoom.
Snack-Bar (snahk bahr)	The same as at home.

Meal times *Horas de comer*

Breakfast (*o pequeno almoço* – oo per**kay**noo ahl**moa**ssoo – in Portugal, *o café da manhã* – oa kah**feh** dah mah**nyahng** – in Brazil) is usually served from 7 to 10 a.m.

Lunch (*o almoço* – oo ahl**moa**ssoo) is generally served from 12.30 to 14.30 p.m. in both Portugal and Brazil.

Dinner (*o jantar* – oo zhahng**tahr**) is served from about 7.30 to 9.30 p.m., except in a Portuguese *casa de fados,* where the show is likely to start around 10 p.m., so dinner is served later. In Brazil dinner time is from 8 to 11 p.m.

Eating habits *Hábitos de comer*

Most Portuguese start the day with a light breakfast and save their appetite for lunch. The latter generally consists of soup, fish or meat, and a dessert. For those with a sweet tooth, the afternoon coffee or tea accompanied by all kinds of delicious pastries, is the peak of the day, and it's also the moment for an ice-cream. To round off the day, the Portuguese have another two or three-course meal. You'll have no problem satisfying your appetite, especially as the portions are simply gargantuan.

Brazilian eating habits more or less follow the Portuguese pattern. Breakfast is, however, a bit heartier, and salad might replace the soup at other meals. Brazilians like to linger over the meal, so don't be surprised if service is slow—you're expected to take your time.

Portuguese cuisine   *Cozinha portuguesa*

Portuguese cuisine is not the most sophisticated in the world, but there is no shortage of freshly-picked vegetables and fruit, or fish and seafood straight from the sea. The *bacalhau,* dried cod, served with boiled potatoes, remains the favourite national dish, followed by custards and all kinds of pastries. Pork comes in many guises, as do chicken and veal. As for the wines, some of them are world famous and certainly worth trying.

Brazilian cuisine has adopted many elements from that of Portugal, refined it with the use of new spices and exotic fruit, and also added a great variety of barbecued meat.

O que deseja?	What would you like?
Recomendo-lhe isto.	I recommend this.
O que deseja beber?	What would you like to drink?
Não temos ...	We haven't got ...
Quer ...?	Do you want ...?

Hungry?   *Tem fome?*

I'm hungry/thirsty.	**Tenho fome/sede.**	taynyoo fommer/sayder
Can you recommend a good restaurant?	**Pode recomendar--me um bom restaurante?**	podder rerkoomayng-dahr mer oong bawng rishtowrahngter
Are there any inexpensive restaurants around here?	**Há restaurantes baratos aqui perto?**	ah rishtowrahngtish berrahtoosh erkee pehrtoo
I'd like to reserve a table for 4.	**Queria reservar uma mesa para 4 pessoas.**	kerreeer rerzerrvahr oomer mayzer perrer 4 perssoaersh
We'll come at 8.	**Viremos às 8.**	virraymoosh ahsh 8

If you want to be sure of getting a table in a well-known restaurant or a *casa de fados,* it may be better to telephone in advance.

Could we have a table ...?	Pode dar-nos uma mesa ...?	podder dahr noosh oomer mayzer
in the corner	num canto	noong kahngtoo
by the window	perto da janela	pehrtoo der zhernehler
outside	lá fora	lah forrer
on the terrace	na esplanada	ner ishplernahder
in a non-smoking area	numa zona para não-fumadores	noomer zoaner perrer nahng^w foomerdoarersh

Asking and ordering — *Pedidos e encomendas*

Waiter/Waitress!	Se faz favor!	ser fash fervoar
I'd like something to eat/drink.	Queria comer/beber alguma coisa.	kerreeer koomayr/berbayr ahlgoomer koyzer
May I have the menu, please?	Pode trazer-me a ementa [o cardápio], por favor?	podder trerzayr mer er immayngter [oa kahrdah-pyoa] poor fervoar
Do you have ...?	Tem ...?	tahng^y
a set menu	uma refeição a preço fixo	oomer rerfayssahng^w er prayssoo feeksoo
local dishes	pratos regionais	prahtoosh rerzhyoonighsh
What do you recommend?	O que me recomenda?	oo ker mer rerkoomayngder
I'd like ...	Queria ...	kerreeer
Could we have a/an ..., please?	Podia trazer-nos ... por favor?	poodeeer trerzayr noosh ... poor fervoar
ashtray	um cinzeiro	oong seengzayroo
cup	uma chávena [xícara]	oomer shahverner [sheekahrah]
fork	um garfo	oong gahrfoo
glass	um copo	oong koppoo
knife	uma faca	oomer fahker
napkin (serviette)	um guardanapo	oong gwerrdernahpoo
plate	um prato	oong prahtoo
spoon	uma colher	oomer koolyehr
May I have some ...?	Pode trazer-me ...?	podder trerzayr mer
bread	pão	pahng^w
butter	manteiga	mahngtayger
lemon	limão	limmahng^w
mustard	mostarda	mooshtahrder
olive oil	azeite	erzayter
pepper	pimenta	pimmayngter

salt	**sal**	sahl
sugar	**açúcar**	erssookerr
vinegar	**vinagre**	vinnahgrer

Some useful expressions for dieters and special requirements:

I'm on a diet.	**Estou a dieta.**	ishtoa er dyehter
I don't drink alcohol.	**Não bebo bebidas alcoólicas.**	nahng^w bayboo berbeedersh ahlkwollikkersh
I mustn't eat food containing ...	**Não devo comer alimentos que contenham ...**	nahng^w dayvoo koomayr erlimmayngtoosh ker kawngtaynyahng^w
flour/fat	**farinha/gordura**	ferreenyer/goordoorer
salt/sugar	**sal/açúcar**	sahl/erssookerr
Do you have ... for diabetics?	**Tem ... para diabéticos?**	tahng^y ... perrer dyerbehtikkoosh
cakes	**bolos**	boaloosh
fruit juice	**sumo [suco] de fruta**	soomoo [sookoa] der frooter
a special menu	**uma ementa [um cardápio] especial**	oomer immayngter [oong kahrdahpyoa] ishperssyahl
Do you have vegetarian dishes?	**Tem pratos vegetarianos?**	tahng^y prahtoosh verzherterryernoosh
Could I have ... instead of the dessert?	**Pode dar-me ... em vez da sobremesa?**	podder dahr mer ... ahng^y vaysh der soobrermayzer
Can I have an artificial sweetener?	**Pode dar-me um edulcorante artificial?**	podder dahr mer oong iddoolkoorahngter errtiffissyahl

And ...

I'd like some more, please.	**Queria mais um pouco, se faz favor.**	kerreeer mighsh oong poakoo ser fash fervoar
Can I have more ...?	**Pode dar-me mais ...?**	podder dahr mer mighsh
Just a small portion.	**Só um bocado.**	saw oong bookahdoo
Nothing more, thanks.	**Mais nada, obrigado(a).**	mighsh nahder oabriggahdoo(ah)
Where are the toilets?	**Onde são as casas de banho [os banheiros]?**	awngder sahng^w ersh kahzersh der bernyoo [oass bahnyayroass]

Breakfast *Pequeno almoço [Café da manhã]*

The Portuguese breakfast consists of coffee (black or with milk), rolls, butter and jam. In Brazil, breakfast is usually hearty: fresh fruit juice, fruit, toast and rolls, cake, butter and jam, accompanied by coffee with hot milk.

I'd like breakfast, please.	Queria tomar o pequeno almoço [café da manhã].	kerreeer toomahr oo perkaynoo ahlmoassoo [kahfeh dah mahnyahng]
I'll have a/an/some ...	Queria ...	kerreeer
bacon and eggs	ovos estrelados com toucinho	ovvoosh ishtrerlahdoosh kawng toasseenyoo
boiled egg	um ovo cozido	oong oavoo koozeedoo
soft/hard	quente/cozido	kayngter/koozeedoo
cereal	cereais	serryighsh
eggs	ovos	ovvoosh
fried eggs	ovos estrelados	ovvoosh ishtrerlahdoosh
scrambled eggs	ovos mexidos	ovvoosh mersheedoosh
fruit juice	sumo [suco] de fruta	soomoo [sookoa] der frooter
grapefruit	toranja	toorahngzher
orange	laranja	lerrahngzher
ham and eggs	ovos estrelados com presunto	ovvoosh ishtrerlahdoosh kawng prerzoongtoo
jam	doce de fruta [geléia]	doasser der frooter [zhaylayah]
marmalade	doce [geléia] de laranja	doasser [zhaylayah] der lerrahngzher
toast	torradas	toorrahdersh
May I have some ...?	Pode trazer-me ...?	podder trerzayr mer
bread	pão	pahng^w
butter	manteiga	mahngtayger
(hot) chocolate	chocolate (quente)	shookoolahter (kayngter)
coffee	café	kerfeh
decaffeinated	sem cafeína	sahng^y kerfeheener
black	sem leite	sahng^y layter
with milk	com leite	kawng layter
honey	mel	mehl
(cold/hot) milk	leite (frio/quente)	layter (freeoo/kayngter)
rolls	papo-secos [pãezinhos]	pahpoo saykoosh [pahng^yzeenyoass]
tea	chá	shah
with milk/lemon	com leite/limão	kawng layter/limmahng^w
(hot) water	água (quente)	ahgwer (kayngter)

What's on the menu?   *O que há na ementa [cardápio]?*

Most Portuguese and Brazilian restaurants display a menu (*ementa* in Portugal, *cardápio* in Brazil); a set menu is rarely offered. *A prato do dia* (**prah**too doo **dee**er—dish of the day) usually offers you a good meal at a fair price. *Especialidade da casa* written next to a dish listed on the menu tells you that the dish is a speciality of the restaurant.

Under the headings below you'll find alphabetical lists of dishes that might be offered on a Portuguese menu with their English equivalent. You can simply show the book to the waiter. If you want some fruit, for instance, let *him* point to what's available on the appropriate list. Use pages 36 and 37 for ordering in general.

	page	
Starters (Appetizers)	41	**Acepipes [Salgadinhos]**
Salads	42	**Saladas**
Eggs	42	**Ovos**
Soups	43	**Sopas**
Fish and seafood	44	**Peixes e mariscos**
Meat	46	**Carnes**
Game and poultry	48	**Caça e criação**
Vegetables	49	**Legumes**
Potatoes, rice, noodles	50	**Batatas, arroz, massa**
Cheese	51	**Queijos**
Fruit	52	**Frutas**
Dessert—Pastries	53	**Sobremesas—Pastelaria**
Drinks	55	**Bebidas**
Wine	56	**Vinhos**
Nonalcoholic drinks	59	**Bebidas não alcoólicas**
Hot beverages	60	**Bebidas quentes**
Snacks—Picnic	63	**Refeições leves—Piquenique**

Reading the menu *Para ler a ementa [o cardápio]*

Especialidades da casa	Specialities of the house
Especialidades regionais	Local specialities
Prato do dia	Dish of the day
À .../À moda de ...	... style
Caseiro(a)	Home-made
À escolha	Of your choice
Só por encomenda	Made to order
Da época	In season

acepipes	ersserpeepersh	starters (appetizers)
aperitivos	erperritteevoosh	aperitifs
arroz	erroash	rice
bacalhau	berkerlyow	cod
bebidas	berbeedersh	drinks
caça	kahsser	game
carnes	kahrnersh	meat
crustáceos	krooshtahssyoosh	shellfish
doces	doassersh	desserts
frango	frahnggoo	chicken
fruta	frooter	fruit
gelados	zherlahdoosh	ice-creams
legumes	lergoomersh	vegetables
mariscos	merreeshkoosh	seafood
ovos	ovvoosh	eggs
petiscos	perteeshkoosh	starters (appetizers)
peixes	payshersh	fish
primeiro prato	primmayroo prahtoo	first course
prato principal	prahtoo preengsippahl	main course
pratos frios	prahtoosh freeoosh	cold dishes
queijos	kayzhoosh	cheese
refrigerantes	rerfrizzherrahngtish	soft drinks
saladas	serlahdersh	salads
salgadinhos	sahlgahdeenyoass	starters (appetizers) (Braz.)
sopas	soapersh	soups
sobremesas	soabrermayzersh	dessert
sorvetes	soarvehtiss	ice-creams (Braz.)
sucos	sookoass	fruit juice (Braz.)
sumos	soomoosh	fruit juice
vinhos	veenyoosh	wine

Starters (Appetizers)   *Acepipes [Salgadinhos]*

If you feel like something to whet your appetite, choose carefully, for the Portuguese appetizer can be filling. Starters may also be listed on the menu under *Petiscos*.

I'd like an appetizer.	**Queria uns acepipes [salgadinhos].**	kerreeer oongsh ersserpeepersh [sahlgahdeenyoass]
What do you recommend?	**O que me recomenda?**	oo ker mer rerkoomayngder
acepipes variados	ersserpeepersh verryahdoosh	assorted appetizers
anchovas	ahngshoaversh	anchovies
atum	ertoong	tuna (tunny)
azeitonas recheadas/pretas/ de Elvas	erzaytoanersh rershyahdersh/pray- tersh/der ehlversh	olives stuffed/black/green
camarões	kermerrawng'sh	shrimp
caracóis à Algarvia	kerrerkoysh ah ahlgerrveeer	snails flavoured with oregano
carnes frias	kahrnersh freeersh	assorted cold cuts
chocos com tinta	shokkoosh kawng teengter	cuttlefish cooked in their own ink
espargos	ishpahrgoosh	asparagus
melão com presunto	merlahng^w kawng prerzoongtoo	melon with ham
moelas	mwehlersh	spicy stew of chicken stomach
ostras do Algarve	oashtrersh doo ahlgahrver	oysters baked in butter and dry wine
paio	pighoo	smoked, rolled pork fillet
pikles	peeklersh	pickled vegetables
pipis	pippeesh	spicy giblet stew
presunto	prerzoongtoo	cured ham
requeijão	rerkayzhahng^w	curd cheese
salgadinhos variados	sahlgahdeenyoass vahryahdoass	assorted appetizers (Braz.)
sardinhas	serrdeenyersh	sardines

amêijoas na cata-
plana
(ermayzhwersh ner
kerterplerner)

clams with smoked ham, *chouriço* and pimento steamed in a pan shaped like a big nutshell

chouriço
(shoareessoo)

smoked pork sausage flavoured with paprika and garlic

linguiça frita
(leenggweesser freeter)

very thin *chouriço* cut in slices and deep-fried in butter

pimentos assados
(pimmayngtoosh erssahdoosh)

sweet peppers, roasted and served cold with olive oil and vinegar

rissóis de camarão
(rissoysh der kermerrahng^w)

deep-fried pastry envelopes filled with shrimp

santola recheada
(sahngtoller rershyahder)

spider-crab stuffed with its own meat, generally seasoned with mustard, curry powder, lemon juice and white wine

Salads *Saladas*

A green or mixed salad is seldom served with meals. You'll have to order it separately. Other salads may be ordered as a first course.

What salads do you have?	**Que saladas tem?**	ker serlahdersh tahng^y
salada	serlahder	salad
de alface	der ahlfahsser	green
de atum	der ertoong	tuna (tunny) and potato
de feijão frade	der fayzhahng^w frahder	black-eyed bean
mista	meeshter	tomato and lettuce
russa	roosser	diced vegetable
de tomate	der toomahter	tomato

Eggs *Ovos*

ovos	ovvossh	eggs
cozidos	koozeedoosh	boiled
escalfados	ishkahlfahdoosh	poached
estrelados	ishtrerlahdoosh	fried
mexidos	mersheedoosh	scrambled
verdes	vayrdersh	stuffed with boiled yolks, onions and parsley, and fried
omelete	ommerlehter	omelet
de camarão	der kermerrahng^w	shrimp
de chouriço	der shoareessoo	smoked sausage
de espargos	der ishpahrgoosh	asparagus

Soups *Sopas*

Portuguese meals often start with soup, a fairly substantial dish based on potatoes.

I'd like some soup.	**Queria uma sopa.**	kerreeer oomer soaper
açorda à Alentejana	erssoarder ah erlayngterzherner	bread soup with garlic and herbs
canja	kahngzher	chicken soup with rice
sopa	soaper	soup
à pescador	ah pishkerdoar	fish soup
de abóbora	der erbobboorer	pumpkin soup
de agriões	der ergryawng^{y}sh	potato and watercress soup
de camarão	der kermerrahng^w	shrimp soup
de cenoura	der sernoarer	carrot soup
de ervilhas	der irrveelyersh	green pea soup
de favas	der fahversh	broad bean soup
de feijão	der fayzhahng^w	red kidney bean and cabbage soup
de feijão frade	der fayzhahng^w frahder	black-eyed bean soup
de feijão verde	der fayzhahng^w vayrder	potato and runner bean soup
de grão	der grahng^w	chick-pea soup
de grelos	der grayloosh	turnip sprout soup
de hortaliça	der orrterleesser	vegetable soup
de rabo de boi	der rahboo der boy	oxtail
transmontana	trahngshmawngterner	vegetable soup with bacon and bread

caldo verde
(kahldoo vayrder)
thick potato and kale soup with smoked sausage

gaspacho
(gershpahshoo)
chilled soup with diced tomatoes, sweet peppers, onions, cucumber and croutons

migas de bacalhau
(meegersh der berkerlyow)
dried cod soup flavoured with garlic and thickened with bread

sopa de cozido
(soaper der koozeedoo)
meat broth with vegetables and macaroni

sopa de tomate
(soaper der toomahter)
tomato soup with poached eggs and bread

sopa seca
(soaper sayker)
thick soup with beef, chicken, ham, smoked sausage, cabbage and bread

Fish and seafood *Peixes e mariscos*

While touring in coastal areas, don't miss the opportunity to sample some of the wide variety of fresh fish and seafood. The Portuguese are fond of boiled fish dishes served with cabbage and boiled potatoes—doused with oil and vinegar.

I'd like some fish.	**Queria peixe.**	keerreeer paysher
What kind of seafood do you have?	**Que espécies de mariscos tem?**	ker ishpehssish der merreeshkoosh tahng^y
amêijoas	ermayzhwersh	clams
atum	ertoong	tuna (tunny)
bacalhau	berkerlyow	cod, usually dried
berbigão	berrbiggahng^w	type of cockle
besugo	berzoogoo	sunfish
camarões	kermerrawng^ysh	shrimp
camarões grandes	kermerrawng^yss grahngdiss	king prawns (Braz.)
caranguejo	kerrahnggayzhoo	crab
carapau	kerrerpow	horse mackerel
cavala	kervahler	mackerel
chocos	shokkoosh	cuttlefish
congro	kawnggroo	conger eel
eiró	ayraw	eel
enguia	aynggheeer	eel
espadarte	ishperdahrter	swordfish
gambas	gahngbersh	king prawns
lagosta	lergoashter	spiny lobster
lagostins	lergooshteengsh	Norway lobster
lampreia	lahngprayer	lamprey
lavagante	lervergahngter	lobster
linguado	leenggwahdoo	sole
lulas	loolersh	squid
mexilhões	mershillyawng^ysh	mussels
ostras	oashtrersh	oysters
pargo	pahrgoo	bream
peixe-agulha	paysher ergoolyer	garfish
peixe-espada	paysher ishpahder	cutlass fish
pescada	pishkahder	whiting
polvo	poalvoo	octopus
robalo	roobahloo	sea bass
salmão (fumado)	sahlmahng^w (foomahdoo)	(smoked) salmon
santola	sahngtoller	spider-crab
sardinhas	serrdeenyersh	sardines
truta	trooter	trout

Here are some of the ways you may want the fish served:

baked	**no forno**	noo foarnoo
fried	**frito**	freetoo
grilled (broiled)	**grelhado**	grilyahdhoo
marinated	**marinado**	merrinnahdoo
poached	**escaldado**	ishkahldahdoo
smoked	**fumado [defumado]**	foomahdoo [dayfoo-mahdoa]
steamed	**cozido ao vapor**	koozeedoo ow verpoar

Bacalhau (dried, salted cod) dishes are among the most famous Portuguese specialities. Here are the names of a few of the more common preparations you're likely to find:

bacalhau à Brás
(berkerlyow ah brahsh)
strips of dried cod fried with onions and potatoes, cooked in beaten eggs

bacalhau à Gomes de Sá
(berkerlyow ah goamersh der sah)
dried cod with olives, garlic, onions, parsley and hard-boiled eggs

bacalhau podre
(berkerlyow poadrer)
a baked dish, in which layers of cod, fried in butter, alternate with layers of sliced, fried potatoes; topped with breadcrumbs and grated cheese

bacalhau com leite de coco
(bahkahlyow kawng layti dee koakoa)
cod stewed in coconut milk (Braz.)

And try some of these specialities:

caldeirada
(kahldayrahder)
several kinds of fish simmered with onions, tomatoes, potatoes, and olive oil

lulas recheadas
(loolersh rershyahdersh)
squid cooked with a stuffing of egg yolk, minced ham, onion and·tomato sauce

moqueca de peixe
(mokkaykah dee payshi)
stew made of fish, shellfish or shrimp with coconut milk, *dendê* oil (yellow palm oil) and other seasonings (Braz.)

vatapá
(vahtahpah)
fish and shrimp (dried and fresh) in a paste made of rice flour or breadcrumbs, coconut milk, *dendê* oil, peanuts, cashew nuts and other seasonings (Braz.)

Meat   *Carnes*

In Portugal, *bife* (from the English word beef) turns out to be the word for steak even when referring to veal, pork or fish. Veal and pork *bifes* taste better than beef *bifes* most of the time. And you may try some lamb *costeletas* (chops) which are delicious. While in Brazil, don't miss the barbecue specialities.

I'd like some ...	Queria ...	kerreeer
beef	**carne de vaca**	kahrner der vahker
lamb	**borrego**	boorraygoo
pork	**carne de porco**	kahrner der poarkoo
veal	**vitela**	vittehler
bife	"beef"	steak
cabrito	kerbreetoo	kid
carneiro	kerrnayroo	mutton
carnes frias	kahrnersh freeersh	assorted cold cuts
chispe	sheeshper	pig's trotter (foot)
chouriço	shoareessoo	smoked sausage
costeleta	kooshterlayter	chop, cutlet
fígado	feegerdoo	liver
filé	filleh	steak (Braz.)
leitão	laytahng^w	suck(l)ing pig
língua	leenggwer	tongue
medalhão	merderlyahng^w	a tenderloin steak
presunto	prerzoongtoo	cured ham
presunto cru	prerzoongtoo kroo	dried ham
rins	reengsh	kidneys
salsicha	sahlseesher	sausage
toucinho	toasseenyoo	bacon

bife na frigideira
(beefer ner frizhiddayrer)

beefsteak fried in butter, white wine and garlic, served with ham and fried bread

carne de porco à Alentejana
(kahrner der poarkoo ah erlayngterzherner)

chopped pork cooked with clams, tomatoes and onions

carne de sol com feijão verde
(kahrni di soll kawng fayzhahng^w vayrdi)

meat dried in the sun (jerky) with green beans (Braz.)

cozido à Portuguesa
(koozeedoo ah poortoogayzer)
boiled beef, bacon, smoked sausage and vegetables, served with rice

churrasco misto
(shoorrahskoa meestoa)
mixed barbecue (beef, sausage and pork) (Braz.)

ensopado de cabrito
(ayngsoopahdoo der kerbreetoo)
stew made of kid and vegetables, served on slices of bread

feijoada
(fayzhwahder)
Brazil's national dish. Black beans cooked with bacon, dried and salted pork, jerky and sausage. You eat it with rice, slices of orange and *farofa,* manioc flour roasted in butter or oil

iscas à Portuguesa
(eeshkersh ah poortoogayzer)
sliced liver marinated in white wine with garlic and herbs and then fried

rojões à moda do Minho
(roozhawngᵞsh ah modder doo meenyoo
chopped pork, marinated in dry white wine with onions and herbs and then fried

sarapatel
(sahrahpahtehl)
porc or mutton stew, thickened with blood (Braz.)

tripas à moda do Porto
(treepersh ah modder doo poartoo)
tripe cooked with assorted pork products, navy beans and chicken, served with rice

baked	**no forno**	noo foarnoo
barbecued	**na brasa**	ner brahzer
boiled	**cozido**	koozeedoo
braised	**estufado**	ishtoofahdoo
breaded	**panado**	pernahdoo
fried	**frito**	freetoo
grilled (broiled)	**grelhado**	grillyahdoo
minced	**picado**	pikkahdoo
roasted	**assado**	erssahdoo
stewed	**guisado**	gizzahdoo
stuffed	**recheado**	rershyahdoo
underdone (rare)	**mal passado**	mahl perssahdoo
medium	**meio passado**	mayoo perssahdoo
well-done	**bem passado**	bahngᵞ perssahdoo

Game and poultry   *Caça e criação*

In both Portugal and Brazil, chicken is a favourite dish, prepared in dozens of ways. The Portuguese may surprise you with the great choice of game and poultry dishes available in various regions.

I'd like some game.	Queria caça.	kerreeer kahsser
borracho	boorrahshoo	squab
capão	kerpahng[w]	capon
codorna	koddoarnah	quail (Braz.)
codorniz	koodoorneesh	quail
coelho	kwaylyoo	rabbit
faisão	fighzahng[w]	pheasant
frango assado	frahnggoo erssahdoo	roast chicken
galinha	gerleenyer	stewing chicken
peito de galinha	paytoo der gerleenyer	chicken breast
perna de galinha	pehrner der gerleenyer	chicken leg
galinhola	gerlinyoller	woodcock
ganso	gahngsoo	goose
javali	zherverlee	wild boar
lebre	lehbrer	hare
pato	pahtoo	duck
perdiz	perrdeesh	partridge
peru	perroo	turkey
pombo	pawngboo	pigeon
veado	vyahdoo	venison

arroz de frango
(erroash der **frahng**goo)
fried chicken with white wine, ham and rice in a casserole

coelho assado
(kwaylyoo erssahdoo)
roast rabbit with onions, white wine and seasoning

galeto com polenta
(gahlaytoa kawng pollayngtah)
fried chicken with polenta (Braz.)

frango na púcara
(frahnggoo ner pookerrer)
chicken stewed in Port wine and cognac, then fried with almonds cooked in wine sauce

pato no tucupi
(pahtoa noa tookoopee)
roast duck with *tucupi,* a manioc juice (Braz.)

xinxim de galinha
(sheeng**sheeng** di gahleenyah)
chicken cooked in a sauce of dried shrimp, peanuts and parsley (Braz.)

Vegetables *Legumes*

Portuguese	Pronunciation	English
aspargos	ahspahrgoass	asparagus (Braz.)
abóbora	erbobboorer	pumpkin
agriões	ergryawng^ysh	watercress
aipo	ighpoo	celery
alcachofra	ahlkershoffrer	artichoke
alface	ahlfahsser	lettuce
alho porro	ahlyoo poarroo	leek
batatas	bertahtersh	potatoes
batata doce	bertahter doasser	sweet potato
berinjela	berreengzhehler	aubergine (eggplant)
brócolos	brokkooloosh	broccoli
beterraba	berterrahber	beetroot
cebolas	serboalersh	onions
cenouras	sernoarersh	carrots
chicória	shikkorryer	endive (Am. chicory)
chuchu	shooshoo	type of rutabaga (Braz.)
cogumelos	koogoomehloosh	mushrooms
couve-flor	koaver floar	cauliflower
couve lombarda	koaver lawngbahrder	savoy cabbage
couve portuguesa	koaver poortoogayzer	kale
couve roxa	koaver roasher	red cabbage
ervilhas	irrveelyersh	peas
espargos	ishpahrgoosh	asparagus
espinafres	ishpinnahfrersh	spinach
favas	fahversh	broad beans
feijão	fayzhahng^w	kidney beans
feijão verde	fayzhahng^w vayrder	runner (green) beans
grão	grahng^w	chick peas
grelos	grayloosh	turnip sprouts
lentilhas	layngteelyersh	lentils
milho	meelyoo	sweet corn (corn)
nabiças	nerbeessersh	turnip greens
nabos	nahboosh	turnips
palmito	pahlmeetoa	palm hearts (Braz.)
pepino	perpeenoo	cucumber
pepinos de conserva	perpeenoosh der kawngsehrver	gherkins (pickles)
pimentos	pimmayngtoosh	sweet peppers
quiabo	kyahboa	okra (Braz.)
rabanetes	rerbernaytish	radishes
repolho	rerpoalyoo	white cabbage
tomates	toomahtish	tomatoes
túberas	tooberrersh	truffles
vagens	vahzhahng^ysh	runner (green) beans

And if you're touring in Brazil, try one of these delicious vegetable dishes:

acarajé (ahkahrahzheh)	grated beans fried in *dendê* (palm) oil, served with pepper sauce, onions and shrimp	
tutu à mineira (tootoo ah minnayrah)	a dish made of beans, manioc flour, pork, cabbage, fried eggs and browned rashers of streaky bacon	

Potatoes, rice and noodles *Batatas, arroz e massa*

In Portugal many dishes are served with both rice and potatoes.

arroz	erroash	rice
de alhos	der ahlyoosh	with garlic
de cabidela	der kerbiddehler	with chicken blood
de cenoura	der sernoarer	with carrots
de cozido	der koozeedoo	cooked in a meat stock
de feijão	der fayzhahng^w	with red or white beans
de grelos	der grayloosh	with turnip sprouts
de manteiga	der mahngtayger	with butter
de tomate	der toomahter	with tomato
batatas	bertahtersh	potatoes
cozidas (com pele)	koozeedersh (kawng pehler)	boiled (in their jackets)
fritas	freetersh	chips (french fries)
palha	pahlyer	matchsticks
massa	mahsser	pasta
esparguete	ishpahrgehter	spaghetti
[espaguete]	[ispahgehti]	
macarrão	merkerrahng^w	macaroni

As for the seasoning ...

açafrão	ersserfrahng^w	saffron
alcaparras	ahlkerpahrrersh	capers
alho	ahlyoo	garlic
azeite	erzayter	olive oil
baunilha	bowneelyer	vanilla
canela	kernehler	cinnamon
caril	kerreel	curry powder
coentros	kwayngtroosh	coriander

colorau	kooloorow	paprika
cominhos	koomeenyoosh	caraway
condimentos	kawngdimmayngtoosh	seasoning
cravinhos	krerveenyoosh	cloves
erva-doce	ehrver doasser	aniseed
gengibre	zhayngzheebrer	ginger
hortelã	orrterlahng	mint
louro	loaroo	bay leaf
manjericão	mahngzherrikkahng^w	basil
mostarda	mooshtahrder	mustard
noz-moscada	nosh mooshkahder	nutmeg
orégão	orrehgahng^w	oregano
pimenta	pimmaynger	pepper
piri-piri	pirri pirri	pimiento
rosmaninho	roozhmerneenyoo	rosemary
sal	sahl	salt
salsa	sahlser	parsley
tomilho	toomeelyoo	thyme
vinagre	vinnahgrer	vinegar

Cheese   *Queijos*

Portuguese cheeses are usually a mixture of sheep's and goat's milk, or cow's and goat's milk. Brazil also produces some cheese, which you're expected to eat as a dessert, accompanied by preserves or sweets—*goiabada,* a paste made of guava, for instance. A cheeseboard is seldom served in Portuguese or Brazilian restaurants.

I'd like some cheese.   **Queria queijo.**   kerreeer kayzhoo

creamy	Queijo da Serra, Azeitão, Évora, Castelo Branco, Serpa, Requeijão (a Brazilian cheese produced in Minas Gerais)
goat's milk cheese	Cabreiro (must be eaten fresh), Queijo de Minas (Brazilian, delicious with *goiabada*)
cow's milk cheese	São João, São Jorge, Ilha (from the Azores Islands), Queijo do Sertão (Brazilian)

Fruit *Frutas*

Do you have fresh fruit?	**Tem fruta fresca?**	tayng frooter frayshker
I'd like a (fresh) fruit cocktail.	**Queria uma salada de fruta (fresca).**	kerreeer oomer serlahdher der frooter (frayshker)
abacaxi	ahbahkahshee	pineapple (Braz.)
alperces	ahlpehrsersh	apricots
ameixas	ermayshersh	plums
ameixas secas	ermayshersh saykersh	prunes
amêndoas	ermayngdwersh	almonds
amendoins	ermayngdweengsh	peanuts
amoras	ermorrersh	blackberries
ananás	ernernahsh	pineapple
avelãs	erverlahngsh	hazelnuts
banana	bernerner	banana
caqui	kahkee	persimmon (Braz.)
castanhas	kershternyersh	chestnuts
cerejas	serrayzhersh	cherries
coco	koakoa	coconut (Braz.)
caju	kahzhoo	cashew nut (Braz.)
damascos	dahmahskoass	apricots (Braz.)
figos	feegoosh	figs
framboesas	frahngbwayzersh	raspberries
goiaba	goyahbah	guava (Braz.)
laranja	lerrahngzher	orange
lima	leemer	lime
limão	limmahng^w	lemon
limão verde	limmahng^w vayrdi	lime (Braz.)
maçã	merssahng	apple
mamão	mahmahng^w	papaya (Braz.)
manga	mahnggah	mango (Braz.)
maracujá	mahrahkoozhah	passion fruit (Braz.)
melancia	merlahngseeer	watermelon
melão	merlahng^w	melon
morangos	moorahnggoosh	strawberries
nêsperas	nayshperrersh	crab apple
nozes	nozzersh	walnuts
passas (de uvas)	pahssersh (der ooversh)	sultanas/raisins
pêra	payrer	pear
pêssego	payssergoo	peach
tâmaras	termerrersh	dates
tangerinas	tahngzherreenersh	tangerines
toranja	toorahngzher	grapefruit
uvas	ooversh	grapes
umbu	oongboo	a tropical fruit (Braz.)

Desserts—Pastries *Sobremesas—Pastelaria*

Cakes, custards and sweets—usually made of egg yolks
(Portugal) or grated coconut (Brazil)—are part of every
meal. You'll probably find them a bit too sweet. You can
also try some ice-cream (*gelado*—zher**lah**doo—in Portugal,
called *sorvete*—sor**veh**ti—in Brazil).

I'd like a dessert, please.	Queria uma sobre-mesa, se faz favor.	kerreeer oomer soobrer-mayzer ser fash fervoar
What do you recommend?	O que me reco-menda?	oo ker mer rerkoomayngder
Something light, please.	Uma coisa leve, por favor.	oomer koyzer lehver poor fervoar
Just a small portion.	Só um bocado.	saw oong bookahdoo

aletria	erlertreeer	vermicelli pudding
arroz doce	erroash doasser	rice pudding
goiabada	goyahbahdah	thick paste made of guavas (Braz.)
leite-creme	layter krehmer	custard, often with caramel topping
marmelada	merrmerlahder	thick paste made of quinces
mousse de chocolate	moosser der shookoolahter	chocolate pudding
ovos moles de Aveiro	ovvoosh mollersh der ahvayroo	beaten egg yolks cooked in syrup
pudim flan	poodeeng flahng	caramel custard

baba-de-moça (bahbah di moassah)	dessert made of egg yolk, coconut milk and syrup (Braz.)
barriga-de-freira (berreeger der frayrer)	dessert made of egg yolk, bread and syrup
canjica (kahngzheekah)	dessert made of grated sweet corn and coconut milk (Braz.)
farófias (ferroffyersh)	beaten egg white poached in milk, topped with cinnamon and egg custard
fios de ovos (feeoosh der ovvoosh)	fine golden strands of egg yolk cooked in syrup
pudim Molotov (poodeeng mollottoff)	fluffy eggwhite mousse immersed in caramel sauce

And here are some pastries and biscuits (cookies) you can have with your coffee or tea:

arrufada de Coimbra	erroofahder der kweengbrer	raised dough cake flavoured with cinnamon
bolinhos de amêndoa	booleenyoosh der ermayngdwer	almond biscuits
bolinhos de canela	booleenyoosh der kernehler	cinnamon biscuits
bolo de arroz	boaloo der erroash	rice cake
bolo inglês	boaloo eengglaysh	cake with candied fruit
bolo podre	boaloo poadrer	cake flavoured with honey and cinnamon
broas castelares	broaersh kershter-lahrersh	sweet-potato biscuits
broas de mel	broaersh der mehl	cornflour and honey biscuits
cavacas	kervahkersh	glazed biscuits
cocadas	koakahdahss	coconut macaroons (Braz.)
massapães	mahsserpahng^ysh	almond macaroons
mil-folhas	meel foalyersh	cream slice (napoleon)
pão-de-ló	pahng^w der law	tea bread
papos-de-anjo	pahpoosh der ahngzhoo	egg yolk macaroons
pastel de coco	pershtehl der koakoo	coconut pastry
pastel de feijão	pershtehl der fayzhahng^w	bean pastry
pastel de nata/ de Belém	pershtehl der nahter/ der berlahng^y	small cream tart
queijada	kayzhahder	small cottage-cheese tart
tarte de amêndoa	tahrter der ermayngdwer	almond tart

bolo de chila do Algarve (boaloo der sheeler doo ahlgahrver)	cake made of pumpkin jam, grated almonds, egg yolks and sugar
pastel de Tentúgal (pershtehl der tayngtoogerl)	very thin flaky pastry filled with beaten egg yolks cooked in syrup
torta de laranja (torrter der lerrahngzher)	swiss roll made of eggs, sugar and orange juice

Aperitifs *Aperitivos*

The Portuguese like to sip an aperitif before dinner, some drink vermouth while others prefer a dry Port or Madeira, or a *Moscatel de Setúbal* served chilled. Brazilians are likely to drink a *batida,* a blend of spirit distilled from sugar-cane, ice, sugar and fruit juice, or a *caipirinha* (see page 59).

I'd like a dry Madeira, please.	**Queria um vinho da Madeira seco, se faz favor.**	kerreeer oong veenyoo der merdayrer saykoo ser fash fervoar
Please bring me a vermouth.	**Por favor, traga-me um vermute.**	por fervoar trahger mer oong vehrmooter

> **À SUA SAÚDE!**
> (ah sooer serooder)
> YOUR HEALTH!/CHEERS!

Beer *Cerveja*

Beer is a popular drink in Portugal and in Brazil. It is good and always served very cold. You may like to sample some of the local brews, for instance Sagres in Portugal and *Antártica* in Brazil. In Portugal beer is often served with *tremoços* (trer**mo**ssoosh—salted lupine seeds) or *amendoins* (ermayng**dweengsh**—peanuts).

I'd like a beer, please.	**Queria uma cerveja, se faz favor.**	kerreeer oomer serrvayzher ser fash fervoar
a dark beer	**uma cerveja preta**	oomer serrvayzher prayter
a draught beer	**uma imperial [um chope]**	oomer eengperrryahl [oong shoppi]
a lager	**uma cerveja (branca)**	oomer serrvayzher (brahngker)
Please bring me a ... of beer.	**Por favor, traga-mè ... de cerveja.**	poor fervoar trahger mer ... der serrvayzher
bottle	**uma garrafa**	oomer gerrahfer
glass	**um copo**	oong koppoo
mug (a quart)	**uma caneca**	oomer kernehker
Waiter! Another beer!	**Se faz favor! Outra cerveja!**	ser fash fervoar. oatrer serrvayzher

Wine *Vinhos*

Climatic conditions in Portugal account for the variety in the nature and quality of the wine. Some wine-producing regions are classified and controlled by law, because of the distinguishing characteristics of their wines. This goes for the Douro Valley in northern Portugal (Port wine), and the districts of Dão, Bairrada, Bucelas, Carcavelos, Algarve and Madeira.

Wine production in the Douro Valley dates back to the Crusades. However the wine which we call Port originated later. In 1678, two Englishmen, having just bought the output of a monastery's vineyard, puzzled over how to ship it back to Britain in order that it might arrive in good condition. They hit upon the idea of adding a little brandy to each of the casks. Thus the famous Port wine was born.

To ensure the integrity of the wine, the Portuguese Port Wine Institute closely oversees production and shipment. Not only is the growing area for Port wine strictly limited, but constant checks are made on the wine leaving the country to monitor colour, bouquet and quality.

The Portuguese seem to prefer the drier, lighter types as aperitifs or dessert wines. You'll notice that a much more popular wine than Port is the light, white *Moscatel* from the Setúbal area, south of Lisbon. It's often drunk before meals.

The *vinhos verdes* (red or white) are called *verdes* (green) because the grapes, slightly underripe, are sour and contain little sugar. They have a low percentage of alcohol and originate from the Minho region, northwest of Portugal.

Brazilian wines are produced in the southern part of the country. This region turns out some good red wines, and white wines too. Brazilians, however—probably because of the hot climate—prefer beer or an exotic and refreshing long drink.

The chart below will help to identify some of the good regional wines. Fine provincial cooking is well accompanied by good local wine whereas exquisite cuisine calls for a noble wine.

Type of wine	Examples	Accompanies
dry, light white	Most of the white *vinhos verdes; Porca de Murça* and *Pérola* from the Douro region; *Bucelas; Óbidos* and *Alcobaça* from the Estremadura region	fish, seafood, appetizers, cheese
dry white	Madeira wines such as *Sercial* and medium-dry *Verdelho*	desserts, sometimes served as an aperitif
sweet white	*Moscatel* from the Setúbal region; wines from the Carcavelos and Favaios regions. Look also for bottles labelled *Grandjó,* from the Douro region	all kinds of desserts *Moscatel de Setúbal* is often taken before meals
rosé	Wines from the Pinhel region, the *Mateus rosé* from the district of Trás-os-Montes	poultry, cold dishes
light-bodied red	Douro *Clarete,* wines from the Lafões region and all red *vinhos verdes*	poultry, meat
full-bodied red	Wines from Colares, Dão, Lagoa and Bairrada regions	meat and game
sweet red	Madeira wines such as *Malmsey* and drier Bual. Port wine from the Douro region	desserts. Can also be used in sauces to impart a delicious flavour to meat
sparkling	Bairrada, especially the *vinhos espumantes naturais* from the Caves da Raposeira	desserts, or as an aperitif

May I have the wine list, please?	**Pode trazer-me a lista dos vinhos, se faz favor?**	podder trerzayr mer er leeshter doosh veenyoosh ser fash fervoar
I'd like a bottle of white/red wine.	**Queria uma garrafa de vinho branco/tinto.**	kerreeer oomer gerrahfer der veenyoo brahngkoo/teengtoo
half a bottle	**meia-garrafa**	mayer gerrahfer
a carafe	**um jarro**	oong zhahrroo
half a litre	**meio-litro**	mayoo leetroo
a glass	**um copo**	oong koppoo
Please bring me another bottle.	**Por favor, traga-me outra garrafa.**	poor fervoar trahger mer oatrer gerrahfer
Where does this wine come from?	**Donde é este vinho?**	dawngder eh ayshter veenyoo

red	tinto	teengtoo
white	branco	brahngkoo
rosé	rosé	rozzay
sparkling	espumante	ishpoomahngter
dry	seco	saykoo
full-bodied	encorpado	ayngkoorpahdoo
light	ligeiro	lizhayroo
sweet	doce	doasser
very dry	extra-seco	ayshtrer saykoo

Other alcoholic drinks *Outras bebidas alcoólicas*

I'd like to try a/an ...	**Queria provar ...**	kerreeer proovahr
anise liqueur	**um anis**	oong erneesh
cognac	**um conhaque**	oong konnyahker
gin and tonic	**um gim tónico**	oong zheeng tonnikkoo
liqueur	**um licor**	oong likkoar
Madeira wine	**um vinho da Madeira**	oong veenyoo der merdayrer
port	**um vinho do Porto**	oong veenyoo doo poartoo
rum	**um rum**	oong roong
sherry	**um Xerez**	oong sherraysh
vermouth	**um vermute**	oong vehrmooter
(double) whisky	**um uísque (duplo)**	oong weeshker (dooploo)
neat (straight)	**puro**	pooroo
on the rocks	**com gelo**	kawng zhayloo
with water/soda	**com água/soda**	kawng ahgwer/sodder

If you'd like to sip a brandy after dinner, try a Portuguese *aguardente velha* like *Borges* or *Constantino*. You may also sample a local *bagaço* (ber**gah**ssoo—spirit made from grape husks), as explosive as the Brazilian *cachaça* (kah**shah**ssah— spirit distilled from sugar-cane). But watch out for the effects!

Here are some other typical Portuguese and Brazilian drinks:

aguardente	ahgwerr**dayng**ter	spirits
de figo	der **fee**goo	fig
de medronho	der merdro**an**yoo	arbutus berry
batida	bah**teed**ah	*cachaça*, fruit juice, sugar, ice (Braz.)
de caju	di kah**zhoo**	cashew nut
de coco	di ko**akoa**	coconut
de maracujá	di mahrahkoo**zhah**	passion-fruit
caipirinha	kighpirr**eeny**ah	*cachaça*, lime, sugar and ice (Braz.)
Cuba libre	koobah **leeb**ri	rum and Coke
ginjinha	zheeng**zheeny**er	spirit distilled from morello cherries

Nonalcoholic drinks	*Bebidas não alcoólicas*	
I'd like a/an ...	**Queria** ...	kerreeer
fruit juice	**um sumo* de fruta**	oong **soo**moo der **froo**ter
grape juice	**um sumo* de uva**	oong **soo**moo der **oo**ver
iced coffee/tea	**um refresco de café/ chá**	oong rerfraysh**koo** der **ker**feh/shah
lemon juice	**uma limonada**	**oo**mer limmoon**ah**der
lemonade	**uma gasosa**	**oo**mer ger**zozz**er
(glass of) milk	**(um copo de) leite**	(oong **koppoo** der) **lay**ter
milk shake	**um batido [milkshake]**	oong ber**teed**oo [milk**shay**ki]
mineral water	**uma água mineral**	**oo**mer **ahg**wer minner**rahl**
fizzy (carbonated)	**com gás**	kawng gash
still	**sem gás**	sahng**ᵞ** gash
orange juice	**um sumo* de laranja**	oong **soo**moo der lerr**ahng**zher
orangeade	**uma laranjada**	**oo**mer lerrahng**zhah**der
pineapple juice	**um sumo* de ananás**	oong **soo**moo der erner**nash**
tonic water	**uma água tónica**	**oo**mer **ahg**wer **tonn**ikker

---

* In Brazil: **suco** (**soo**koa)

Brazilians are very fond of refreshing drinks (*refrescos*—ray-**fray**skoas). Look for the bars advertising *sucos* (juices) with lots of fresh fruit on display. They serve as many as 20 different fruits, squeezed as you watch. Some are very exotic, some quite sweet. Try one!

água de coco	ahgwah di koakoa	coconut juice
caldo de cana	kahldoa di kahnah	sugar-cane juice
guaraná	gwahrahnah	a tropical fruit drink
leite de coco	layti di koakoa	coconut milk
mate	mahti	ice-cold Paraguay tea
milkshake	milkshayki	milk shake
de café	di kahfeh	coffee-flavoured
de limão	di limmahng^w	lemon-flavoured
suco de abacaxi	sookoa di ahbahkahshee	pineapple juice
suco de mamão	sookoa di mahmahng^w	papaya juice
suco de manga	sookoa di mahnggah	mango juice
suco de tamarindo	sookoa di tahmahreengdoa	tamarind juice

Hot beverages *Bebidas quentes*

Drunk anytime of the day—or night—Brazilian *cafezinho* (kahfehzeenyoa), a strong, espresso-type coffee, is served black with a lot of sugar to make it less bitter-tasting.

In Portugal, at the end of lunch or dinner most people order a *bica* (**bee**ker), similar to Brazilian *cafezinho*. With a few drops of milk in it, a *bica* is called a *garoto* (ger**roa**too); and a *galão* (ger**lahng**^{w}) is a white coffee in a tall glass. A diluted black coffee is called a *carioca* (ker**ryo**kker). But you also can ask for:

(hot) chocolate	um chocolate (quente)	oong shookoolahter (kayngter)
(double) coffee	um café (duplo)	oong kerfeh (dooploo)
with milk	com leite	kawng layter
decaffeinated	sem cafeína	sahng^y kerfeheener
tea	um chá	oong shah
cup of tea	uma chávena [xícara] de chá	oomer shahverner [sheekahrah] der shah
with milk/lemon	com leite/limão	kawng layter/limmahng^w

Complaints *Reclamações*

There's a plate/glass missing.	**Falta um prato/ um copo.**	fahlter oong prahtoo/ oong koppoo
I have no knife/ fork/spoon.	**Não tenho faca/ garfo/colher.**	nahng^w taynyoo fahker/ gahrfoo/koolyehr
That's not what I ordered.	**Não é o que eu encomendei.**	nahng^w eh oo ker ehoo ayngkoomayngday
I asked for ...	**Pedi ...**	perdee
There must be some mistake.	**Deve haver um engano.**	dehver ervayr oong aynggernoo
May I change it?	**Não pode trocar?**	nahng^w podder trookahr
I asked for a small portion (for the child).	**Pedi uma dose pequena (para esta criança).**	perdee oomer dozzer perkayner (perrer ehshter kryahngser)
The meat is ...	**A carne está ...**	er kahrner ishtah
overdone	**passada demais**	perssahder dermighsh
underdone	**mal passada**	mahl perssahder
too rare	**mal passada demais**	mahl perssahder dermighsh
too tough	**dura demais**	doorer dermighsh
This is too ...	**Isto está ... demais.**	eeshtoo ishtah ... dermighsh
bitter/salty/sweet	**amargo/salgado/ doce**	ermahrgoo/sahlgahdoo/ doasser
I don't like this.	**Não gosto disto.**	nahng^w goshtoo deeshtoo
The food is cold.	**A comida está fria.**	er koomeeder ishtah freeer
This isn't fresh.	**Isto não está fresco.**	eeshtoo nahng^w ishtah frayshkoo
What's taking you so long?	**Porque demora tanto?**	poorker dermorrer tahngtoo
Have you forgotten our drinks?	**Esqueceu-se das nossas bebidas?**	ishkehssehoo ser dersh nossersh berbeedersh
The wine tastes of cork.	**O vinho sabe a rolha.**	oo veenyoo sahber er roalyer
This isn't clean.	**Isto não está limpo.**	eeshtoo nahng^w ishtah leengpoo
Would you ask the head waiter to come over?	**Pode mandar chamar o chefe de mesa?**	podder mahngdahr shermahr oo shehfer der mayzer

The bill (check) *A conta*

A service charge is generally included automatically in restaurant bills, but if service has been especially good, an extra tip is appropriate and appreciated. Credit cards may be used in an increasing number of restaurants. Signs are posted indicating which cards are accepted.

I'd like to pay.	**Queria pagar.**	kerreeer pergahr
We'd like to pay separately.	**Queríamos pagar separadamente.**	kerreeermoosh pergahr serperrahdermayngter
I think there is a mistake in this bill.	**Creio que se enganou na conta.**	krayoo ker ser aynggernoa ner kawngter
What is this amount for?	**A que corresponde esta importância?**	er ker koorrershpawngder ehshter eengpoortahngsyer
Is service included?	**O serviço está incluído?**	oo serrveessoo ishtah eengklweedoo
Is everything included?	**Está tudo incluído?**	ishtah toodoo eengklweedoo
Do you accept traveller's cheques?	**Aceitam cheques de viagem?**	erssaytahng^w shehkersh der vyahzhahng^y
Can I pay with this credit card?	**Posso pagar com este cartão de crédito?**	possoo pergahr kawng ayshter kerrtahng^w der krehdittoo
Thank you, this is for you.	**Obrigado(a), isto é para si.**	oabriggahdoo(er) eeshtoo eh perrer see
Keep the change.	**Guarde o troco.**	gwahrder oo troakoo
That was a delicious meal.	**A refeição estava deliciosa.**	er rerfayssahng^w ishtahver derlissyozzer
We enjoyed it, thank you.	**Gostámos muito, obrigado(a).**	gooshtahmoosh moong^{y}too oabriggahdoo(er)

SERVIÇO INCLUÍDO
SERVICE INCLUDED

TIPPING, see inside back-cover

Snacks—Picnic *Refeições leves—Piquenique*

You may not feel like having a big meal in a restaurant and may just want a quick bite at a snack-bar. You'll find a selection of small pies and fritters, sandwiches and pastries, and also small dishes *(petiscos)* or salads (see pages 41–42). Since most of the snacks are on display, ordering is easy.

I'll have one of these, please.	**Queria um destes, se faz favor.**	kerreeer oong dayshtish ser fash fervoar
Give me two of these and one of those.	**Dê-me dois destes e um daqueles.**	day mer doysh dayshtish ee oong derkaylersh
to the left/right above/below	**à esquerda/direita por cima/por baixo**	ah ishkayrder/dirrayter poor seemer/poor bighshoo
It's to take away.	**É para levar.**	eh perrer lervahr
I'd like a/some ...	**Queria ...**	kerreeer
chicken	**um frango**	oong frahnggoo
half a roast chicken	**meio-frango assado**	mayoo frahnggoo erssahdoo
chicken pie	**uma empada de galinha**	oomer ayngpahder der gerleenyer
chips (french fries)	**batatas fritas**	bertahtersh freetersh
croquette	**um croquete**	oong krokkehter
cod	**pastel de bacalhau**	pershtehl der berkerlyow
meat	**croquete de carne**	krokkehter der kahrner
hamburger	**um hamburger**	oong ahngboorgehr
hot dog	**um cachorro (quente)**	oong kershoarroo (kayngter)
omelete	**uma omelete**	oomer ommerlehter
pancake	**um crepe [uma panqueca]**	oong krehper [oomah pahngkehkah]
with sugar	**com açúcar**	kawng erssookerr
with jam	**com doce [geléia]**	kawng doasser [zhaylayah]
(small) pie	**um pastel**	oong pershtehl
meat	**de carne**	der kahrner
shrimp	**de camarão**	der kermerrahng[w]
salad	**uma salada**	oomer serlahder
sandwich	**uma [um] sanduíche**	oomer [oong] sahngdweesher
cheese	**de queijo**	der kayzhoo
ham	**de fiambre**	der fyahngbrer
toast	**uma torrada**	oomer toorrahder
toasted sandwich	**uma tosta**	oomer toshter
ham-and-cheese	**tosta mista [um misto quente]**	toshter meeshter [oong meestoa kayngti]

Here's a basic list of food and drink that might come in useful when shopping for a picnic.

Please give me a/an/some ...	Por favor, dê-me ...	poor fervoar day mer
apples	maçãs	merssahngsh
bananas	bananas	bernernersh
biscuits (Br.)	bolachas	boolahshersh
beer	cerveja	serrvayzher
bread	pão	pahng^w
brown	escuro	ishkooroo
wholemeal (-wheat)	integral	eengtergrahl
butter	manteiga	mahngtayger
cake	um bolo	oong boaloo
cheese	queijo	kayzhoo
chips (Am.)	batatas fritas	bertahtersh freetersh
chocolate bar	uma tablete de chocolate	oomer tahblehter der shookoolahter
coffee	café	kerfeh
instant	instantâneo	eengshtahngternyoo
cold cuts	carnes frias	kahrnersh freeersh
cookies	bolachas	boolahshersh
crisps	batatas fritas	bertahtersh freetersh
eggs	ovos	ovvoosh
frankfurters	salsichas	sahlseeshersh
gherkins (pickles)	pepinos de conserva	perpeenoosh der kawngsehrver
grapes	uvas	ooversh
ham	fiambre	fyahngbrer
ice-cream	gelado [sorvete]	zherlahdoo [sorvehti]
lemon	um limão	oong limmahng^w
milk	leite	layter
mustard	mostarda	mooshtahrder
oranges	laranjas	lerrahngzhersh
pastries	bolos	boaloosh
pepper	pimenta	pimmayngter
roll	um papo-seco [pãozinho]	oong pahpoo saykoo [pahng^wzeenyoa]
salami	salame	serlermer
salt	sal	sahl
sausage	um chouriço	oong shoareessoo
soft drink	um refrigerante	oong rerfrizzherrahngter
sugar	açúcar	ersookerr
tea	chá	shah
tomatoes	tomates	toomahtish
yoghurt	iogurte	yoggoorter

Travelling around

In Brazil, where air transport is almost as common as bus travel in Portugal, the following expressions might be useful.

Plane *Avião*

Is there a flight to Rio de Janeiro?	**Há um voo para o Rio de Janeiro?**	ah oong **vo**aoo perrer oo reeoo der zhernayroo
Is it a direct flight?	**É um voo directo?**	eh oong **vo**aoo dirrehtoo
When's the next flight to São Paulo?	**A que horas é o próximo avião para São Paulo?**	er ker orrersh eh oo **pross**immoo ervyahng[w] perrer sahng[w] powloo
Can I make a connection to Brasília?	**Tenho correspon-dência [conexão] para Brasília?**	taynyoo koorrershpawng-dayngsyer [konnehk**sahng**[w]] perrer brerzeelyer
I'd like a ticket to Recife.	**Quero um bilhete para Recife.**	kehroo oong billyayter perrer rer**ssee**fer
single (one-way) return (roundtrip)	**ida** **ida e volta**	eeder eeder ee **vol**lter
What time do we take off?	**A que horas sai o avião?**	er ker orrersh sigh oo ervyahng[w]
What time do I have to check in?	**A que horas devo apresentar-me?**	er ker orrersh **day**voo erprerzayng**tahr** mer
Is there a bus to the airport?	**Há um autocarro [ônibus] para o aeroporto?**	ah oong owto**kkah**rroo [oanibbooss] perrer oo erehroppoartoo
What's the flight number?	**Qual é o número do voo?**	kwahl eh oo **noo**merroo doo **vo**aoo
At what time do we arrive?	**A que horas chegamos?**	er ker orrersh sherger**moosh**
I'd like to … my reservation.	**Queria … a marca-ção do meu lugar.**	kerreeer … er merrker-**ssahng**[w] doo mehoo loo**gahr**
cancel change confirm	**anular** **mudar** **confirmar**	ernoo**lahr** moo**dahr** kawngfirr**mahr**

CHEGADA ARRIVAL	**PARTIDA** DEPARTURE

Train *Comboio [trem]*

The Portuguese railway, *Caminhos de Ferro Portugueses (C.P.)*, handles practically all rail services. The trains are fast and generally run on time on the main lines. They offer first and second class seats. The Brazilian railways, *Estrada de Ferro Central do Brasil (E.F.C.B.)*, are, with the exception of a few lines, not recommended for passengers.

Lisboa-Expresso, TER (lizhboaer ishprehssoo, tehr)	Express train linking Lisbon with Madrid, reservation compulsory, surcharge payable
Lusitânia-Expresso (loozitternyer ishprehssoo)	Express train, links Lisbon to Madrid, early booking advisable
Sud-Express (sood ishprehss)	Express train, links Lisbon to Paris, early booking advisable
Internacional (eengterrnerssyoonahl)	A direct train; for a trip abroad you'll have to book a seat in advance, as only one carriage crosses the border.
Rápido (rahpiddoo)	Direct train, stops only at main stations, early booking advisable
Automotora (owtoamootoarer)	Small diesel train used on short runs
Correio (koorrayoo)	Long-distance postal train, stops at all stations, also takes passengers

To the railway station *Para a estação*

Lisbon has four principal railway stations. International services and trains for northern Portugal leave from Santa Apolónia station. Commuter trains for the western suburbs and Estoril and Cascais leave from Cais do Sodré. Trains for Sintra and the west depart from Rossio station. And the fourth station, Sul e Sueste, has ferryboats which cross the Tagus for trains that go on as far as the Algarve.

Taxi!	**Táxi!**	tahksi
Take me to ... station.	**Leve-me à estação de ...**	lehver mer ah ishter-ssahng^w der

| Is this the railway station for trains to ...? | É esta a estação dos comboios [trens] para ...? | eh eshter er ishter-ssahng^w doosh kawng-boyoosh [trahng^yss] perrer |
| How much is that? | Quanto é? | kwahngtoo eh |

ENTRADA	ENTRANCE
SAÍDA	EXIT
ACESSO AOS CAIS [ÀS PLATAFORMAS]	TO THE PLATFORMS
INFORMAÇÕES	INFORMATION

Where's the ...? *Onde é ...?*

Where is/are the ...?	Onde é/são ...?	awngder eh/sahng^w
booking office	a marcação de lugares	er merrkerssahng^w der loogahrersh
currency exchange office	o câmbio	oo kahngbyoo
left-luggage office (baggage check)	o depósito da bagagem	oo derpozzittoo der bergahzhahng^y
lost property (lost and found) office	a secção dos perdidos e achados	er sehksahng^w doosh perrdeedoosh ee ershahdoosh
luggage lockers	o depósito da bagagem auto-mático	oo derpozzittoo der bergahzhahng^y owtoomahtikkoo
newsstand	o quiosque [a banca] de jornais	oo kyoshker [ah bahngkah] der zhoornighsh
reservations office	a marcação de lugares	er merrkerssahng^w der loogahrersh
restaurant	o restaurante	oo rishtowrahngter
snack bar	o snack-bar [a lanchonete]	oo "snack bar" [ah lahngshoanehti]
ticket office	a bilheteira [a bilheteria]	er billyertayrer [ah billyaytayreeah]
waiting room	a sala de espera	er sahler der ishpehrer
Where are the toilets?	Onde são as casas de banho [os banheiros]?	awngder sahng^w ersh kahzersh der bernyoo [oass bahnyayroass]

TAXI, see page 21

Inquiries *Informações*

When is the ... train to Faro?	Quando é o ... comboio* para Faro?	kwahngdoo eh oo ... kawngboyoo perrer fahroo
first/last/next	primeiro/último/ próximo	primmayroo/ooltimmoo/ prossimmoo
What time does the train to Braga leave?	A que horas parte o comboio* para Braga?	er ker orrersh pahrter oo kawngboyoo perrer brahger
What's the fare to Oporto?	Qual é o preço do bilhete para o Porto?	kwahl eh oo prayssoo doo billyayter perrer oo poartoo
Is it a through train?	É um comboio* directo?	eh oong kawngboyoo dirrehtoo
Must I pay a surcharge?	Tenho de pagar um suplemento?	taynyoo der pergahr oong sooplermayngtoo
Is there a connection to ...?	Há correspondência [conexão] para ...?	ah koorrershpawngdayng-syer [konnehksahng^w] perrer
Do I have to change trains?	Tenho de mudar de comboio*?	taynyoo der moodahr der kawngboyoo
Is there sufficient time to change?	Dá tempo para mudar?	dah tayngpoo perrer moodahr
Is the train running on time?	O comboio* sai à tabela?	oo kawngboyoo sigh ah terbehler
What time does the train arrive in Lisbon?	A que horas chega o comboio* a Lisboa?	er ker orrersh shayger oo kawngboyoo er lizhboaer
Is there a dining-car on the train?	O comboio* tem restaurante?	oo kawngboyoo tahng^y rishtowrahngter
Does the train stop in Obidos?	O comboio* pára em Óbidos?	oo kawngboyoo pahrer ahng^y obbiddoosh
What track does the train to Sintra leave from?	Qual é a linha do comboio* para Sintra?	kwahl eh er leenyer doo kawngboyoo perrer seengtrer
What platform does the train from Sintra arrive at?	Qual é o cais [a plataforma] do comboio* de Sintra?	kwahl eh oo kighsh [ah plahtahforrmah] doo kawngboyoo der seengtrer
I'd like to buy a timetable.	Queria comprar um horário.	kerreeer kawngprahr oong orrahryoo

---

* In Brazil: **trem** [trahng^y]

É um comboio [trem] directo.	It's a through train.
Tem de mudar em ...	You have to change at ...
Mude em ... e apanhe [pegue] um comboio [trem] regional.	Change at ... and get a local train.
O cais [a plataforma] 3 fica ...	Platform 3 is ...
ali/lá em cima à esquerda/à direita	over there/upstairs on the left/on the right
Há um comboio [trem] para ... às ...	There's a train to ... at ...
O seu comboio [trem] sai da linha 5.	Your train will leave from track 5.
Há um atraso de ... minutos.	There'll be a delay of ... minutes.
Primeira classe à frente/ ao meio/atrás.	First class at the front/in the middle/at the end.

Tickets *Bilhetes*

I'd like a ticket to Oporto.	**Quero um bilhete para o Porto.**	kehroo oong billyayter perrer oo poartoo
single (one-way)	**ida**	eeder
return (roundtrip)	**ida e volta**	eeder ee vollter
first class	**primeira classe**	primmayrer klahsser
second class	**segunda classe**	sergoongder klahsser
half price	**meio-bilhete**	mayoo billyayter
with surcharge	**com suplemento**	kawng sooplermayngtoo

Reservation *Marcação de lugares*

I want to reserve a ...	**Queria marcar ...**	kerreeer merrkahr
seat (by the window)	**um lugar (junto à janela)**	oong loogahr (zhoongtoo ah zhernehler)
berth	**um beliche**	oong berleesher
upper	**superior**	sooperryoar
lower	**inferior**	eengferryoar
berth in the sleeping car	**um lugar na carruagem-camas [no vagão-leitos]**	oong loogahr ner kerrwah-zhahng^v kermersh [noa vahgahng^w laytoass]

NUMBERS, see page 147

Excursões

All aboard *Partida*

Is this the right platform for the train to Faro?	É este o cais [a plataforma] do comboio* para Faro?	eh **ays**hter oo **kigh**sh [ah plahtah**forr**mah] doo kawng**boy**oo **perr**er **fah**roo
Is this the train to Madrid?	É este o comboio* para Madrid?	eh **ays**hter oo kawng**boy**oo **perr**er merd**reed**
Excuse me. May I get by?	Com licença. Posso passar?	kawng li**ssayng**ser. **poss**oo perr**ssahr**
Is this seat taken?	Este lugar está ocupado?	**ays**hter loo**gahr** ish**tah** okkoo**pah**doo

FUMADORES	NÃO FUMADORES
SMOKER	NONSMOKER

I think that's my seat.	Acho que esse é o meu lugar.	**ah**shoo ker **ays**ser eh oo **meh**oo loo**gahr**
Would you let me know before we get to Coimbra?	Pode avisar-me quando chegarmos a Coimbra?	**pod**der erviz**zahr** mer **kwahng**doo sher**gahr**moosh er **kweeng**brer
What station is this?	Que estação é esta?	ker ishter**ssahng**ʷ eh **ehsh**ter
How long does the train stop here?	Quanto tempo vai demorar o comboio* aqui?	**kwahng**too **tayng**poo vigh dermoo**rahr** oo kawng**boy**oo er**kee**
When do we get to Lisbon?	Quando chegamos a Lisboa?	**kwahng**doo sher**ger**moosh er lizh**boa**er

Sleeping *Para dormir*

Are there any free compartments in the sleeping car?	Há compartimentos livres na carruagem-camas [no vagão-leitos].	ah kawngperrtim**mayng**toosh **leev**rersh ner ker**rwah**zhahngʸ **ker**mersh [noa vah**gahng**ʷ **lay**toass]
Where's the sleeping car?	Onde fica a carruagem-camas [o vagão-leitos]?	**awng**der **feek**er er ker**rwah**zhahngʸ **ker**mersh [oa vah**gahng**ʷ **lay**toass]
Where's my berth?	Onde fica o meu beliche?	**awng**der **feek**er oo **meh**oo ber**lee**sher

---

* In Brazil: **trem** [trahngʸ]

I'd like a lower/upper berth.	Queria um beliche inferior/superior.	kerreeer oong berleesher eengferryoar/sooperryoar
Would you make up our berths?	Pode preparar-nos os beliches?	podder prerperrahr noosh oosh berleeshersh
Would you wake me at 7 o'clock?	Pode acordar-me às 7 horas?	podder erkoordahr mer ahsh 7 orrersh

Eating *Para comer*

You can get snacks and drinks in the buffet car and a full meal in the dining car. If the train is crowded there may be two sittings.

| Where's the dining car/buffet car? | Onde é a carruagem--restaurante/cantina? | awngder eh er kerrwah-zhahng^y rishtowrahngter/kahngteener |

Baggage and porters. *Bagagens e carregadores*

Porter!	Carregador!	kerrergerdoar
Can you help me with my luggage?	Pode ajudar-me a levar a bagagem?	podder erzhoodahr mer er lervahr er bergahzhahng^y
Where are the luggage trolleys (carts)?	Onde estão os carrinhos da bagagem?	awngder ishtahng^w oosh kerreenyoosh der bergahzhahng^y
Where are the luggage lockers?	Onde é o depósito da bagagem automá-tico?	awngder eh oo derpozzit-too der bergahzhahng^y owtoomahtikkoo
Where's the left-luggage office (baggage check)?	Onde é o depósito da bagagem?	awngder eh oo derpozzit-too der bergahzhahng^y
I'd like to leave my luggage, please.	Queria depositar a minha bagagem, se faz favor.	kerreeer derpoozittahr er meenyer bergahzhahng^y ser fahsh fervoar
I'd like to register (check) my luggage.	Queria despachar a minha bagagem.	kerreeer dishpershahr er meenyer bergahzhahng^y

---

DESPACHO DE BAGAGENS
REGISTERING (CHECKING) BAGGAGE

PORTERS, see also page 18

Coach (long-distance bus) *Camioneta [ônibus]*

Inter-city bus and coach services are frequent and cover most of Portugal. Some coaches are run by the Portuguese Transport Company, *Rodoviária Nacional (R.N.)*, others are private. In Brazil coach travel is cheap, but time-consuming.

Where's the coach terminal (bus station)?	**Onde é o terminal das camionetas [dos ônibus]?**	awngder eh oo terrminnahl dersh kahmyooneetersh [doass oanibbooss]
When's the next inter-city bus to ...?	**A que horas é o próximo expresso para ...?**	er ker orrersh eh oo prossimmoo ishprehssoo perrer
Does this coach stop in ...?	**Esta camioneta [este ônibus] pára em ...?**	ehshter kahmyoonehter [aysti oanibbooss] pahrer ahng^y
How long does the journey (trip) take?	**Quanto tempo demora a viagem?**	kwahngtoo tayngpoo dermorrer er vyahzhahng^y

Note: Most of the phrases on the previous pages can be used or adapted for travelling on local transport.

Bus—Tram (streetcar) *Autocarro [ônibus]—Eléctrico [bonde]*

I'd like a booklet of tickets/tourist pass.	**Queria uma caderneta de bilhetes/um passe para turistas.**	kerreeer oomer kerderrnayter der billyaytersh/ oong pahsser perrer tooreeshtersh
Which tram (streetcar) goes to the town centre?	**Qual é o eléctrico [bonde] que vai para o centro da cidade?**	kwahl eh oo illehtrikkoo [bawngdi] ker vigh perrer oo sayngtroo der siddahder
Where can I get a bus to ...?	**Onde posso apanhar [pegar] um autocarro [ônibus] para ...?**	awngder possoo erpernyahr [paygahr] oong owtokkah- rroo [oanibbooss] perrer
Which bus do I take for ...?	**Que autocarro [ôni- bus] devo apanhar [pegar] para ...?**	ker owtokkahrroo [oani- bbooss] dayvoo erpernyahr [paygahr] perrer
Where's the bus stop?	**Onde é a paragem do autocarro [parada de ônibus]?**	awngder eh er perrah- zhahng^y doo owtokkahrroo [pahrahdah di oanibbooss]

When is the ... bus to ...?	A que horas é o ... autocarro [ônibus] para ...?	er ker orrersh eh oo ... owtokkahrroo [oanibbooss] perrer
first/last/next	primeiro/último/próximo	primmayroo/ooltimmoo/prossimmoo
How much is the fare to ...?	Qual é o preço do bilhete para ...?	kwahl eh oo prayssoo doo billyayter perrer
Do I have to change buses?	É preciso mudar de autocarro [ônibus]?	eh prersseezoo moodahr der owtokkahrroo [oanibbooss]
How many bus stops are there to ...?	Quantas paragens [paradas] há até ...?	kwahngtersh perrahzhahngᵛsh [pahrahdahss] ah erteh
Will you tell me when to get off?	Pode avisar-me quando devo descer?	podder ervizzahr mer kwahngdoo dayvoo dishsayr
I want to get off at ...	Quero descer no(a) ...	kehroo dishsayr noo(er)

**PARAGEM DE AUTOCARROS
[PARADA DE ÔNIBUS]**   BUS STOP

Underground (subway) *Metropolitano/Metro*

The underground in Lisbon has two main lines which join at Pombal Square. The fare is the same irrespective of the distance you travel. São Paulo and Rio de Janeiro also have underground systems.

Where's the nearest underground (subway) station?	Onde é a estação de metro mais próxima?	awngder eh er ishterssahngᵂ der mehtroo mighsh prossimmer?
Does this train go to ...?	Este metro vai para ...?	ayshter mehtroo vigh perrer
Where do I change for ...?	Onde devo mudar para ...?	awngder dayvoo moodahr perrer
Is the next station ...?	A próxima estação é ...?	er prossimmer ishterssahngᵂ eh
Which line should I take for ...?	Que linha devo tomar para ...?	ker leenyer dayvoo toomahr perrer

Boat service   *Barcos*

When does the next boat to ... leave?	Quando sai o próximo barco para ...?	kwahngdoo sigh oo prossimmoo bahrkoo perrer
Where's the embarkation point?	Onde é o cais de embarque?	awngder eh oo kighsh der ayngbahrker
How long does the crossing take?	Quanto tempo leva a travessia?	kwahngtoo tayngpoo lehver er trerversseeer
At which port(s) do we stop?	Em que porto(s) paramos?	ahng^y ker poartoo(sh) perrermoosh
I'd like to take a cruise.	Gostava de fazer um cruzeiro.	gooshtahver der ferzayr oong kroozayroo
bay	a baía	er bereeer
cabin	a cabine	er kahbeener
single/double	individual/dupla	eengdivviddwahl/doopler
deck	o convés	oo kawngvehsh
ferry	o ferry-boat	oo "ferry-boat"
harbour	o porto	oo poartoo
hovercraft	o hovercraft	oo "hovercraft"
hydrofoil	o hidroplano [aerobarco]	oo iddropplernoo [ahehrobbahrkoa]
life belt	o cinto de salvação	oo seengtoo der sahlverssahng^w
life boat	o bote salva-vidas	oo botter sahlver veedersh
ship	o navio	oo nerveeoo
steamer	o vapor	oo verpoar

Other means of transport   *Outros meios de transporte*

bicycle	a bicicleta	er bissikklehter
cable car	o teleférico	oo terlerfehrikkoo
funicular	o elevador	oo illerverdoar
helicopter	o helicóptero	oo illikkopterroo
lift (elevator)	o elevador	oo illerverdoar
moped	a bicicleta motorizada	er bissikklehter mootoorizzahder
motorbike	a motocicleta	er mottossikklehter
scooter	a scooter	er "scooter"

Or perhaps you prefer:

to hitchhike	pedir boleia [carona]	perdeer boolayer [kahroanah]
to walk	andar a pé	ahngdahr er peh

Car *Automóvel*

Roads in Portugal are classified by numbers, the lower the better. Some motorways (expressway) and bridges are subject to tolls *(a portagem)*. On winding mountain roads it's compulsory to sound your horn. Seat belts *(o cinto de segurança)* are obligatory unless you're in a built-up area. In southern Brazil roads are good, the traffic, however, is very intense, and driving requires good nerves.

Where's the nearest filling station?	Qual é a estação de serviço mais próxima?	kwahl eh er ishterssahng^w der serrveessoo mighsh prossimmer
Full tank, please.	Encha o depósito, se faz favor.	ayngsher oo derpozzittoo ser fash fervoar
Give me ... litres of petrol (gasoline).	Dê-me ...litros de gasolina.	day mer ... leetroosh der gerzooleener
super (premium)/ regular/unleaded/ diesel	super/normal sem chumbo/ gasóleo	soopehr/norrmahl/sahng^y shoongboo/gahzollyoo
Please check the ...	Verifique ...	verriffeeker
battery	a bateria	er berterreeer
brake fluid	o líquido dos travões [freios]	oo leekiddoo doosh trer-vawng^ysh [frayoass]
oil/water	o óleo/a água	oo ollyoo/er ahgwer
Would you check the tyre pressure?	Pode verificar a pressão dos pneus?	podder verriffikkahr er prerssahng^w doosh pnehoosh
1.6 front, 1.8 rear.	23 à frente, 26 atrás.	23 ah frayngter 26 ertrahsh
Please check the spare tyre, too.	Verifique também o pneu sobresselente, se faz favor.	verriffeeker tahngbahng^y oo pnehoo soobrersser-layngter ser fash fervoar
Can you mend this puncture (fix this flat)?	Pode consertar este furo?	podder kawngserrtahr ayshter fooroo
Would you change the ..., please?	Pode mudar ...?	podder moodahr
bulb	a lâmpada	er lahngperder
fan belt	a correia da ventoinha	er koorrayer der vayngtweenyer

CAR HIRE, see page 20

spark(ing) plugs	as velas	ersh **vehlersh**
tyre	o pneu	oo **pnehoo**
wipers	os limpa-vidros	oosh **leengper veedroosh**
Would you clean the windscreen (windshield)?	Pode limpar o pára-brisas?	podder leeng**pahr** oo **pahrer breezersh**

Asking the way—Street directions   *Para perguntar o caminho*

Can you tell me the way to ...?	Pode indicar-me o caminho para ...?	podder eeng**dikkahr** mer oo ker**meenyoo** perrer
How do I get to ...?	Como se vai para ...?	**koamoo** ser vigh perrer
Are we on the right road for ...?	É esta a estrada para ...?	eh **ehshter** er ish**trahder** perrer
How far is the next village?	A que distância fica a próxima povoação?	er ker dish**tahngsyer** **feeker** er **prossimmer** poovwers**sahng**w
Is there a road with little traffic?	Há alguma estrada com pouco trânsito?	ah ahl**goomer** ish**trahder** kawng **poakoo trahng**zittoo
How far is it to ... from here?	A que distância estamos de ...?	er ker dish**tahngsyer** ish**termoosh** der
Is there a motorway (expressway)?	Há uma auto-estrada?	ah **oomer** owto ish**trahder**
How long does it take by car/on foot?	Quanto tempo se leva de carro/a pé?	**kwahng**too **tayng**poo ser **lehver** der **kahr**roo/er peh
Can I drive to the centre of town?	Posso ir de carro até ao centro da cidade?	**posso** eer der **kahr**roo er**teh** ow **sayng**troo der sid**dah**der
Can you tell me where ... is?	Pode dizer-me onde fica ...?	podder dizz**ayr** mer **awng**der **feeker**
How can I find this place/address?	Como posso encontrar este lugar/ endereço?	**koamoo** posso ayng**kawng**trahr **aysh**ter loo**gahr**/ ayngderr**ayssoo**
Where's this?	Onde fica isto?	**awng**der **feeker eesh**too
Can you show me on the map where I am?	Pode mostrar-me no mapa onde estou?	podder moosh**trahr** mer noo **mah**per **awng**der ish**toa**
Can you show me on the map where ... is?	Pode mostrar-me no mapa onde fica ...?	podder moosh**trahr** mer noo **mah**per **awng**der **feeker**

Enganou-se na estrada.	You're on the wrong road.
Vá sempre em frente.	Go straight ahead.
É ali à esquerda/à direita.	It's down there on the left/right.
em frente de/atrás de ... ao lado de/depois de ...	opposite/behind ... next to/after ...
norte/sul/(l)este/oeste	north/south/east/west
Vá até ao primeiro/ segundo cruzamento.	Go to the first/second crossroads (intersection).
Vire à esquerda nos semáforos.	Turn left at the traffic lights.
Vire à direita na próxima esquina.	Turn right at the next corner.
Apanhe a estrada para ...	Take the ... road to.
É uma rua de sentido único.	It's a one-way street.
Tem de voltar atrás até ...	You have to go back to ...
Siga a direcção Sul Ponte.	Follow signs for Sul Ponte.

Parking *Estacionamento*

Where can I park?	Onde posso estacionar?	awngder possoo ishterssyoonahr
Is there a car park nearby?	Há um parque de automóveis aqui perto?	ah oong pahrker der owtoomovvaysh erkee pehrtoo
May I park here?	Posso estacionar aqui?	possoo ishterssyoonahr erkee
How long can I park here?	Quanto tempo posso ficar aqui estacionado?	kwahngtoo tayngpoo possoo fikkahr erkee ishterssyoonahdoo
What's the charge per hour?	Qual é o preço à hora?	kwahl eh oo prayssoo ah orrer
Do you have some change for the parking meter?	Tem dinheiro trocado para o parcómetro?	tahng^y dinnyayroo trookahdoo perrer oo perrkommertroo

Breakdown—Road assistance   *Avarias—Asistência na estrada*

Where's the nearest garage?	**Onde é a garagem mais próxima?**	awngder eh er gerrah-zhahng^y mighsh prossimmer

Where's the nearest garage? — **Onde é a garagem mais próxima?** — awngder eh er gerrahzhahng^y mighsh prossimmer

Excuse me. My car has broken down. — **Desculpe. O meu carro avariou-se.** — dishkoolper. oo mehoo kahrroo erverryoa ser

I've had a break-down at ... — **Tive uma avaria em ...** — teever oomer erverreeer ahng^y

Can you send a mechanic? — **Pode mandar-me um mecânico?** — podder mahngdahr mer oong merkernikkoo

My car won't start. — **O motor não pega.** — oo mootoar nahng^w pehger

The battery is dead. — **A bateria está descarregada.** — er berterreeer ishtah dishkerrergahder

I've run out of petrol (gasoline). — **Acabou-se-me a gasolina.** — erkerboa ser mer er gerzooleener

I have a flat tyre. — **Tenho um pneu vazio.** — taynyoo oong pnehoo verzeeoo

The engine is over-heating. — **O motor aquece demais.** — oo mootoar erkehsser dermighsh

There is something wrong with the ... — **Há um defeito qualquer ...** — ah oong derfaytoo kwahlkehr

brakes — **nos travões [freios]** — noosh trervawng^ysh [frayoass]

carburettor — **no carburador** — noo kerrboorerdoar

exhaust pipe — **no tubo de escape** — noo tooboo der ishkahper

radiator — **no radiador** — noo rerdyerdoar

steering wheel — **no volante** — noo voolahngter

wheel — **numa roda** — noomer rodder

Can you send a breakdown van (tow truck)? — **Pode mandar-me um pronto-socorro?** — podder mahngdahr mer oong prawngtoo sookoarroo

How long will you be? — **Quanto tempo vai demorar?** — kwahngtoo tayngpoo vigh dermoorahr

Accident—Police   *Accidentes—Polícia*

Please call the police. — **Por favor, chame a polícia.** — poor fervoar shermer er pooleessyer

There's been an accident. It's about 2 km. from ... — **Houve um acidente. A cerca de 2 km de ...** — oaver oong erssiddayngter. er sayrker der 2 killommertroosh der

Where is there a telephone?	Onde há um telefone?	awngder ah oong terlerfonner
Call a doctor/an ambulance quickly.	Chame um médico/ uma ambulância, depressa.	shermer oong mehdikkoo/ oomer ahngboolahngsyer derprehsser
There are people injured.	Há feridos.	ah ferreedoosh
Here's my driving licence.	Aqui está a minha carta de condução [carteira de motorista].	erkee ishtah er meenyer kahrter der kawngdoo- ssahng^w [kahrtayrah di moatoareestah]
What's your name and address?	Qual é o seu nome e endereço?	kwahl eh oo sehoo noamer ee ayngderrayssoo
What's your insurance company?	Qual é a sua com- panhia de seguros?	kwahl eh er sooer kawng- pernyeeer der sergooroosh

Road signs *Sinais de trânsito*

AFROUXE	Slow down
BERMAS ALTAS	Soft shoulder
CUIDADO	Caution
CURVAS	Bends (curves)
DESCIDA PERIGOSA	Steep hill
DESVIO	Diversion (detour)
DEVAGAR	Slow
ESTACIONAMENTO PERMITIDO/PROIBIDO	Parking allowed/ No parking
OBRAS	Road works (men working)
PASSAGEM DE NÍVEL	Level (railroad) crossing
PEDÁGIO (Braz.)	Toll
PEDESTRES (Braz.)	Pedestrians
PEÕES	Pedestrians
PORTAGEM	Toll
... PROIBIDO	No ...
QUEDA DE PEDRAS	Falling rocks
SAÍDA DE CAMI[NH]ÕES	Lorry (truck) exit
SIGA PELA DIREITA	Keep right
SEM SAÍDA	No through road
SEMÁFOROS	Traffic lights ahead
SILÊNCIO	Silence zone
TRABALHOS	Road works (men working)
TRÂNSITO PROIBIDO	Road closed
VEÍCULOS PESADOS	Heavy vehicles

Sightseeing

Where's the tourist office?	Onde é o turismo?	awngder eh oo tooreezhmoo
What are the main points of interest?	O que há de mais interessante para se ver?	oo ker ah der mighsh eeng-terrerssahngter perrer ser vayr
We're here for ...	Ficamos aqui ...	fikkermoosh erkee
only a few hours	só algumas horas	saw ahlgoomersh orrersh
a day	um dia	oong deeer
a week	uma semana	oomer sermerner
Can you recommend a sightseeing tour/ an excursion?	Pode recomendar-me um circuito turístico/uma excursão?	podder rerkoomayngdahr mer oong sirrkooytoo tooreeshtikkoo/oomer ishkoorsahng^w
Where's the point of departure?	De onde é a partida?	der awngder eh er perrteeder
Will the bus pick us up at the hotel?	A camioneta [o ônibus] vem buscar--nos ao hotel?	er kahmyoonehter [oa oanibbooss] vahng^y boosh-kahr noosh ow ottehl
How much does the tour cost?	Quanto custa a excursão?	kwahngtoo kooshter er ishkoorsahng^w
What time does the tour start?	A que horas começa a excursão?	er ker orrersh koomehsser er ishkoorsahng^w
Is lunch included?	O almoço está incluído?	oo ahlmoassoo ishtah eengklweedoo
What time do we get back?	A que horas regressamos?	er ker orrersh rergrerssermoosh
Do we have free time in ...?	Temos algum tempo livre em ...?	taymoosh ahlgoong tayng-poo leevrer ahng^y
Is there an English-speaking guide?	Há algum guia que fale inglês?	ah ahlgoong gheeer ker fahler eengglaysh
I'd like to hire a private guide for ...	Queria um guia particular por ...	kerreeer oong gheeer perrtikkoolahr poor
half a day	meio-dia	mayoo deeer
a full day	um dia inteiro	oong deeer eengtayroo

Where is/are the ...?	Onde fica/ficam ...?	awngder feeker/feekahng^w
aquarium	o aquário	oo erkwahryoo
art gallery	a galeria de arte	er gerlerreeer der ahrter
artists' quarter	o bairro dos artistas	oo bighrroo doosh errteeshtersh
basilica	a basílica	er berzeelikker
botanical gardens	o jardim botânico	oo zherrdeeng booternikkoo
building	o edifício	oo iddiffeessyoo
bullring	a praça de touros	er prahsser der toaroosh
business district	o centro de negócios	oo sayngtroo der nergossyoosh
castle	o castelo	oo kershtehloo
cathedral	a sé/catedral	er seh/kerterdrahl
cemetery	o cemitério	oo sermittehryoo
city centre	o centro da cidade	oo sayngtroo der siddahder
chapel	a capela	er kerpehler
church	a igreja	er iggrayzher
concert hall	a sala de concertos	er sahler der kawngsayrtoosh
convent	o convento	oo kawngvayngtoo
court house	o palácio de justiça	oo perlahssyoo der zhooshteesser
downtown area	o centro da cidade	oo sayngtroo der siddahder
exhibition	a exposição	er ishpoozissahng^w
factory	a fábrica	er fahbrikker
fair	a feira	er fayrer
flea market	a feira da ladra	er fayrer der lahdrer
fortress	a fortaleza	er foorterlayzer
fountain	a fonte	er fawngter
gardens	o jardim	oo zherrdeeng
harbour	o porto	oo poartoo
library	a biblioteca	er bibblyootehker
market	o mercado	oo merrkahdoo
memorial	o monumento comemorativo	oo moonoomayngtoo koomermoorerteevoo
monastery	o mosteiro	oo mooshtayroo
monument	o monumento	oo moonoomayngtoo
museum	o museu	oo moozehoo
old town	a cidade velha	er siddahder vehlyer
opera house	o teatro da ópera	oo tyahtroo der opperrer
palace	o palácio	oo perlahssyoo
park	o parque	oo pahrker
parliament building	a assembleia nacional	er erssayngblayer nerssyoonahl
planetarium	o planetário	oo plernertahryoo
ruins	as ruínas	ersh rweenersh

shopping area	a zona comercial	er zoaner koomerrsyahl
square	a praça	er prahsser
stadium	o estádio	oo ishtahdyoo
statue	a estátua	er ishtahtwer
stock exchange	a bolsa	er boalser
theatre	o teatro	oo tyahtroo
tomb	o túmulo	oo toomooloo
tower	a torre	er toarrer
town hall	a câmara municipal	er kermerrer moonissippahl
university	a universidade	er oonivverrsiddahder
zoo	o jardim zoológico	oo zherrdeeng zoolozhikkoo

Admission À entrada

Is ... open on Sundays?	... está aberto aos domingos?	ishtah erbehrtoo owsh doomeenggoosh
What are the opening hours?	Quais são as horas de abertura?	kwighsh sahngʷ ersh orrersh der erberrtoorer
When does it close?	A que horas fecha?	er ker orrersh faysher
How much is the entrance fee?	Quanto custa a entrada [o ingresso]?	kwahngtoo kooshter er ayngtrahder [oo eenggrehssoa]
Is there any reduction for ...?	Há desconto para ...?	ah dishkawngtoo perrer
children	crianças	kryahngssersh
the disabled	deficientes físicos	derfissyayngtish feezikkoosh
groups	grupos	groopoosh
pensioners	reformados [aposentados]	rerfoormahdoosh [ahpoozayngtahdoass]
students	estudantes	ishtoodahngtish
Have you a guide-book (in English)?	Tem um guia (em inglês)?	tahngʸ oong gheeer (ahngʸ eengglaysh)
Can I buy a catalogue?	Posso comprar um catálogo?	possoo kawngprahr oong kertahloogoo
Is it all right to take pictures?	É permitido tirar fotografias?	eh perrmitteedoo tirrahr footoogrerfeeersh

| ENTRADA LIVRE | ADMISSION FREE |
| É PROIBIDO TIRAR FOTOGRAFIAS | NO CAMERAS ALLOWED |

Who—What—When? *Quem—Que—Quando?*

What's that building?	**Que edifício é aquele?**	ker iddi**ffees**syoo eh er**kay**ler
Who was the ...?	**Quem foi ...?**	kahng^y foy
architect	**o arquitecto**	oo errkit**teh**too
artist	**o artista**	oo errt**ees**hter
painter	**o pintor**	oo peeng**toar**
sculptor	**o esculptor**	oo ishkool**toar**
Who built it?	**Quem o construiu?**	kahng^y oo kawngsht**rwee**oo
Who painted that picture?	**Quem pintou aquele quadro?**	kahng^y peeng**toa** er**kay**ler **kwah**droo
When did he live?	**Em que época viveu?**	ahng^y ker **eh**pooker vi**vveh**oo
When was it built?	**Quando foi construído?**	**kwahng**doo foy kawngsht**rwee**doo
Where's the house where ... lived?	**Onde fica a casa onde viveu ...?**	**awng**der **fee**ker er **kah**zer **awng**der vi**vveh**oo
We're interested in ...	**Estamos interessa-dos em ...**	ish**ter**moosh eengterrer-**ssah**doosh ahng^y
antiques	**antiguidades**	ahngtigg**wid**dahdersh
archaeology	**arqueologia**	errkyooloo**zhee**er
art	**arte**	**ah**rter
botany	**botânica**	boo**ter**nikker
ceramics	**cerâmica**	serrer**mik**ker
coins	**numismática**	noomizh**mah**tikker
fine arts	**belas-artes**	**beh**lersh **ah**rtish
furniture	**mobiliário**	moobil**lyah**ryoo
geology	**geologia**	zhyooloo**zhee**er
handicrafts	**artesanato**	errterzer**nah**too
history	**história**	ish**tor**ryer
maritime history	**história marítima**	ish**tor**ryer merree**tim**mer
medicine	**medicina**	merdi**ssee**ner
music	**música**	**moo**zikker
natural history	**ciências naturais**	**syayng**syersh nertoo**righ**sh
ornithology	**ornitologia**	orrnittooloo**zhee**er
painting	**pintura**	peeng**too**rer
pottery	**olaria**	oller**reer**
religion	**religião**	rerlizh**yahng**^w
sculpture	**escultura**	ishkool**too**rer
zoology	**zoologia**	zoo-ooloo**zhee**er
Where's the ... department?	**Onde é a secção de ...?**	**awng**der eh er seh**ksahng**^w der

It's ...	É ...	eh
amazing	**espantoso**	ishpahng**toa**zoo
awful	**horroroso**	orroo**roa**zoo
beautiful	**lindo**	**leeng**doo
gloomy	**lúgubre**	**loo**goobrer
impressive	**impressionante**	eengprerssyoo**nahng**ter
interesting	**interessante**	eengterrer**ssahng**ter
magnificent	**magnífico**	merg**nee**fikkoo
pretty	**bonito**	boo**nee**too
strange	**estranho**	ish**trern**yoo
superb	**estupendo**	ishtoo**payng**doo
terrifying	**pavoroso**	pervoo**roa**zoo
tremendous	**tremendo**	trer**mayng**doo
ugly	**feio**	**fay**oo

Religious services *Serviços religiosos*

Portugal, predominantly Roman Catholic, is rich in cathe-drals and churches worth visiting. Fátima—probably the most famous pilgrimage centre in the Iberian peninsula—is about 130 km. north-east of Lisbon. Brazil is also largely Roman Catholic. Most places are open for the public to view except, of course, during mass. If you're interested in taking photographs, you should get permission first.

Is there a ... near here?	**Há ... aqui perto?**	ah ... erkee pehrtoo
Catholic church	**uma igreja católica**	oomer iggrayzher kertollikker
Protestant church	**uma igreja protestante**	oomer iggrayzher prootishtahngter
mosque	**uma mesquita**	oomer mishkeeter
synagogue	**uma sinagoga**	oomer sinnergogger
At what time is ...?	**A que horas é ...?**	er ker orrersh eh
mass/the service	**a missa/ o culto**	er meesser/oo kooltoo
Where can I find a ... who speaks English?	**Onde posso encon-trar um ... que fale inglês?**	awngder possoo ayngkawng-trahr oong ... ker fahler eengglaysh
priest/minister	**padre/pastor**	pahdrer/pershtoar
rabbi	**rabino**	rerbeenoo
I'd like to visit the church.	**Queria visitar a igreja.**	kerreeer vizzittahr er iggrayzher

In the countryside *No campo*

Is there a scenic route to ...?	**Há algum itinerário turístico para ...?**	ah ahlgoong ittinnerrah-ryoo tooreeshtikkoo perrer
How far is it to ...?	**A que distância fica ...?**	er ker dishtahngsyer feeker
Can we walk?	**Podemos ir a pé?**	poodaymoosh eer er peh
How high is that mountain?	**Qual é a altitude daquela montanha?**	kwahl eh er ahltittooder derkehler mawngternyer
What's the name of that ...?	**Qual é o nome ...?**	kwahl eh oo noamer
animal/bird	**daquele animal/ pássaro**	derkayler ernimmahl/ pahsserroo
flower/tree	**daquela flor/árvore**	derkehler floar/ahrvoorer

Landmarks *Pontos de referência*

bridge	**a ponte**	er pawngter
cliff	**a falésia**	er ferlehzyer
coast	**a costa**	er koshter
farm	**a quinta [fazenda]**	er keengter [fahzayngdah]
field	**o campo**	oo kahngpoo
footpath	**o caminho pedestre**	oo kermeenyoo perdehshtrer
forest	**a floresta**	er floorehshter
garden	**o jardim**	oo zherrdeeng
hill	**a colina**	er kooleener
house	**a casa**	er kahzer
lake	**o lago**	oo lahgoo
meadow	**o prado**	oo prahdoo
mountain range	**a serra**	er sehrrer
path	**o caminho**	oo kermeenyoo
peak	**o pico/cume**	oo peekoo/koomer
rain forest	**a selva**	er sehlver
river	**o rio**	oo reeoo
road	**a estrada**	er ishtrahder
sea	**o mar**	oo mahr
spring	**a nascente**	er nershsayngter
valley	**o vale**	oo vahler
village	**a aldeia**	er ahldayer
vineyard	**a vinha**	er veenyer
wall	**o muro**	oo mooroo
waterfall	**a cascada**	er kershkahder
windmill	**o moinho**	oo mweenyoo
wood	**a mata**	er mahter

ASKING THE WAY, see page 76

Relaxing

Cinema (movies) — Theatre   Cinema — Teatro

In Portugal, films are usually shown in the original language, with Portuguese subtitles. Separate performances are the rule, beginning about 3 p.m., with the last show at around 9.30 p.m. In Brazil showings are normally continuous, starting at 2 p.m.

In Portuguese theatres, there are matinées and two evening performances on Sundays. Revues are very popular.

You can find out what's playing from newspapers and billboards.

What's on at the cinema tonight?	O que dão no cinema hoje à noite?	oo ker dahng^w noo sinnaymer oazher ah noyter
What's playing at the ... theatre?	O que está em cena no teatro ...?	oo ker ishtah ahng^y sayner noo tyahtroo
What sort of play is it?	Que género de peça é?	ker zhehnerroo der pehsser eh
Who's it by?	Quem é o autor?	kahng^y eh oo owtoar
Can you recommend (a) ...?	Pode recomendar--me ...?	podder rerkoomayngdahr mer
good film	um bom filme	oong bawng feelmer
comedy	uma comédia	oomer koomehdyer
musical	uma comédia musical	oomer koomehdyer moozikkahl
revue	uma revista	oomer rerveeshter
Where's that film directed by ... being shown?	Em que cinema está sendo exibido o filme de ...?	ahng^y ker sinnaymer ishtah sayngdoo izzibbeedoo oo feelmer der
Who's in it?	Quem são os actores?	kahng^y sahng^w oosh ahtoarersh
Who's playing the lead?	Quem desempenha o papel principal?	kahng^y derzayngpaynyer oo perpehl preengsippahl
Who's the director?	Quem é o realizador?	kahng^y eh oo ryerlizzerdoar
At which theatre is that play by ... being performed?	Em que teatro está sendo representada a peça de ...?	ahng^y ker tyahtroo ishtah sayngdoo rerprerzayngtahder er pehsser der

Is there a sound-and-light show on somewhere?	Há algum espectáculo de luzes e som em qualquer lado?	ah ahlgoong ishpehtahkooloo der loozersh ee sawng ahng^Y kwahlkehr lahdoo
What time does it begin/finish?	A que horas começa/acaba?	er ker orrersh koomehsser/erkahber
Are there any seats for tonight?	Há ainda bilhetes para hoje à noite?	ah ereengder billyaytish perrer oazher ah noyter
How much are the seats?	Qual é o preço dos lugares?	kwahl eh oo prayssoo doosh loogahrersh
I'd like to reserve 2 seats for the show on Friday evening.	Quero reservar 2 lugares para o espectáculo de sexta-feira à noite.	kehroo rerzerrvahr 2 loogahrersh perrer oo ishpehtahkooloo der sayshter fayrer ah noyter
Can I have a ticket for the matinée on Tuesday?	Pode dar-me um bilhete para a matinée de terça--feira?	podder dahr mer oong billyayter perrer er mahtinneh der tayrser fayrer
I'd like a seat in the stalls (orchestra).	Quero um lugar na plateia.	kehroo oong loogahr ner plertayer
Not too far back.	Não muito atrás.	nahng^w moong^Ytoo ertrahsh
Somewhere in the middle.	Mais ou menos ao meio.	mighsh oa maynoosh ow mayoo
How much are the seats in the circle (mezzanine)?	Qual é o preço dos lugares no balcão?	kwahl eh oo prayssoo doosh loogahrersh noo bahlkahng^w
May I have a programme, please?	Pode dar-me um programa?	podder dahr mer oong proogrermer
Where's the cloakroom?	Onde é o vestiário?	awngder eh oo vishtyahryoo

👉	👈
Lamento, mas a lotação está esgotada.	I'm sorry, we're sold out.
Restam apenas alguns lugares no balcão.	There are only a few seats left in the circle (mezzanine).
Pode mostrar-me o bilhete?	May I see your ticket?
Este é o seu lugar.	This is your seat.

DAYS OF THE WEEK, see page 151

Opera—Ballet—Concert   *Ópera—Ballet—Concerto*

Can you recommend a/an ...?	**Pode recomendar--me ...?**	podder rerkoomayng**dahr** mer
ballet	**um ballet**	oong **bahleh**
concert	**um concerto**	oong kawng**sayr**too
opera	**uma ópera**	oomer **opperrer**
operetta	**uma opereta**	oomer **opperrayter**
Where's the opera house/the concert hall?	**Onde fica o teatro da ópera/a sala de concertos?**	**awng**der feeker oo **tyah**troo der **opperrer**/er **sahler** der kawng**sayr**toosh
What's on at the opera tonight?	**O que está em cena na ópera hoje à noite?**	oo ker ishtah ahng^y **sayner** ner **opperrer oazher** ah **noyter**
Who's singing/dancing?	**Quem canta/dança?**	kahng^y **kahng**ter/**dahng**ser
Which orchestra is playing?	**Qual é a orquestra?**	kwahl eh er orr**kehsh**trer
What are they playing?	**O que vão tocar?**	oo ker vahng^w too**kahr**
Who's the conductor/soloist?	**Quem é o chefe [regente] de orquestra/o solista?**	kahng^y eh oo **shehfer** [**rayzhayng**ti] der orr**kehsh**trer/oo soo**leesh**ter

Fado—Nightclubs—Discos   *Fado—Boîtes—Discotecas*

In Portugal, you will find the usual range of nightclubs and discotheques along the coast and in large towns. You can have a night out in a casino, or visit a *casa de fados,* an intimate, late-night restaurant where your meal is accompanied by the haunting melodies of the *fado,* the national folk song. Gambling is illegal in Brazil, but having fun isn't. There are many nightclubs, particularly in Rio de Janeiro.

Can you recommend a good nightclub?	**Pode recomendar-me uma boa boîte/casa de fados?**	podder rerkoomayng**dahr** mer oomer **boaer bwahter**/**kah**zer der **fah**doosh
Is there a floor show?	**Há variedades?**	ah verryer**dah**dish
Is evening dress required?	**É preciso traje de noite?**	eh prer**ssee**zoo **trah**zher der **noy**ter

Where can we go dancing?	Onde podemos ir dançar?	awngder poodaymoosh eer dahngsahr
Is there a disco-theque in town?	Há alguma discoteca na cidade?	ah ahlgoomer dishkoo-tehker ner siddahder
Would you like to dance?	Quer dançar?	kehr dahngsahr
I'd like to see some folk dancing.	Gostava de ver danças folclóricas.	gooshtahver der vayr dahngsersh follklorrikkersh
Where's the casino?	Onde é o casino?	awngder eh oo kerzeenoo

Bullfight *A tourada*

The Portuguese version of the bullfight *(corrida à Portuguesa* or *tourada)* is quite different from the Spanish *corrida*. In Spain, the fashion has always been to fight the bull on foot whereas in Portugal the characteristic style is on horseback, and killing the bull is actually forbidden.

The best (and most expensive) seats are located in the shade *(sombra)* and in the front rows *(barreira)*. Next come the *sol e sombra* (sun and shade) seats.

Bullfighting takes place—from Easter to October—almost every Sunday afternoon in many places.

| I'd like to see a bullfight. | Queria ver uma tourada. | kerreeer vayr oomer toarahder |
| I want a seat in the shade/in the sun. | Queria um lugar à sombra/ao sol. | kerreeer oong loogahr ah sawngbrer/ow sol |

Sports *Desportos [esportes]*

The Portuguese and Brazilians are great football (soccer) fans. Portugal is well known for its splendid golf courses.

| Is there a football (soccer) match any-where this Saturday? | Há algum jogo de futebol no sábado? | ah ahlgoong zhoagoo der footerboll no sahberdoo |
| Which teams are playing? | Quais são as equipas que jogam? | kwighsh sahng^w ersh ikkeepersh ker zhoggahng^w |

Can you get me a ticket?	Pode arranjar-me [arrumar-me] um bilhete?	podder errahngzhahr mer [ahrroomahr mi] oong billyayter

basketball	o basquetebol	oo bahshkehtboll
boxing	o boxe	oo boks
car racing	as corridas de automóveis	ersh koorreedersh der owtoomovvaysh
cycling	o ciclismo	oo sikkleezhmoo
football (soccer)	o futebol	oo footerboll
(horseback) riding	a equitação	er ikkitterssahng[w]
horse racing	as corridas de cavalos	ersh koorreedersh der kervahloosh
swimming	a natação	er nerterssahng[w]
tennis	o ténis	oo tehnish
volleyball	o voleibol	oo vollayboll

I'd like to see a boxing match.	Gostava de ver um combate de boxe.	gooshtahver der vayr oong kawngbahter der boks
What's the admission charge?	Quanto custa a entrada [o ingresso]?	kwahngtoo kooshter er ayngtrahder [oa eenggrehssoa]
Where's the nearest golf course?	Onde é o campo de golfe mais próximo?	awngder eh oo kahngpoo der goalfer mighsh prossimmoo
Where are the tennis courts?	Onde são os campos de ténis?	awngder sahng[w] oosh kahngpoosh der tehnish
What's the charge per ...?	Qual é o preço por ...?	kwahl eh oo prayssoo poor
day/round/hour	dia/jogo/hora	deeer/zhoagoo/orrer
Can I hire (rent) golf clubs/rackets?	Posso alugar clubes de golfe/raquetes?	possoo erloogahr kloobersh der goalfer/rahkehtish
Where's the race course (track)?	Onde é o hipódromo?	awngder eh oo ippoddroomoo
Is there any good fishing/hunting around here?	Há algum bom lugar para pescar/caçar aqui perto?	ah ahlgoong bawng loogahr perrer pishkahr/kerssahr erkee pehrtoo
Do I need a permit?	É preciso licença?	eh prersseezoo lissayngser
Where can I get one?	Onde posso arranjar [arrumar] uma?	awngder possoo errahngzhahr [ahrroomahr] oomer
Is there a swimming pool here?	Há aqui uma piscina?	ah erkee oomer pishseener

Is it open-air or indoor?	É ao ar livre ou coberta?	eh ow ahr **leev**rer oa koo**behr**ter
Is it heated?	É aquecida?	eh erkehs**seed**er
What's the temperature of the water?	Qual é a temperatura da água?	kwahl eh er tayngperrer**toor**er der **ahg**wer

On the beach   *Na praia*

Is it safe for swimming?	Pode-se nadar sem perigo?	**podd**er ser ner**dahr** sahng^y perree**goo**
Is there a lifeguard?	Há um banheiro [salva-vidas]?	ah oong bern**yay**roo [**sahl**vah **veed**ahss]
Is it safe for children?	Não há perigo para as crianças?	nahng^w ah perree**goo** perrer ersh kryahng**sersh**
The sea is calm.	O mar é calmo.	oo mahr eh **kahl**moo
There are some big waves.	Há ondas grandes.	ah **awng**dersh **grahng**dish
Are there any dangerous currents?	Há correntes perigosas?	ah koor**rayng**tish perrig**gozz**ersh
What time is high tide/low tide?	A que horas é a maré alta/maré baixa?	er ker **orr**ersh eh er **mer**reh **ahl**ter/**merr**eh **bighsh**er
I want to hire a/an/some ...	Quero alugar ...	**kehr**oo erloo**gahr**
bathing hut (cabana)	uma barraca	**oom**er ber**rahk**er
deck chair	uma cadeira de encosto	**oom**er ker**dayr**er der ayng**koash**too
motorboat	um barco a motor	oong **bahr**koo er **moo**toar
rowing boat	um barco a remos	oong **bahr**koo er **reh**moosh
sailing boat	um barco à vela	oong **bahr**koo ah **veh**ler
skin-diving equipment	um equipamento para pesca submarina	oong ikkipper**mayng**too perrer **pehsh**ker soob**merr**ee**ner**
sunshade (umbrella)	um chapéu de sol	oong sher**peh**oo der soll
surfboard	uma prancha de surf	**oom**er **prahng**sher der serrf
waterskis	uns esquis aquáticos	oongsh ish**keesh** erk**wah**tik**koosh**
windsurfer	uma prancha à vela	**oom**er **prahng**sher ah **veh**ler

| PRAIA PRIVADA | PRIVATE BEACH |
| É PROIBIDO TOMAR BANHO | NO SWIMMING |

Making friends

Introductions *Apresentações*

May I introduce ...?	**Posso apresentar--lhe ...?**	possoo erprerzayngtahr lyer
John, this is ...	**João, apresento--lhe ...**	zhwahng[w] erprerzayngtoo lyer
My name is ...	**Chamo-me ...**	shermoo mer
Pleased to meet you.	**Muito prazer em conhecê-lo(la).**	moong[y]too prerzayr ahng[y] koonyerssay loo(ler)
What's your name?	**Como se chama?**	koamoo ser shermer
How are you?	**Como está?**	koamoo ishtah
Fine, thanks. And you?	**Bem, obrigado(a). E o Senhor (a Senhora)?**	bahng[y] oabriggahdoo(er). ee oo sinnyoar (er sinnyoarer)

Follow up *Para quebrar o silêncio*

How long have you been here?	**Há quanto tempo está aqui?**	ah kwahngtoo tayngpoo ishtah erkee
We've been here a week.	**Estamos aqui há uma semana.**	ishtermoosh erkee ah oomer sermerner
Are you enjoying your stay?	**Gosta de estar cá?**	goshter der ishtahr kah
Yes, I like it very much.	**Sim, gosto muito.**	seeng goshtoo moong[y]too
I like the land-scape/region a lot.	**Gosto muito da paisagem/região.**	goshtoo moong[y]too der pighzahzhahng[y]/rerzhyahng[w]
What do you think of the country/people?	**O que é que acha do país/das pessoas?**	oo ker eh ker ahsher doo pereesh/dersh perssoaersh
Where do you come from?	**Donde é?**	dawngder eh
I'm from ...	**Sou de ...**	soa der
What nationality are you?	**De que nacionalidade é?**	der ker nerssyoonerliddahder eh

COUNTRIES, see page 146

I'm ...	Sou ...	soa
American	americano	ermerrikkernoo
British	británico	britternikkoo
Canadian	canadiano	kernerdyernoo
English	inglês	eengglaysh
Irish	irlandês	irrlahngdaysh

Are you on your own?	Está sozinho(a)?	ishtah sawzeenyoo(er)

I'm with my ...	Estou com ...	ishtoa kawng
wife	a minha mulher	er meenyer moolyehr
husband	o meu marido	oo mehoo merreedoo
family	a minha família	er meenyer fermeelyer
children	os meus filhos	oosh mehoosh feelyoosh
parents	os meus pais	oosh mehoosh pighsh
boyfriend/girlfriend	o meu namorado/a	oo mehoo nermoorahdoo/er
	minha namorada	meenyer nermoorahder

grandfather/	o avô/	oo ervoa/
grandmother	a avó	er ervaw
father/mother	o pai/a mãe	oo pigh/er mahng^y
son/daughter	o filho/a filha	oo feelyoo/er feelyer
brother/sister	o irmão/a irmã	oo irrmahng^w/er irrmahng
uncle/aunt	o tio/a tia	oo teeoo/er teeer
nephew/niece	o sobrinho/	oo soobreenyoo/
	a sobrinha	er soobreenyer
cousin	o primo/ a prima	oo preemoo/er preemer

Are you married/ single?	É casado(a)/ solteiro(a)?	eh kerzahdoo(er)/ solltayroo(er)
Do you have children?	Tem filhos?	tahng^y feelyoosh
What do you do?	Qual é a sua profissão?	kwahl eh er sooer proofissahng^w
I'm a student.	Sou estudante.	soa ishtoodahngter
What are you studying?	O que é que está a estudar?	oo ker eh ker ishtah er ishtoodahr
I'm here on a business trip.	Estou aqui em viagem de negócios.	ishtoa erkee ahng^y vyah-zhahng^y der nergossyoosh
Do you travel a lot?	Viaja muito?	vyahzher moong^{y}too
Do you play chess/ cards?	Joga xadrez/às cartas?	zhogger sherdraysh/ahsh kahrtersh

The weather *O tempo*

What a lovely day!	**Que lindo dia!**	ker leengdoo deeer
What awful weather!	**Que tempo horrível!**	ker tayngpoo orreevehl
Isn't it cold/ hot today?	**Que frio/calor está hoje!**	ker freeoo/kerloar ishtah oazher
Is it usually as warm as this?	**Está sempre assim tanto calor?**	ishtah sayngprer ersseeng tahngtoo kerloar
Do you think it's going to ...?	**Acha que vai ...?**	ahsher ker vigh
be a nice day rain	**estar bom tempo chover**	ishtahr bawng tayngpoo shoovayr
What is the weather forecast?	**Quais são as previsões do tempo?**	kwighsh sahngʷ ersh prer-vizzawngʸsh doo tayngpoo

cloud	**a nuvem**	er noovahngʸ
fog	**o nevoeiro**	oo nervwayroo
ice	**o gelo**	oo zhayloo
lightning	**o relâmpago**	oo rerlahngpergoo
moon	**a lua**	er looer
rain	**a chuva**	er shoover
sky	**o céu**	oo sehoo
star	**a estrela**	er ishtrayler
sun	**o sol**	oo soll
thunder	**o trovão**	oo troovahngʷ
thunderstorm	**a trovoada**	er troovwahder
wind	**o vento**	oo vayngtoo

Invitations *Convites*

Would you like to have dinner with us on ...?	**Quer jantar connosco ...?**	kehr zhahngtahr koanoashkoo
May I invite you for lunch?	**Posso convidá-lo(la) para almoçar?**	possoo kawngviddah loo (ler) perrer ahlmoossahr
Can you come round for a drink this evening?	**Pode cá vir hoje à noite tomar uma bebida?**	podder kah veer oazher ah noyter toomahr oomer berbeeder
There's a party. Are you coming?	**Há uma festa. Quer vir?**	ah oomer fehshter. kehr veer

DAYS OF THE WEEK, see page 151

That's very kind of you.	É muito amável da sua parte.	eh moong^ytoo ermahvehl der sooer pahrter
Great. I'd love to come.	Óptimo. Virei com muito prazer.	ottimmoo. virray kawng moong^ytoo prerzayr
What time shall we come?	A que horas vimos?	er ker orrersh veemoosh
May I bring a friend/ a girlfriend?	Posso trazer um amigo/uma amiga?	possoo trerzayr oong ermeegoo/oomer ermeeger
I'm afraid we've got to leave now.	Lamento, mas temos de nos ir já embora.	lermayngtoo mersh tay-moosh der noosh eer zhah ayngborrer
Next time you must come to visit us.	Para a próxima vez, são vocês que vêm ver-nos.	perrer er prossimmer vaysh sahng^w vossaysh ker vahng^yahng^y vayr noosh
Thanks for the evening. It was great.	Obrigado(a) pela festa. Foi óptima.	oabriggahdoo(er) payler fehshter. foy ottimmer

Dating *Encontros*

Do you mind if I smoke?	Importa-se que eu fume?	eengporrter ser ker ehoo foomer
Would you like a cigarette?	Quer um cigarro?	kehr oong siggahrroo
Do you have a light, please?	Tem lume, por favor?	tahng^y loomer poor fervoar
Why are you laughing?	Porque está a rir?	poorker ishtah er reér
Is my pronunciation that bad?	A minha pronúncia é assim tão má?	er meenyer proonoongsyer eh ersseeng tahng^w mah
Do you mind if I sit here?	Importa-se que eu me sente aqui?	eengporrter ser ker ehoo mer sayngter erkee
Can I get you a drink?	Posso oferecer-lhe uma bebida?	possoo offerrerssayr lyer oomer berbeeder
Are you waiting for someone?	Está à espera de alguém?	ishtah ah ishpehrer der ahlgahng^y
Are you free this evening?	Está livre hoje à noite?	ishtah leevrer oazher ah noyter
Would you like to go out with me tonight?	Quer sair comigo hoje à noite?	kehr sereer koomeegoo oazher ah noyter

Would you like to go dancing?	Quer ir dançar?	kehr eer dahng**sahr**
I know a good discotheque.	Conheço uma boa discoteca.	koonyayssoo oomer boaer dishkootehker
Shall we go to the cinema (movies)?	Vamos ao cinema?	vermoosh ow sinnaymer
Would you like to go for a drive?	Quer ir dar um passeio de carro?	kehr eer dahr oong perssayoo der **kahr**rroo
Where shall we meet?	Onde nos encontramos?	awngder noosh ayngkawngtrermoosh
I'll pick you up at your hotel.	Vou buscá-la ao seu hotel.	voa booshkah ler ow sehoo ottehl
Where are you staying?	Onde está hospedado?	awngder ishtah oshperdahdoo
I'll call for you at 8.	Vou buscá-la às 8.	voa booshkah ler ash 8
May I take you home?	Posso acompanhá-la a casa?	possoo erkawngpernyah ler er kahzer
Can I see you again tomorrow?	Posso voltar a vê-la amanhã?	possoo volltahr er vay ler ahmernyahng
I hope we'll meet again.	Espero que nos voltemos a ver.	ishpehroo ker noosh volltaymoosh er vayr

... and you might answer:

I'd love to, thank you.	Com muito prazer, obrigado(a).	kawng **moong**ʸtoo prerzayr oabriggahdoo(er)
Thank you, but I'm busy.	Obrigado(a), mas tenho que fazer.	oabriggahdoo(er) mersh taynyoo ker ferzayr
No, I'm not interested, thank you.	Obrigado(a), mas não estou interessada.	oabriggahdoo(er) mersh nahngʷ ishtoa eengterressahder
Leave me alone, please!	Deixe-me em paz, se faz favor!	daysher mer ahngʸ pash ser fash fervoar
Thank you, it's been a wonderful evening.	Obrigado(a), passei uma noite maravilhosa.	oabriggahdoo(er) perssay oomer noyter merrervillyozzer
I've enjoyed myself.	Diverti-me muito.	divverrtee mer **moong**ʸtoo

Shopping Guide

This shopping guide is designed to help you find what you want with ease, accuracy and speed. It features:

1. A list of all major shops, stores and services (p. 98).

2. Some general expressions required when shopping to allow you to be specific and selective (p. 100).

3. Full details of the shops and services most likely to concern you. Here you'll find advice, alphabetical lists of items, and conversion charts listed under the headings below.

		page
Bookshop/ Stationer's	books, magazines, newspapers, stationery	104
Camping equipment	all items required for camping	106
Chemist's (drugstore)	medicine, first-aid, cosmetics, toilet articles	108
Clothing	clothes and accessories, shoes	112
Electrical appliances	radios, cassette-recorders, shavers	119
Grocery	some general expressions, weights, measures and packaging	120
Jeweller's/ Watchmaker's	jewellery, watches, watch repairs	121
Optician	glasses, lenses, binoculars	123
Photography	cameras, films, developing, accessories	124
Tobacconist's	smoker's supplies	126
Miscellaneous	souvenirs, records, cassettes, toys	127

LAUNDRY, see page 29/HAIRDRESSER'S, see page 30

Shops, stores and services *Lojas e serviços*

Most shops are open from about 9 a.m. to 7 p.m., with a lunch break from 1 to 3 p.m. Very few remain open on Saturday afternoon. Brazilian stores are open from 8 a.m. to 9 p.m. and close at noon on Saturdays.

Where's the nearest ...?	Onde é ... mais próximo(a)?	awngder eh ... mighsh prossimmoo(er)
antique shop	o antiquário	oo ahngtikkwahryoo
art gallery	a galeria de arte	er gerlerreeer der ahrter
baker's	a padaria	er pahderreeer
bank	o banco	oo bahngkoo
barber's	o barbeiro	oo berrbayroo
beauty salon	o instituto de beleza	oo eengshtittootoo der berlayzer
bookshop	a livraria	er livvrerreeer
butcher's	o talho [açougue]	oo tahlyoo [ahssoaghi]
cake shop	a pastelaria	er pershterlerreeer
camera shop	a loja de artigos fotográficos	er lozher der errteegoosh footoograhfikkoosh
chemist's	a farmácia	er ferrmahssyer
dairy	a leitaria	er layterreeer
delicatessen	a salsicharia	er sahlsisherreeer
dentist	o dentista	oo dayngteeshter
department store	o grande armazém	oo grahngder ahrmerzahng^y
drugstore	a farmácia	er ferrmahssyer
dry cleaner's	a lavandaria a seco	er lervahngderreeer er saykoo
electrician	o electricista	oo illehtrisseeshter
fishmonger's	a peixaria	er paysherreeer
florist's	a florista	er flooreeshter
furrier's	a casa de peles	er kahzer der pehlersh
greengrocer's	o lugar de frutas e legumes [a quitanda]	oo loogahr der frootersh ee lergoomersh [ah kittahngdah]
grocery	a mercearia	er merrsyerreeer
hairdresser's (ladies/men)	o cabeleireiro (para senhoras/homens)	oo kerberlayrayroo (perrer sinnyoarersh/ommahng^ysh
hardware store	a loja de ferrajens	er lozher der ferrah-zhahng^ysh
health food shop	a loja de produtos dietéticos	er lozher der proodoo-toosh dyaytehtikkoosh
hospital	o hospital	oo oshpittahl
ironmonger's	a loja de ferragens	er lozher der ferrah-zhahng^ysh

jeweller's	a ourivesaria	er oarivverzerreeer
launderette	a lavandaria automática	er lervahngderreeer owtoomahtikker
laundry	a lavandaria	er lervahngderreeer
library	a biblioteca	er bibblyootehker
market	o mercado	oo merrkahdoo
newsstand	o quiosque [a banca] de jornais	oo kyoshker [ah bahngkah] der zhoornighsh
optician	o oculista	oo okkooleeshter
pastry shop	a pastelaria	er pershterlerreeer
photographer	o fotógrafo	oo footoggrerfoo
police station	o posto da polícia	oo poashtoo der pooleessyer
post office	a estação de correios	er ishterssahng^w der koorrayoosh
second-hand shop	a loja de velharias	er lozher der vehlyerreeersh
shoemaker's (repairs)	o sapateiro	oo serpertayroo
shoe shop	a sapataria	er serperterreeer
shopping centre	o centro comercial	oo sayngtroo koomerrsyahl
souvenir shop	a loja de lembranças	er lozher der layngbrahngsersh
sporting goods shop	a loja de artigos desportivos [esportivos]	er lozher der errteegoosh dishpoorteevoosh [aysporrteevoass]
stationer's	a papelaria	er perperlerreeer
supermarket	o supermercado	oo soopehrmerrkahdoo
telegraph office	estação telegráfica	ishterssahng^w terlergrahfikker
tobacconist's	a tabacaria	er terberkerreeer
toy shop	a loja de brinquedos	er lozher der breengkaydoosh
travel agency	a agência de viagens	er erzhayngsyer der vyahzhahng^{y}sh
vegetable store	o lugar de frutas e e legumes [a quitanda]	oo loogahr der frootersh ee lergoomersh [ah kittahngdah]
veterinarian	o veterinário	oo verterrinnahryoo
watchmaker's	a relojoaria	er rerloozhwerreeer
wine merchant's	o comerciante de vinhos	oo koomerrsyahngter der veenyoosh

ENTRADA	ENTRANCE
SAÍDA	EXIT
SAÍDA DE EMERGÊNCIA	EMERGENCY EXIT

General expressions *Expressões gerais*

Where? *Onde?*

Where's there a good ...?	Onde há um bom/ uma boa ...?	awngder ah oong bawng/ oomer boaer
Where can I find a ...?	Onde posso encontrar um/uma ...?	awngder possoo ayng-kawngtrahr oong/oomer
Where's the main shopping area?	Onde é a zona comercial?	awngder eh er zoaner koomerrsyahl
Is it far from here?	É longe daqui?	eh lawngzher derkee
How do I get there?	Como posso ir até lá?	koamoo possoo eer erteh lah

SALDOS **SALE**

Service *Serviços*

Can you help me?	Pode ajudar-me?	podder erzhoodahr mer
I'm just looking.	Estou só a ver.	ishtoa saw er vayr
Do you sell ...?	Vende ...?	vayngder
I want to buy ...	Quero comprar ...	kehroo kawngprahr
Can you show me some ...?	Pode mostrar-me ...?	podder mooshtrahr mer
Do you have any ...?	Tem ...?	tahng^v
Where's the ... department?	Onde é a secção ...?	awngder eh er sehksahng^w
Where is the lift (elevator)/escalator?	Onde é o elevador/ a escada rolante?	awngder eh oo illerverdoar/ er ishkahder roolahngter

That one *Aquele*

Can you show me ...?	Pode mostrar-me ...?	podder mooshtrahr mer
this/that	isto/aquilo	eeshtoo/erkeeloo
the one in the window/in the display case	o que está na vitrina/na banca	oo ker ishtah ner vittreener/ ner bahngker

Defining the article   *Descrição do artigo*

I'd like a ... one.	Quero um ...	kehroo oong
big	grande	grahngder
cheap	barato	berrahtoo
dark	escuro	ishkooroo
good	bom	bawng
heavy	pesado	perzahdoo
large	grande	grahngder
light (weight)	leve	lehver
light (colour)	claro	klahroo
oval	oval	ovvahl
rectangular	rectangular	rehtahnggoolahr
round	redondo	rerdawngdoo
small	pequeno	perkaynoo
square	quadrado	kwerdrahdoo
sturdy	resistente	rerzishtayngter

Preference   *Preferências*

Can you show me some more?	Pode mostrar-me mais alguns?	podder mooshtrahr mer mighsh ahlgoongsh
Haven't you anything ...?	Não tem nada ...?	nahng^w tahng^y nahder
cheaper/better	mais barato/melhor	mighsh berrahtoo/millyor
larger/smaller [menor]	maior/mais pequeno [menor]	mayor/mighsh perkaynoo [mehnor]

How much?   *Quanto custa?*

How much is this?	Quanto custa isto?	kwahngtoo kooshter eeshtoo
How much are they?	Quanto custam?	kwahngtoo kooshtahng^w
I don't understand.	Não compreendo.	nahng^w kawngpryayngdoo
Please write it down.	Pode escrever num papel?	podder ishkrervayr noong perpehl
I don't want anything too expensive.	Não quero nada muito caro.	nahng^w kehroo nahder moong^y too kahroo
I don't want to spend more than ... escudos/cruzados.	Não quero gastar mais que ... escudos/ cruzados.	nahng^w kehroo gershtahr mighsh ker ... ishkoodoosh/ kroozahdoass

COLOURS, see page 113

Decision *Decisão*

| It's not quite what I want. | Não é bem o que quero. | nahng^w eh bahng^w oo ker kehroo |

It's not quite what I want. — Não é bem o que quero. — nahng^w eh bahng^w oo ker kehroo

No, I don't like it. — Não, não gosto. — nahng^w nahng^w goshtoo

I'll take it. — Fico com ele. — feekoo kawng ayler

Ordering *Encomenda*

Can you order it for me? — Pode encomendar--mo? — podder ayngkoomayngdahr moo

How long will it take? — Quanto tempo demora? — kwahngtoo tayngpoo dermorrer

Delivery *Entrega*

I'll take it with me. — Levo-o já. — lehvoo oo zhah

Deliver it to the ... Hotel. — Mande entregá-lo no Hotel ... — mahngder ayngtrergah loo noo ottehl

Please send it to this address. — Mande-o para este endereço, por favor. — mahngder oo perrer ayshter ayngderrayssoo poor fervoar

Will I have any difficulty with the customs? — Terei dificuldades na alfândega? — terray diffikkooldah-dersh ner ahlfahngderger

Paying *Pagamento*

How much is it? — Quanto é? — kwahngtoo eh

Can I pay by traveller's cheque? — Posso pagar com cheques de viagem? — possoo pergahr kawng shehkersh der vyahzhahng^y

Do you accept dollars/pounds? — Aceitam dólares/libras? — erssaytahng^w dollerrsh/leebrersh

Do you accept credit cards? — Aceitam cartões de crédito? — erssaytahng^w kerrtawng^ysh der krehdittoo

Do I have to pay the VAT (sales tax)? — Tenho de pagar o IVA? — taynyoo der pergahr oo eever

Isn't there a mistake in the bill? — Não se enganou na conta? — nahng^w ser aynggernoa ner kawngter

Anything else? *Mais alguma coisa?*

No, thanks, that's all.	**Não, obrigado(a)*, é tudo.**	nahng^w oabrig**gah**doo/er eh **too**doo
Yes, I'd like ...	**Sim, quero ...**	seeng **keh**roo
Show me ...	**Mostre-me ...**	**mosh**trer mer
May I have a bag, please?	**Pode dar-me um saco, por favor?**	**pod**der dahr mer oong **sah**koo poor fer**voar**
Could you wrap it up for me, please?	**Pode embrulhar, se faz favor?**	**pod**der ayngbroo**lyahr** ser fahsh fer**voar**

Dissatisfied? *Insatisfeito?*

Can you exchange this, please?	**Pode trocar isto?**	**pod**der troo**kahr eesh**too
I want to return this.	**Quero devolver isto.**	**keh**roo dervoll**vayr eesh**too
I'd like a refund. Here's the receipt.	**Quero que me reembolsem. Aqui está o recibo.**	**keh**roo ker mer ryayng-**boal**sahng^y. er**kee** ish**tah** oo rer**ssee**boo

---

Em que posso servi-lo(la)?	Can I help you?
O que deseja?	What would you like?
Que ... deseja?	What ... would you like?
cor/forma **qualidade/quantidade**	colour/shape quality/quantity
Lamento, mas não temos.	I'm sorry, we haven't any.
Esse artigo está esgotado.	We're out of stock.
Deseja que o encomendemos?	Shall we order it for you?
Quer levá-lo já ou deseja que lho enviemos?	Will you take it with you or shall we send it?
Mais alguma coisa?	Anything else?
São ... escudos/cruzados.	That's ... escudos/cruzados.
A caixa é ali.	The cash desk is over there.

---

* A woman would say **obrigada**.

Bookshop—Stationer's *Livraria—Papelaria*

In Portugal and Brazil, bookshops and stationer's are usually separate, though the latter will often sell paperbacks. Newspapers and magazines are sold at newsstands.

Where's the nearest ...?	**Onde é ... mais próximo(a)?**	awngder eh ... mighsh prossimmoo(er)
bookshop	**a livraria**	er livvrerreeer
stationer's	**a papelaria**	er perperlerreeer
newsstand	**o quiosque [a banca] de jornais**	oo kyoshker [ah bahngkah] der zhoornighsh
Where can I buy an English-language newspaper?	**Onde posso comprar um jornal em inglês?**	awngder possoo kawngprahr oong zhoornahl ahng^y eengglaysh
Where do you keep the English books?	**Onde estão os livros em inglês?**	awngder ishtahng^w oosh leevroosh ahng^y eengglaysh
Do you have second-hand books?	**Tem livros em segunda mão?**	tahng^y leevroosh ahng^y sergoongder mahng^w
I want to buy a/an/some ...	**Quero comprar ...**	kehroo kawngprahr
address book	**um livrinho de endereços**	oong livvreenyoo der ayngderrayssoosh
ball-point pen	**uma esferográfica**	oomer ishfehroggrahfikker
book	**um livro**	oong leevroo
calendar	**um calendário**	oong kerlayngdahryoo
cellophane tape	**fita adesiva**	feeter erderzeever
crayons	**lápis de cor**	lahpish der koar
dictionary	**um dicionário**	oong dissyoonahryoo
Portuguese-English pocket	**português-inglês de bolso**	poortoogaysh eengglaysh der boalsoo
drawing paper	**papel de desenho**	perpehl der derzaynyoo
drawing pins	**pioneses [tachas]**	pyoonehzersh [tahshahss]
envelopes	**uns envelopes**	oongsh ayngverloppish
eraser	**uma borracha**	oomer boorrahsher
exercise book	**um caderno**	oong kerdehrnoo
felt-tip pen	**uma caneta feltro**	oomer kernayter fayltroo
fountain pen	**uma caneta de tinta permanente***	oomer kernayter der teengter perrmernayngter
glue	**cola**	koller
grammar book	**uma gramática**	oomer grermahtikker

---

* In Brazil: **uma caneta-tinteiro** (oomah kahnaytah teengtayroa)

guidebook	um guia turístico	oong **gheer** too**reesht**tikkoo
ink	tinta	teengter
red/blue	vermelha/azul	verr**may**lyer/er**zool**
(adhesive) labels	etiquetas	it**tikk**aytersh
	(autocolantes)	(owtokkoo**lahng**tish)
magazine	uma revista	oomer rer**veesh**ter
map	um mapa	oong **mahp**er
map of the town	uma planta da	oomer **plahng**ter der
	cidade	sid**dah**der
road map of ...	um mapa das	oong **mahp**er dersh
	estradas de ...	ish**trah**dersh der
mechanical pencil	uma lapiseira	oomer ler**pizz**ayrer
newspaper	um jornal	oong **zhoor**nahl er**mer**ri-
American/English	americano/inglês	**kker**noo/eeng**glaysh**
notebook	um bloco de	oong **blokk**oo der
	apontamentos	erpawng**termayng**toosh
note paper	papel de carta	per**pehl** der **kahr**ter
paintbox	uma caixa de tintas	oomer **kighsh**er der
		teengtersh
paper	papel	per**pehl**
paperback	um livro de bolso	oong **leev**roo der **boal**soo
paperclips	clipes	**klee**pish
paper napkins	guardanapos de	gwerr**der**nah**poosh** der
	papel	per**pehl**
paste	cola	**koll**er
pen	uma caneta	oomer ker**nay**ter
pencil	um lápis	oong **lah**pish
pencil sharpener	um apara-lápis	oong erpahrer **lah**pish
	[apontador]	[ahpawngtah**doar**]
playing cards	cartas de jogar	**kahr**tersh der **zhoo**gahr
pocket calculator	uma calculadora	oomer kahlkooler**doar**er
	de bolso	der **boal**soo
postcard	um bilhete postal	oong bil**lyay**ter poosh**tahl**
propelling pencil	uma lapiseira	oomer ler**pizz**ayrer
refill (for a pen)	uma carga (para	oomer **kahr**ger (perrer
	caneta)	ker**nay**ter
rubber	uma borracha	oomer boor**rahsh**er
ruler	uma régua	oomer **reh**gwer
staples	agrafos [grampos]	er**grah**foosh [**grahng**poass]
string	cordel [barbante]	koor**dehl** [bahr**bahng**ti]
thumbtacks	pioneses [tachas]	pyoo**neh**zersh [**tah**shahss]
travel guide	um guia turístico	oong **gheer** too**reesh**tikkoo
typewriter ribbon	uma fita para má-	oomer **fee**ter perrer **mah**-
	quina de escrever	kinner der ish**krer**vayr
typing paper	papel para máquina	per**pehl** perrer **mah**kinner
	de escrever	der ish**krer**vayr
writing pad	um bloco de papel	oong **blokk**oo der per**pehl**

Camping equipment *Equipamento de campismo*

I'd like a/an/some ...	Queria ...	kerreeer
backpack	uma mochila	oomer moosheeler
bottle-opener	um abre-garrafas [abridor de garrafas]	oong ahrer gerrahfersh [ahbriddoar di gahrrahfahss]
butane gas	gás butano	gahsh booternoo
campbed	uma cama de campismo	oomer kermer der kahngpeezhmoo
can opener	um abre-latas [abridor de latas]	oong ahrer lahtersh [ahbriddoar di lahtersh]
candles	velas	vehlersh
(folding) chair	uma cadeira (de fechar)	oomer kerdayrer (der fishahr)
charcoal	carvão de lenha	kerrvahng^w der laynyer
clothes pegs	molas da roupa	mollersh der roaper
compass	uma bússola	oomer boossooler
cool box	uma mala frigorífica	oomer mahler friggooreefikker
corkscrew	um saca-rolhas	oong sahker roalyersh
deck chair	uma cadeira de encosto	oomer kerdayrer der ayngkoashtoo
dishwashing detergent	detergente para a louça	derterrzhayngter perrer er loasser
first-aid kit	um estojo de primeiros-socorros	oong ishtoazhoo der primmayroosh sookorroosh
fishing tackle	apetrechos de pesca	erpertrayshoosh der pehshker
flashlight	uma lanterna de bolso	oomer lahngtehrner der boalsoo
food box	uma caixa para alimentos	oomer kighsher perrer erlimmayngtoosh
frying pan	uma frigideira	oomer frizhiddayrer
groundsheet	um tapete	oong terpayter
hammer	um martelo	oong merrtehloo
hammock	uma cama de rede [uma rede]	oomer kermer der rayder [oomer raydi]
ice pack	uma placa frigorífica	oomer plahker friggooreefikker
kerosene	petróleo	pertrollyoo
lantern	uma lanterna	oomer lahngtehrner
matches	fósforos	foshfooroosh
mattress	um colchão	oong koalshahng^w
methylated spirits	álcool desnaturado	ahlkoll dizhnertoorahdoo
mosquito net	um mosquiteiro	oong mooshkittayroo

CAMPING, see page 32

paraffin	petróleo	pertrollyoo
penknife	um canivete	oong kernivvehter
picnic basket	um cesto de piquenique	oong sayshtoo der pikkerneeker
plastic bag	um saco de plástico	oong sahkoo der plahshtikkoo
rope	uma corda	oomer korrder
rucksack	uma mochila	oomer moosheeler
saucepan	um tacho	oong tahshoo
sleeping bag	um saco-cama	oong sahkoo kermer
(folding) table	uma mesa (de fechar)	oomer mayzer der fishahr
tent	uma tenda	oomer tayngder
tent pegs	umas estacas de tenda	oomersh ishtahkersh der tayngder
tent pole	um mastro de tenda	oong mahshtroo der tayngder
tinfoil	papel de alumínio	perpehl der erloomeenyoo
tin opener	um abre-latas [abridor de latas]	oong ahbrer lahtersh [ahbriddoar di lahtahss]
torch	uma lanterna de bolso	oomer lahngtehrner der boalsoo
vacuum flask	um termo [uma garrafa térmica]	oong tayrmoo [oomah gahrrahfah tehrmikkah]
washing powder	detergente para a roupa	derterrzhayngter perrer er roaper
water flask	um cantil	oong kahngteel
wood alcohol	álcool desnaturado	ahlkoll dizhnertoorahdoo

Crockery *Louça*

cups	chávenas [xícaras]	shahvernersh [sheekahrahss]
mugs	canecas	kernehkersh
plates	pratos	prahtoosh
saucers	pires	peerersh
tumblers	copos	koppoosh

Cutlery *Talheres*

forks	garfos	gahrfoosh
knives	facas	fahkersh
spoons	colheres	koolyehrersh
teaspoons	colheres de chá	koolyehrersh der shah
(made of) plastic/ stainless steel	(de) plástico/ aço inoxidável	(der) plahshtikkoo/ ahssoo innoksiddahvehl

Chemist's (drugstore)   *Farmácia*

Portuguese chemists' don't normally stock the great range of goods you would find in Britain or the U.S., for example photographic equipment or books. For perfume, makeup, etc., you must go to a *perfumaria* (perrfoomer**reee**r). Otherwise, toilet and household articles can be bought from a *drogaria* (drooger**reee**r).

This section is divided into two parts:

1. Pharmaceutical—medicine, first-aid, etc.
2. Toiletry—toilet articles, cosmetics

General   *Generalidades*

Where's the nearest (all-night) chemist's?	**Onde fica a farmácia (de serviço) mais próxima?**	awngder feeker er ferrmahssyer (der serrvee-ssoo) mighsh prossimmer
What time does the chemist's open/close?	**A que horas abre/fecha a farmácia?**	er ker orrersh ahbrer/faysher er ferrmahssyer

1—Pharmaceutical   *Produtos farmacêuticos*

I want something for ...	**Quero qualquer coisa para ...**	kehroo kwahlkehr koayzer perrer
a cold	**a constipação [o resfriado]**	er kawngshtipperssahng^w [oo raysfryahdoa]
a cough	**a tosse**	er tosser
hay fever	**a febre dos fenos**	er fehbrer doosh faynoosh
insect bites	**as picadas de insectos**	ersh pikkahdersh der eengsehtoosh
sunburn	**as queimaduras do sol**	ersh kaymerdoorersh doo soll
travel sickness	**o enjoo (da viagem)**	oo ayngzhoaoo (der vyah-zhahng^y)
an upset stomach	**a indigestão**	er eengdizhershtahng^w
Can you make up this prescription for me?	**Pode aviar-me esta receita?**	podder ervyahr mer ehster rerssayter
Can I get it without a prescription?	**É preciso receita médica?**	eh prersseezoo rerssayter mehdikker
Shall I wait?	**Tenho que esperar?**	taynyoo ker ishperrahr

DOCTOR, see page 137

Can I have a/an/some ...?	Pode dar-me ...?	podder dahr mer
analgesic	um analgésico	oong ernahlzhehzikkoo
antiseptic cream	uma pomada anti-séptica	oomer poomahder ahngti sehtikker
aspirin	aspirinas	ershpirreenersh
(elastic) bandage	uma ligadura [atadura] (elástica)	oomer liggerdoorer [ahtahdoorah] (illahshtikker)
Band-Aids	pensos rápidos [bandaids]	payngsoosh rahpiddoosh [bahngdaydss]
contraceptives	contraceptivos	kawngtrerssehteevoosh
corn plasters	pensos para os calos	payngsoosh perrer oosh kahloosh
cotton wool (absorbent cotton)	algodão hidrófilo	ahlgoodahng^w iddroffilloo
cough drops	pastilhas para a tosse	pershteelyersh perrer er tosser
disinfectant	um desinfectante	oong derzeengfehtahngter
Elastoplast	pensos rápidos [bandaids]	payngsoosh rahpiddoosh [bahngdaydss]
eye drops	gotas para os olhos	goatersh perrer oosh ollyoosh
gauze	gaze	gahzer
insect repellent/spray	um produto insectífugo/spray insecticida	oong proodootoo eengsehteefoogoo/"spray" eengsehtisseeder
iodine	tintura de iodo	teengtoorer der yoadoo
laxative	um laxativo	oong lersherteevoo
mouthwash	um gargarejo	oong gerrgerrayzhoo
nose drops	gotas para o nariz	goatersh perrer oo nerreesh
sanitary towels (napkins)	pensos higiénicos [toalhas higiénicas]	payngsoosh izhyehnikkoosh [twahlyahss izhyehnikkahss]
suppositories	supositórios	soopoozittorryoosh
... tablets	comprimidos ...	kawngprimmeedoosh
tampons	tampões higiénicos	tahngpawng^{y}sh izhyehnikkoosh
thermometer	um termómetro	oong terrmommertroo
throat lozenges	pastilhas para a garganta	pershteelyersh perrer er gerrgahngter
vitamin pills	vitaminas	vittermeenersh

VENENO	POISON
PARA USO EXTERNO	FOR EXTERNAL USE ONLY

2 — Toiletry   *Produtos de higiene e cosméticos*

I'd like a/an/some ...	Queria ...	kerreeer
after-shave lotion	uma loção para depois da barba	oomer loossahng^w perrer derpoysh der bahrber
blusher	um blusher	oong "blusher"
bubble bath	um banho de espuma	oong bernyoo der ishpoomer
cosmetic	um cosmético	oong koozhmehteekoo
cream	um creme	oong krehmer
cleansing cream	creme de limpeza	krehmer der leengpayzer
foundation cream	creme de base	krehmer der bahzer
moisturizing cream	creme hidratante	krehmer iddrrertahngter
night cream	creme de noite	krehmer der noyter
cuticle remover	um produto para tirar as cutículas	oong proodootoo perrer tirrahr ersh kooteekoolersh
deodorant	um desodorizante [desodorante]	oong derzoddoorizzahngter [dayzoadoarahngti]
emery board	uma lima [lixa] de unhas	oomer leemer [leeshah] der oonyersh
eyebrow pencil	um lápis para os olhos	oong lahpish perrer oosh ollyoosh
eye shadow	uma sombra para os olhos	oomer sawngbrer perrer oosh ollyoosh
face powder	pó de arroz	paw der erroash
foot/hand cream	um creme para os pés/as mãos	oong krehmer perrer oosh pehsh/ersh mahng^wsh
lipsalve	um bâton para o cieiro	oong bahtawng perrer oo syayroo
lipstick	um bâton	oong bahtawng
make-up remover pads	discos de algodão	deeshkoosh der ahlgoo-dahng^w
nail brush	uma escova de unhas	oomer ishkoaver der oonyersh
nail clippers	um corta-unhas	oong korrter oonyersh
nail file	uma lima [lixa] de unhas	oomer leemer [leeshah] der oonyersh
nail polish	um verniz [esmalte] de unhas	oong verrneesh [ismahlti] der oonyersh
nail polish remover	um dissolvente de verniz [esmalte]	oong dissollvayngter der verrneesh [ismahlti]
nail scissors	uma tesoura de unhas	oomer terzoarer der oonyersh
perfume	um perfume	oong perrfoomer
powder	pó	paw
razor	uma gilete [um barbeador]	oomer zhillehter [oong bahrbyahdoar]

razor blades	lâminas de barbear	lerminnersh der berrbyahr
safety pins	alfinetes-de-ama	ahlfinnaytersh der ermer
shaving cream	um creme da barba	oong krehmer der bahrber
soap	um sabonete	oong serboonayter
sponge	uma esponja	oomer ishpawngzher
sun-tan cream/oil	um creme/óleo para bronzear	oong krehmer/ollyoo perrer brawngzyahr
talcum powder	pó de talco	paw der tahlkoo
tissues	lenços de papel	layngsoosh der perpehl
toilet paper	papel higiénico	perpehl izhyehnikkoo
toilet water	uma água-de-colónia	oomer ahgwer der koolonnyer
toothbrush	uma escova de dentes	oomer ishkoaver der dayngtish
toothpaste	uma pasta de dentes	oomer pahshter der dayngtish
towel	uma toalha	oomer twahlyer
tweezers	uma pinça para depilar	oomer peengser perrer derpillahr

For your hair *Para o cabelo*

bobby pins	ganchos [grampos]	gahngshoosh [grahngpoass]
comb	um pente	oong payngter
dry shampoo	um shampoo [xampu] seco	oong shahngpoa [shahngpoo] saykoo
hairbrush	uma escova de cabelo	oomer ishkoaver der kerbayloo
hairgrips	ganchos [grampos]	gahngshoosh [grahngpoass]
hair lotion	uma loção capilar	oomer loossahng^w kerpillahr
hair slide	um travessão [clipe]	oong trerverssahng^w [kleepi]
hair spray	laca [laquê]	lahker [lahkay]
setting lotion	um fixador	oong fikserdoar
shampoo for dry/greasy (oily) hair	um shampoo [xampu] para cabelo seco/ oleoso	oong shahngpoa [shahng-poo] perrer kerbayloo saykoo/ollyoazoo
tint	um produto colorante	oong proodootoo kooloorahngter
wig	uma peruca	oomer perrooker

For the baby *Para o bebé [nenê]*

baby food	comida para bebé [nenê]	koomeeder perrer behbeh [naynay]
dummy (pacifier)	uma chupeta	oomer shoopayter
feeding bottle	um biberon	oong bibberrawng
nappies (diapers)	fraldas	frahldersh

Clothing *Vestuário*

If you want to buy something specific, prepare yourself in advance. Look at the list of clothing on page 116. Get some idea of the colour, material and size you want. They're all listed on the next few pages.

General *Generalidades*

I'd like ...	**Queria ...**	kerreeer
I want ... for a 10-year-old boy/girl.	**Quero ... para um menino/uma menina de 10 anos.**	kehroo ... perrer oong merneenoo/oomer mernee-ner der 10 ernoosh
I want something like this.	**Quero qualquer coisa neste género.**	kehroo kwahlkehr koyzer nayshter zhehnerroo
I like the one in the window.	**Gosto do que está na vitrina.**	goshtoo doo ker ishtah ner vittreener
How much is that per metre?	**A como [Quanto] é o metro?**	er koamoo [kwahngtoo] eh oo mehtroo

1 centimetre (cm.)	= 0.39 in.	1 inch =	2.54 cm.
1 metre (m.)	= 39.37 in.	1 foot =	30.5 cm.
10 metres	= 32.81 ft.	1 yard =	0.91 m.

Colour *Cores*

I want a darker/lighter shade.	**Quero um tom mais escuro/mais claro.**	kehroo oong tawng mighsh ishkooroo/mighsh klahroo
I want something to match this.	**Quero qualquer coisa que condiga com isto.**	kehroo kwahlkehr koyzer ker kawngdeeger kawng eeshtoo
I don't like the colour/pattern.	**Não gosto da cor/do padrão.**	nahng^w goshtoo der koar/doo perdrahng^w

liso
(leezoo)

às riscas
(ahsh reesh-kersh)

às bolas
(ahsh bollersh)

xadrez
(sherdraysh)

estampado
(ishtahng-pahdoo)

beige	bege	behzher
black	preto	praytoo
blue	azul	erzool
brown	castanho [marrom]	kershternyoo [mahrrawng]
fawn	castanho dourado	kershternyoo doarahdoo
golden	dourado	doarahdoo
green	verde	vayrder
grey	cinzento	seengzayngtoo
mauve	lilás	lillahsh
orange	cor-de-laranja	koar der lerrahngzher
pink	cor-de-rosa	koar der rozzer
purple	roxo	roashoo
red	vermelho	verrmaylyoo
scarlet	escarlate	ishkerrlahter
silver	prateado	prertyahdoo
turquoise	azul-turquesa	erzool toorkayzer
white	branco	brahngkoo
yellow	amarelo	ermerrehloo
light ...	... claro	... klahroo
dark ...	... escuro	... ishkooroo

Fabrics *Tecidos*

Do you have anything in ...?	Tem alguma coisa de ...?	tahng^y ahlgoomer koyzer der
Is that ...?	É ...?	eh
handmade	feito à mão	faytoo ah mahng^w
imported	importado	eengpoortahdoo
made here	feito aqui	faytoo erkee
pure cotton/wool	algodão puro/ pura lã	ahlgoodahng^w pooroo/ poorer lahng
synthetic	sintético	seengtehtikkoo
colourfast	de cor fixa	der koar feekser
Is it hand washable/ machine washable?	Pode lavar-se à mão/ à máquina?	podder lervahr ser ah mahng^w/ah mahkinner
Will it shrink?	Não encolhe?	nahng^w ayngkollyer
Is it wrinkle-resistant?	Não amarrota?	nahng^w ermerrotter
I want something thinner.	Quero qualquer coisa mais fina.	kehroo kwahlkehr koyzer mighsh feener
Do you have anything of better quality?	Tem uma qualidade melhor?	tahng^y oomer kwerliddahder millyor

cambric	cambraia	kahngbrighder
camel-hair	pêlo de camelo	payloo der kermayloo
chiffon	chiffon	shiffawng
corduroy	bombazina	bawngberzeener
cotton	algodão	ahlgoodahng^w
crepe	crepe	krehper
denim	sarja	sahrzher
felt	feltro	fayltroo
flannel	flanela	flernehler
gabardine	gabardine	gerbahrdeener
lace	renda	rayngder
leather	cabedal [couro]	kerberdahl [koaroo]
linen	linho	leenyoo
poplin	popelina	popperleener
satin	cetim	serteeng
silk	seda	sayder
suede	camurça	kermoorser
terrycloth	pano turco	pernoo toorkoo
	[tecido felpudo]	[taysseedoa fehlpoodoa]
velvet	veludo	verloodoo
velveteen	veludo de algodão	verloodoo der
		ahlgoodahng^w
wool	lã	lahng
worsted	lã cardada	lahng kerrdahder

Size *Medidas*

Sizes can vary from one manufacturer to another, so be sure to try on shoes and clothing before you buy.

I take size 38.	O meu número é o 38.	oo mehoo noomerroo eh oo 38
Could you measure me?	Pode tirar-me as medidas?	podder tirrahr mer ersh merdeedersh
I don't know the Portuguese/ Brazilian sizes.	Não conheço as medidas portuguesas/ brasileiras.	nahng^w koonyayssoo ersh merdeedersh poortoogay-zersh/brahzillayrahss
Can I try it on?	Posso provar?	possoo proovahr
Where's the fitting room?	Onde é a cabine de provas?	awngder eh er kahbeener der provversh
Is there a mirror?	Há um espelho?	ah oong ishpaylyoo

It fits very well.	Fica muito bem.	feeker moong^ytoo bahng^y
It doesn't fit.	Não fica bem.	nahng^w feeker bahng^y
It's too ...	Está muito ...	ishtah moong^ytoo
short/long	curto/comprido	koortoo/kawngpreedoo
tight/loose	apertado/largo	erperrtahdoo/lahrgoo
How long will it take to alter?	Quanto tempo leva para modificar?	kwahngtoo tayngpoo lehver perrer moodiffikkahr

Women   *Senhoras*

Dresses/Suits					
American	8	10	12	14	16	18
British	10	12	14	16	18	20
Portuguese	36	38	40	42	44	46
Brazilian	38	40	42	44	46	48

Stockings				Shoes			
American British	8–8½	9–9½	10–10½	4½ 3	5½ 4	6½ 5	7½ 6
Portuguese Brazilian	36–38	38–40	40–42	36	37	38	39

Men   *Homens*

Suits/Overcoats						Shirts			
American British	36	38	40	42	44	46	15	16	17	18
Portuguese Brazilian	46	48	50	52	54	56	38	41	43	45

Shoes					
American British		5	6	7	8	8½
Portuguese Brazilian		38	39	41	42	43

NUMBERS, see page 147

Clothes and accessories   *Roupas e acessórios*

I'd like a/an/some ...	Queria ...	kerreeer
bathing cap	uma touca de banho	oomer toaker der bernyoo
bathing suit	um fato [maiô] de banho	oong fahtoo [mighoa] der bernyoo
blouse	uma blusa	oomer bloozer
bra	um soutien	oong sootyahng
braces	uns suspensórios	oongsh sooshpayngsorryoosh
briefs	umas calças [calcinhas]	oomersh kahlsersh [kahlseenyahss]
cap	um boné	oong bonneh
cardigan	um casaco de malha	oong kerzahkoo der mahlyer
coat	um casaco comprido	oong kerzahkoo kawng-preedoo
dress	um vestido	oong vershteedoo
evening dress (woman's)	um vestido de noite	oong vershteedoo der noyter
girdle	uma cinta	oomer seengter
gloves	umas luvas	oomersh looversh
handbag	uma mala de mão [bolsa]	oomer mahler der mahngʷ [boalsah]
hat	um chapéu	oong sherpehoo
jacket	um casaco	oong kerzahkoo
jeans	uns jeans	oongsh "jeans"
nightdress	uma camisa de dormir [camisola]	oomer kermeezer der doormeer [kahmizzollah]
pair of ...	um par de ...	oong pahr der
panties	umas calças [calcinhas]	oomersh kahlsersh [kahlseenyahss]
pants (Am.)	umas calças compridas	oomersh kahlsersh kawng-preedersh
panty girdle	uma cinta-calça	oomer seengter kahlser
panty hose	um collant	oong collahng
pullover	uma camisola de malha [um pulôver]	oomer kermizzoller der mahlyer [oong pooloavehr]
roll-neck (turtle-neck)	de gola alta	der goller ahlter
round-neck/V-neck	de decote redondo/em bico	der derkotter rerdawng-doo/ahngʸ beekoo
with long/short sleeves	de mangas compridas/curtas	der mahnggersh kawng-preedersh/koortersh
sleeveless	sem mangas	sahngʸ mahnggersh
pyjamas	um pijama	oong pizhermer

raincoat	uma capa da chuva	oomer kahper der shoover
scarf	um lenço de pescoço	oong layngsoo der pishkoassoo
shirt	uma camisa	oomer kermeezer
shorts	uns calções	oongsh kahlsawngᵛsh
skirt	uma saia	oomer sigher
slip	uma saia de baixo	oomer sigher der bighshoo
socks	umas peúgas [meias curtas]	oomersh pyoogersh [mayahss koortahss]
stockings	umas meias	oomersh mayersh
suit (man's)	um fato [terno]	oong fahtoo [tehrnoa]
suit (woman's)	um fato [terno] de saia e casaco	oong fahtoo [tehrnoa] der sigher ee kerzahkoo
suspenders (Am.)	uns suspensórios	oongsh sooshpayngsorryoosh
sweatshirt	uma camisola [um suéter] de algodão	oomer kermizzoller [oong swehtehr] der ahlgoodahngʷ
swimming trunks/ swimsuit	um fato [maiô] de banho	oong fahtoo [mighoa] der bernyoo
T-shirt	uma camiseta	oomer kermizzayter
tie	uma gravata	oomer grervahter
tights	um collant	oong kollahng
tracksuit	um fato de treino [um training]	oong fahtoo der traynoo [oong trayneengg]
trousers	umas calças compridas	oomersh kahlsersh kawngpreedersh
umbrella	um guarda-chuva	oong gwahrder shoover
underpants	umas cuecas	oomersh kwehkersh
undershirt	uma camisola interior [camiseta]	oomer kermizzoller eengterryoar [kahmizzaytah]
vest (Am.)	um colete	oong koolayter
vest (Br.)	uma camisola interior [camiseta]	oomer kermizzoller eengterryoar [kahmizzaytah]
waistcoat	um colete	oong koolayter

belt	um cinto	oong seengtoo
buckle	uma fivela	oomer fivvehler
button	um botão	oong bootahngʷ
collar	um colarinho	oong koolerreenyoo
pocket	um bolso	oong boalsoo
press stud (snap fastener)	um botão de mola [de pressão]	oong bootahngʷ der moller [der prayssahngʷ]
zip (zipper)	um fecho éclair	oong fayshoo ayklehr

Shoes   *Sapatos*

I'd like a pair of ...	**Queria um par de ...**	kerreeer oong pahr der
boots	**botas**	bottersh
moccasins	**mocassins**	mokkahssahngsh
plimsolls (sneakers)	**ténis**	tehnish
sandals	**sandálias**	sahngdahlyersh
shoes	**sapatos**	serpahtoosh
flat	**de salto raso**	der sahltoo rahzoo
with a heel	**de salto alto**	der sahltoo ahltoo
with leather/	**de sola de cabedal**	der soller der kerberdahl
rubber soles	**[couro]/de borracha**	[koaroo]/der boorrahsher
slippers	**chinelos**	shinnehloosh

These are too ...	**Estes são ... demais.**	ayshtish sahng^w ... dermighsh
narrow/wide	**apertados/largos**	erperrtahdoosh/**lahr**goosh
large/small	**grandes/pequenos**	grahngdish/perkaynoosh
Do you have a larger/smaller size?	**Tem um número maior/mais pequeno [menor]?**	tahng^y oong noomerroo mayor/mighsh perkaynoo [mehnor]
Do you have the same in black?	**Tem os mesmos em preto?**	tahng^y oosh mayzhmoosh ahng^y praytoo
cloth	**em tela**	ahng^y tehler
leather	**em cabedal [couro]**	ahng^y kerberdahl [koaroo]
rubber	**em borracha**	ahng^y boorrahsher
suede	**em camurça**	ahng^y kermoorser
Is it genuine leather?	**É cabedal [couro] autêntico?**	eh kerberdahl [koaroo] owtayngtikkoo
I need some shoe polish/shoelaces.	**Preciso de graxa/ atacadores [cordões] de sapatos.**	prersseezoo der grahsher/ erterkerdoarersh [kordawng^{y}sh] der serpahtoosh

Shoes worn out? Here's the key to getting them fixed again:

Can you repair these shoes?	**Pode consertar estes sapatos?**	podder kawngserrtahr ayshtish serpahtoosh
Can you stitch this?	**Pode coser isto?**	podder koozayr eeshtoo
I want new soles and heels.	**Quero que ponha solas e saltos novos.**	kehroo ker poanyer sollersh ee sahltoos novvoosh
When will they be ready?	**Quando estarão prontos?**	kwahngdoo ishterrahng^w prawngtoosh

COLOURS, see page 113

Electrical appliances   *Aparelhos eléctricos*

The standard current in Portugal is 220-volt, 50-cycle A.C.
In most places in Brazil the current is 110-volt, 60-cycles.

What's the voltage?	**Qual é a voltagem?**	kwahl eh er voltahzhahng^y
Do you have a battery for this?	**Tem uma pilha para isto?**	tahng^y oomer peelyer perrer eeshtoo
Can you repair this?	**Pode consertar isto?**	podder kawngserrtahr eeshtoo
Can you show me how it works?	**Pode mostrar-me como funciona?**	podder mooshtrahr mer koamoo foongsyonner
I'd like a/an/some ...	**Queria ...**	kerreeer
adaptor	**um adaptador**	oong erderpterdoar
amplifier	**um amplificador**	oong ahngpliffikkerdoar
bulb	**uma lâmpada**	oomer lahngperder
clock-radio	**um rádio-despertador**	oong rahdyoo dishperrterdoar
electric toothbrush	**uma escova de dentes eléctrica**	oomer ishkoaver der dayngtish illehtrikker
extension lead (cord)	**uma extensão**	oomer ishtayngsahng^w
hair dryer	**um secador de cabelo**	oong serkerdoar der kerbayloo
headphones	**uns auscultadores [fones]**	oongsh owshkoolterdoarersh [fonniss]
(travelling) iron	**um ferro de engomar (de viagem)**	oong fehrroo der aynggoomahr (der vyahzhahng^y)
lamp	**um candeeiro [abajur]**	oong kahngdyayroo [ahbahzhoor]
plug	**uma ficha**	oomer feesher
portable ...	**... portátil**	... poortahtill
radio	**um rádio**	oong rahdyoo
record player	**um gira-discos [toca-discos]**	oong zheerer deeshkoosh [tokkah deeskoass]
shaver	**uma máquina de barbear**	oomer mahkinner der berrbyahr
speakers	**uns alto-falantes**	oongsh ahltoo ferlahngtish
(cassette) tape recorder	**um gravador (de cassetes)**	oong grerverdoar (der kahssehtish)
(colour) television	**uma televisão (a cores)**	oomer terlervizzahng^w (er koarersh)
transformer	**um transformador**	oong trahngshfoormerdoar
video cassette	**uma videocassete**	oomer viddyokkahssehter
video recorder	**um gravador vídeo**	oong grerverdoar veedyoo

Grocery *Mercearia*

I'd like some bread, please.	**Queria pão, se faz favor.**	kerreeer pahng^w ser fahsh fervoar
What sort of cheese do you have?	**Que género de queijo tem?**	ker zhehnerroo der kayzhoo tahng^y
A piece of ...	**Um pedaço ...**	oong perdahssoo
that one	**daquele**	derkayler
the one on the shelf	**do que está na prateleira**	doo ker istah ner prerterlayrer
I'll have one of those, please.	**Dê-me um desses, por favor.**	day mer oong dayssersh poor fervoar
May I help myself?	**Posso servir-me?**	possoo serrveer mer
I'd like ...	**Queria ...**	kerreeer
a kilo of apples	**um quilo de maçãs**	oong keeloo der merssahngsh
half a kilo of tomatoes	**meio-quilo de tomates**	mayoo keeloo der toomahtish
100 grams of butter	**100 gramas de manteiga**	100 grermersh der mahngtayger
a litre of milk	**um litro de leite**	oong leetroo der layter
4 slices of ham	**4 fatias de fiambre**	4 ferteeersh der fyahngbrer
a packet of tea	**um pacote de chá**	oong perkotter der shah
a jar of honey	**um frasco de mel**	oong frahshkoo der mehl
a tin (can) of peaches	**uma lata de pêssegos**	oomer lahter der payssergoosh
a tube of mustard	**um tubo de mostarda**	oong tooboo der mooshtahrder
a box of chocolates	**uma caixa de chocolates**	oomer kighsher der shookoolahtish

---

1 kilogram or kilo (kg.) = 1000 grams (g.)

100 g. = 3.5 oz.	½ kg. = 1.1 lb.
200 g. = 7.0 oz.	1 kg. = 2.2 lb.

1 oz. = 28.35 g.
1 lb. = 453.60 g.

---

1 litre (l.) = 0.88 imp. quarts = 1.06 U.S. quarts

1 imp. quart = 1.14 l.	1 U.S. quart = 0.95 l.
1 imp. gallon = 4.55 l.	1 U.S. gallon = 3.8 l.

FOOD, see also page 63

Jeweller's—Watchmaker's   *Ourivesaria—Relojoaria*

Could I see that, please?	**Posso ver aquilo ali?**	possoo vayr erkeeloo erlee
Do you have anything in gold?	**Tem alguma coisa em ouro?**	tahng^y ahlgoomer koyzer ahng^y oaroo
How many carats is this?	**Quantos quilates tem isto?**	kwahngtoosh killahtish tahng^y eeshtoo
Is this real silver?	**É prata de lei?**	eh prahter der lay
Can you repair this watch?	**Pode consertar este relógio?**	podder kawngserrtahr ayshter rerlozhyoo
I'd like a/an/ some ...	**Queria ...**	kerreeer
alarm clock	**um despertador**	oong dishperrterdoar
bangle	**um bracelete**	oong brahsserlehter
battery	**uma pilha**	oomer peelyer
bracelet	**uma pulseira**	oomer poolsayrer
chain bracelet	**uma corrente de pulso**	oomer koorrayngter der poolsoo
charm bracelet	**uma pulseira de berloques**	oomer poolsayrer der berrlokkersh
brooch	**um broche**	oong brosher
chain	**uma corrente**	oomer koorrayngter
charm	**um berloque**	oong berrlokker
cigarette case	**uma cigarreira**	oomer siggerrayrer
cigarette lighter	**um isqueiro**	oong ishkayroo
clip	**um broche de mola**	oong brosher der moller
clock	**um relógio**	oong rerlozhyoo
cross	**uma cruz**	oomer kroosh
cuff links	**uns botões de punho [abotoaduras]**	oongsh bootawng^ysh der poonyoo [ahboatwah-doorahss]
cutlery	**uns talheres**	oongsh terlyehrersh
earrings	**uns brincos**	oongsh breengkoosh
filigree jewellery	**as filigranas**	ersh filliggrernersh
gem	**uma pedra preciosa**	oomer pehdrer prerssyozzer
jewel box	**um cofre de jóias**	oong koffer der zhoyersh
necklace	**um colar**	oong koolahr
pendant	**um pingente**	oong peengzhayngter
pin	**um alfinete**	oong ahlfinnayter
pocket watch	**um relógio de bolso**	oong rerlozhyoo der boalsoo
powder compact	**uma caixinha de pó de arroz**	oomer kighsheenyer der paw der erroash

ring	um anel	oong ernehl
engagement ring	um anel de noivado	oong ernehl der noyvahdoò
signet ring	um anel de sinete	oong ernehl der sinnayter
wedding ring	uma aliança	oomer erlyahngser
rosary	um rosário	oong roozahryoo
silverware	umas pratas	oomersh prahtersh
tie clip/pin	uma mola/um alfinete de gravata	oomer moller/oong ahlfi-nnayter der grervahter
watch	um relógio	oong rerlozhyoo
automatic	automático	owtoomahtikkoo
digital	digital	dizhittahl
quartz	quartzo	kwahrtzoo
with a second hand	com ponteiro de segundos	kawng pawngtayroo der sergoongdoosh
waterproof	à prova de água	ah provver der ahgwer
watchstrap (watchband)	uma correia de relógio	oomer koorrayer der rerlozhyoo
wristwatch	um relógio de pulso	oong rerlozhyoo der poolsoo

amber	âmbar	ahngberr
amethyst	ametista	ermerteeshter
chromium	cromo	krommoo
copper	cobre	kobbrer
coral	coral	koorahl
crystal	cristal	krishtahl
diamond	diamante	dyermahngter
emerald	esmeralda	izhmerrahlder
enamel	esmalte	izhmahlter
glass	vidro	veedroo
gold	ouro	oaroo
gold-plated	banhado a ouro	bernyahdoo er oaroo
ivory	marfim	merrfeeng
jade	jade	zhahder
onyx	ónix	onniks
pearl	pérola	pehrooler
pewter	estanho	ishternyoo
platinum	platina	plerteener
ruby	rubi	roobee
sapphire	safira	serfeerer
silver	prata	prahter
silver-plated	banhado a prata	bernyahdoo er prahter
stainless steel	aço inoxidável	ahssoo innoksiddahvehl
topaz	topázio	toopahzyoo
turquoise	turqueza	toorkayzer

Optician *Oculista*

I've broken my glasses.	**Parti [Quebrei] os óculos.**	perrtee [kaybray] oosh okkooloosh
Can you repair them for me?	**Pode consertá-los?**	podder kawngserrtah loosh
When will they be ready?	**Quando estarão prontos?**	kwahngdoo ishterrahng^w prawngtoosh
Can you change the lenses?	**Pode mudar as lentes?**	podder moodahr ersh layngtish
I want tinted lenses.	**Quero lentes de cor.**	kehroo layngtish der koar
The frame is broken.	**A armação está partida [quebrada].**	er errmerssahng^w ishtah perrteeder [kaybrahdah]
I'd like a spectacle case.	**Queria uma caixa de óculos.**	kerreeer oomer kighsher der okkooloosh
I'd like to have my eyesight checked.	**Queria fazer um exame à vista.**	kerreeer ferzayr oong izzermer ah veeshter
I'm short-sighted/long-sighted.	**Sou míope/presbita.**	soa meeooper/prershbeeter
I want some contact lenses.	**Quero lentes de contacto.**	kehroo layngtish der kawngtahktoo
I've lost one of my contact lenses.	**Perdi uma lente de contacto.**	perrdee oomer layngter der kawngtahktoo
Could you give me another one?	**Pode dar-me outra?**	podder dahr mer oatrer
I have hard/soft lenses.	**Tenho lentes de contacto rígidas/flexíveis.**	taynyoo layngtish der kawngtahktoo reezhiddersh/ flehkseevaysh
Have you any contact-lens fluid?	**Tem um líquido para lentes de contacto?**	tahng^y oong leekiddoo perrer layngtish der kawngtahktoo
I'd like to buy a pair of sunglasses.	**Queria comprar um par de óculos de sol.**	kerreeer kawngprahr oong pahr der okkooloosh der soll
May I look in a mirror?	**Posso ver-me ao espelho?**	possoo vayr mer ow ishpaylyoo
I'd like to buy a pair of binoculars.	**Queria comprar uns binóculos.**	kerreeer kawngprahr oongsh binnokkooloosh

Photography   *Fotografia*

I want a/an ... camera.	**Quero uma máquina fotográfica ...**	kehroo oomer mahkinner footoograhfikker
automatic	**automática**	owtoomahtikker
inexpensive	**barata**	berrahter
simple	**simples**	seengplersh
Show me some cine (movie) cameras.	**Mostre-me algumas máquinas de filmar.**	moshtrer mer ahlgoomersh mahkinnersh der filmahr
I'd like to have some passport photos taken.	**Queria tirar fotografias de passaporte.**	kerreeer tirrahr footoogrerfeeersh der persserporrter

Film   *Rolos [Filmes]*

I'd like a film for this camera.	**Queria um rolo para esta máquina.**	kerreeer oong roaloo perrer ehshter mahkinner
black and white	**a preto e branco**	er praytoo ee brahngkoo
colour	**a cores**	er koarersh
colour negative	**para negativos a cores**	perrer nergerteevoosh er koarersh
colour slide	**para slides**	perrer slighdersh
cartridge	**um rolo-cassete**	oong roaloo kahssehter
disc film	**um disco-película**	oong deeshkoo perleekooler
roll film	**um rolo**	oong roaloo
video cassette	**uma videocassete**	oomer viddyokkahssehter
24/36 exposures	**24/36 fotografias**	veengter ee kwahtroo/ treengter ee saysh footoogrerfeeersh
this size	**deste tamanho**	dayshter termernyoo
this ASA/DIN number	**este número de ASA/DIN**	ayshter noomerroo der ahzer/deen
artificial light type	**para luz artificial**	perrer loosh errtiffissyahl
daylight type	**para luz do dia**	perrer loosh doo deeer
fast (high-speed)	**ultra-rápido**	ooltrer rahpiddoo
fine grain	**de grão fino**	der grahng^w feenoo

Developing   *Revelação*

What's the charge for processing?	**Quanto custa a revelação?**	kwahngtoo kooshter er rerverlerssahng^w

I'd like ... prints of each negative.	Quero ... cópias de cada negativo.	kehroo ... koppyersh der kerder nergerteevoo
with a mat finish	mates	mahtish
with a glossy finish	brilhantes	brillyahngtish
Will you enlarge this, please?	Pode ampliar isto, por favor?	podder ahngplyahr eeshtoo poor fervoar
When will the photos be ready?	Quando estarão prontas?	kwahngdoo ishterrahngʷ prawngtersh

Accessories and repairs   *Acessórios e consertos*

I'd like a/an/some ...	Quero ...	kehroo
battery	uma pilha	oomer peelyer
cable release	um disparador	oong dishperrerdoar
camera case	uma capa (de máquina fotográfica)	oomer kahper (der mahkinner footoograhfikker)
(electronic) flash	um flash (electrónico)	oong flahsh (illehtronnikkoo)
filter	um filtro	oong feeltroo
for black and white	para preto e branco	perrer praytoo ee brahngkoo
for colour	para cores	perrer koarersh
lens	uma objectiva	oomer obzhehteever
telephoto lens	uma teleobjectiva	oomer tehlehobzhehteever
wide-angle lens	uma objectiva grande angular	oomer obzhehteever grahngder ahnggoolahr
lens cap	uma tampa para a objectiva	oomer tahngper perrer er obzhehteever
Can you repair this camera?	Pode consertar esta máquina?	podder kawngserrtahr ehshter mahkinner
The film is jammed.	O rolo está encravado.	oo roaloo ishtah ayngkrervahdoo
There's something wrong with the ...	Há qualquer avaria ...	ah kwahlkehr erverreeer
exposure counter	no contador	noo kawngterdoar
film winder	no botão de bobinagem	noo bootahngʷ der bobbinnahzhahngʸ
flash attachment	no encaixe do flash	noo ayngkighsher doo flahsh
lens	na objectiva	ner obzhehteever
light meter	no fotómetro	noo footommertroo
rangefinder	no telémetro	noo terlehmertroo
shutter	no obturador	noo obtoorerdoar

NUMBERS, see page 147

Tobacconist's *Tabacaria*

Other than at tobacconist's you can buy cigarettes at newsstands, hotels and bars. Foreign brands are heavily taxed.

A packet of cigarettes, please.	Um maço de cigarros, se faz favor.	oong mahssoo der siggahrroosh ser fahsh fervoar
Do you have any American/English cigarettes?	Tem cigarros americanos/ingleses?	tahng^y siggahrroosh ermerrikkernoosh/eengglayzersh
I'd like a carton.	Queria um pacote.	kerreeer oong perkotter
I'd like a/some ...	Queria ...	kerreeer
candy	rebuçados [balas]	rrerboossahdoosh [bahlahss]
chewing gum	pastilhas elásticas [chicletes]	pershteelyersh illahsh-tikkersh [shikklehtiss]
chewing tobacco	tabaco [fumo] de mascar	terbahkoo [foomoa] der mershkahr
chocolate	chocolate	shookoolahter
cigarette case	uma cigarreira	oomer siggerrayrer
cigarette holder	uma boquilha [piteira]	oomer bookeelyer [pittayrah]
cigarettes	cigarros	siggahrroosh
filter-tipped	com filtro	kawng feeltroo
without filter	sem filtro	sahng^y feeltroo
mild/strong	suaves/fortes	swahversh/forrtish
menthol	mentolados	mayngtoolahdoosh
king-size	gigantes	zhiggahngtish
cigars	charutos	sherrootoosh
lighter	um isqueiro	oong ishkayroo
lighter fluid/gas	gasolina/gás para isqueiro	gerzooleener/gash perrer ishkayroo
matches	fósforos	foshfooroosh
pipe	um cachimbo	oong kersheengboo
pipe cleaners	limpa-cachimbos	oong leengper ker-sheengboosh
pipe tobacco	tabaco [fumo] para cachimbo	terbahkoo [foomoa] perrer kersheengboo
pipe tool	um esgaravatador de cachimbos	oong izhgerrerverter-doar der kersheengboosh
postcard	um bilhete postal	oong billyayter pooshtahl
snuff	rapé	rerpeh
stamps	selos	sayloosh
sweets	rebuçados [balas]	rrerboossahdoosh [bahlahss]
wick	uma torcida	oomer toorseeder

Miscellaneous *Miscelânea*

Souvenirs *Lembranças*

Here are some suggestions for articles which you might like
to bring back as a souvenir or a gift.

I'd like to buy a gift for ...	**Queria comprar um presente para ...**	kerreeer kawngprahr oong prerzayngter perrer
Something typically Portuguese/Brazilian.	**Algo tipicamente português/brasileiro.**	ahlgoo tippikkermayngter poortoogaysh/brahzillayroo
china	**a porcelana**	er poorserlerner
corkware	**os artigos de cortiça**	oosh errteegoosh der koorteesser
costumes	**os trajos típicos**	oosh trahzhoosh teepikkoosh
embroidery	**os bordados**	oosh boordahdoosh
filigree jewellery	**as filigranas**	ersh filliggrernersh
handkerchieves	**os lenços**	oosh layngsoosh
headscarves	**os lenços de pescoço**	oosh layngsoosh der pishkoassoo
lace	**as rendas**	ersh rayngdersh
leatherwork	**os artigos de couro**	oosh errteegoosh der ishternyoo
pottery	**a loiça de barro**	er loysser der bahrroo
rugs	**os tapetes**	oosh terpaytish
tiles	**os azulejos**	oosh erzoolayzhoosh
wickerware	**os artigos de verga**	oosh errteegoosh der vayrger
woodwork	**os artigos de madeira**	oosh errteegosh der merdayrer
woven materials	**os artigos de tear manual [tecelagem]**	oosh errteegoosh der tyahr mernwahl [tayssaylahzhayng^y]

Records—Cassettes *Discos – Cassetes*

Do you have any records by ...?	**Tem discos de ...?**	tahng^y deeshkoosh der
I'd like a ...	**Queria ...**	kerreeer
cassette	**uma cassete**	oomer kahssehter
video cassette	**uma videocassete**	oomer viddyokkahssehter
compact disc	**um disco compacto**	oong deeshkoo kawngpahktoo

L.P. (33 rpm)	**um L.P.** **(33 rotações)**	oong **ehler pay** (33 rooter**ssawng^vsh**)
E.P. (45 rpm)	**um maxi-single** **(45 rotações)**	oong "maxi-single" (45 rooter**ssawng^vsh**)
single	**um single** **(45 rotações)**	oong "single" (45 rooter**ssawng^vsh**)

Do you have any songs by ...?	**Tem canções de ...?**	tahng^y kahng**sawng^vsh** der
Can I listen to this record?	**Posso ouvir este disco?**	possoo oa**veer ays**ter **deesh**koo
chamber music	**música de câmara**	moozikker der **ker**merrer
classical music	**música clássica**	moozikker **klahs**sikker
folk music	**música folclórica**	moozikker folk**lor**rikker
instrumental music	**música instrumental**	moozikker eengshtroo- mayng**tahl**
light music	**música ligeira**	moozikker li**zhay**rer
orchestral music	**música sinfónica**	moozikker seengfonnikker
pop music	**música pop**	moozikker pop

Toys *Brinquedos*

I'd like a toy/ game ...	**Queria um brinquedo/jogo ...**	ker**ree**er oong breeng**kay**doo/**zhoa**goo
for a boy	**para um menino**	perrer oong mer**nee**noo
for a 5-year-old girl	**para uma menina de 5 anos**	perrer **oo**mer mer**nee**ner der 5 er**noosh**
ball	**uma bola**	**oo**mer **bol**ler
beach ball	**um balão**	oong ber**lahng^w**
bucket and spade (pail and shovel)	**um balde e uma pá**	oong **bahl**der ee **oo**mer pah
building blocks (bricks)	**um jogo de construções**	oong **zhoa**goo der kawngshtroo**ssawng^wsh**
card game	**um baralho de cartas**	oong ber**rah**lyoo der **kahr**tersh
chess set	**um jogo de xadrez**	oong **zhoa**goo der sher- **draysh**
doll	**uma boneca**	**oo**mer boo**neh**ker
electronic game	**um jogo electrónico**	oong **zhoa**goo illehtronnikkoo
flippers	**umas barbatanas**	**oo**mersh berrber**ter**nersh
roller skates	**uns patins de rodas**	oongsh per**teengsh** der **rod**dersh

Your money: banks—currency

In Portugal the usual banking hours are from 8.30 to 11.45 a.m. and from 1 to 2.30 or 2.45 p.m., Monday to Friday. In Brazil banking hours are normally from 10 a.m. to 4.30 p.m. Monday to Friday.

You'll find currency exchange offices *(câmbio)* in most Portuguese and Brazilian tourist centres, and they often stay open longer, especially during the summer season, for the benefit of tourists.

The basic unit of currency in Portugal is the *escudo* (ish-**koo**doo) divided into 100 *centavos* (sayng**tah**voosh). *Escudo* is abbreviated to *esc.*

Coins: 50 centavos, 1, 2½, 5, 10, 20, 25 and 50 escudos.
Banknotes: 100, 500, 1,000 and 5,000 escudos.

Brazil's monetary unit is the *cruzado* (kroo**zah**doa), abbreviated Cz$, and introduced into the country in February 1986. While the old currency continues to circulate, visitors should note that its value is one thousandth that of the new currency (1 *cruzado* = 1000 *cruzeiros*—abbreviated Cr$).

Coins: Cz$ 0.01, 0.02, 0.03, 0.10, 0.20, 0.50, 1, 5 and 10.
Banknotes: Cr$ 1,000, 5,000, 10,000, 50,000, 100,000 and 500,000; Cz$ 10, 50, 100, 500 and 1,000.

Credit cards may be used in an increasing number of hotels, restaurants, shops, etc. Signs are posted indicating which cards are accepted.

Traveller's cheques are accepted by hotels, travel agents and many shops, although the exchange rate is invariably better at a bank. Be sure to take your passport with you for identification. You may also cash Eurocheques in Portugal.

Where's the nearest bank?	**Onde é o banco mais próximo?**	awngder eh oo bahngkoo mighsh prossimmoo
Where's the nearest currency exchange office?	**Onde é a agência de câmbio mais próxima?**	awngder eh er erzhayng-syer der kahngbyoo mighsh prossimmer

At the bank   *No banco*

I want to change some dollars/pounds.	Quero trocar dólares/libras.	kehroo trookahr dollersh/leebrersh
I want to cash a traveller's cheque.	Quero levantar um cheque de viagem.	kehroo lervahngtahr oong shehker der vyahzhahng^y
What's the exchange rate?	A como [quanto] está o câmbio?	er koamoo [kwahngtoa] ishtah oo kahngbyoo
How much commission do you charge?	Que comissão cobram?	ker koomissahng^w kobbrahng^w
Can you telex my bank in London?	Pode mandar um telex para o meu banco em Londres?	podder mahngdahr oong tehlehks perrer oo mehoo bahngkoo ahng^y lawngdrersh
I have a/an/some ...	Tenho ...	taynyoo
bank card	um cartão bancário	oong kerrtahng^w bahngkahryoo
credit card	um cartão de crédito	oong kerrtahng^w der krehdittoo
Eurocheques	Eurocheques	ehooroshehkersh
introduction from ...	uma carta de apresentação de ...	oomer kahrter der erprerzayngterssahng^w der ...
letter of credit	uma carta de crédito	oomer kahrter der krehdittoo
I'm expecting some money from New York. Has it arrived?	Estou à espera de dinheiro de Nova Iorque. Já chegou?	ishtoa ah ishpehrer der dinnyayroo der novver york. zhah shergoa
Please give me some ...	Se faz favor, dê-me ...	ser fahsh fervoar day mer
coins	moedas	mwehdersh
notes (bills)	notas	nottersh
small change	dinheiro trocado	dinnyayroo trookahdoo

Deposits—Withdrawals   *Depósitos—Levantamentos*

I want to ...	Quero ...	kehroo
open an account	abrir uma conta	erbreer oomer kawngter
withdraw ... escudos/cruzados	levantar ... escudos/cruzados	lervahngtahr ishkoodoosh/kroozahdoass
Where should I sign?	Onde devo assinar?	awngder dayvoo erssinnahr

NUMBERS, see page 147

I want to deposit this in my account.	Quero depositar isto na minha conta.	kehroo derpoozittahr eeshtoo ner meenyer kawngter

Business terms   *Termos comerciais*

My name is ...	O meu nome é ...	oo mehoo noamer eh
Here's my card.	Aqui está o meu cartão.	erkee ishtah oo mehoo kerrtahng^w
I have an appointment with ...	Tenho um encontro marcado com ...	taynyoo oong ayngkawngtroo merrkahdoo kawng
Can you give me an estimate of the cost?	Pode dar-me uma estimação do custo?	podder dahr mer oomer ishtimmerssahngg^w doo kooshtoo
What's the rate of inflation?	Qual é o índice de inflação?	kwahl eh oo eengdisser der eengflahssahng^w
Can you provide me with an interpreter?	Pode arranjar-me [arrumar-me] um intérprete?	podder errahngzhahr mer [ahrroomahr mi] oong eengtehrprerter
Where can I make photocopies?	Onde posso fazer fotocópias?	awngder possoo ferzayr fottokkoppyersh

amount	a importância	er eengpoortahngsyer
balance	o balanço	oo berlahngsoo
bond	a obrigação	er oabriggerssahng^w
capital	o capital	oo kerpittahl
cheque book	o livro de cheques	oo leevroo der shehkersh
contract	o contrato	oo kawngtrahtoo
discount	o desconto	oo dishkawngtoo
expenses	as despesas	ersh dishpayzersh
interest	o juro	oo zhooroo
investment	o investimento	oo eengvershtimmayngtoo
invoice	a factura	er fahtoorer
loss	a perda	er payrder
mortgage	a hipoteca	er ippootehker
payment	o pagamento	oo pergermayngtoo
percentage	a percentagem	er perrsayngtahzhahng^y
profit	o lucro	oo lookroo
purchase	a compra	er kawngprer
sale	a venda	er vayngder
share	a acção	er ahssahng^w
transfer	a transferência	er trahngshferrayngsyer
value	o valor	oo verloar

At the post office

Post offices in Portugal are indicated by the letters CTT
(Correios e Telecomunicações) and are generally open from
9 a.m. to 6.30 p.m., Monday to Friday; in addition main
offices operate on Saturday mornings until noon. Stamps
can also be bought at tobacconist's and souvenir stands.
Letter boxes (mailboxes) on the street follow the British
pillar-box design; they're painted red, too.

In Brazil, post offices bear a sign ECT *(Empresa Brasileira
de Correios e Telégrafos)* and are generally open from
8 a.m. to 6 p.m. Monday to Friday, till noon on Saturdays. Streetcorner letter boxes are yellow.

Where's the nearest post office?	**Onde fica a estação de correios mais próxima?**	awngder feeker er ishter-ssahng^w der koorrayoosh mighsh prossimmer
What time does the post office open/close?	**A que horas abre/fecha o correio?**	er ker orrersh ahbrer/faysher oo koorrayoo
A stamp for this letter/postcard, please.	**Um selo para esta carta/este bilhete postal, por favor.**	oong sayloo perrer ehshter kahrter/ayshter billyayter pooshtahl poor fervoar
A ... escudo stamp, please.	**Um selo de ... escudos, por favor.**	oong sayloo der ... ish-koodoosh poor fervoar
What's the postage for a letter to London?	**Qual é a franquia de uma carta para Londres?**	kwahl eh er frahngkeeer der oomer kahrter perrer lawngdrersh
What's the postage for a postcard to Los Angeles?	**Qual é a franquia de um bilhete postal para Los Angeles?**	kwahl eh er frahngkeeer der oong billyayter pooshtahl perrer "Los Angeles"
Where's the letter box (mailbox)?	**Onde é a caixa do correio?**	awngder eh er kighsher doo koorrayoo

I want to send this parcel.	Quero enviar esta encomenda [este pacote].	kehroo ayngvyahr ehshter ayngkoomayngder [aysti] pahkotti]
I want to send this by ...	Quero mandar isto ...	kehroo mahngdahr eeshtoo
airmail	por avião	poor ervyahng^w
express (special delivery)	por expresso	poor ishprehssoo
registered mail	registado	rerzhishtahdoo
At which counter can I cash an international money order?	Em que guiché posso levantar um vale de correio internacional?	ahng^y ker ghisheh possoo lervahngtahr oong vahler der koorrayoo eengterrnerssyoonahl
Where's the poste restante (general delivery)?	Onde é a posta restante?	awngder eh er poshter rishtahngter
Is there any post (mail) for me? My name is ...	Há correio para mim? O meu nome é ...	ah koorrayoo perrer meeng. oo mehoo noamer eh

SELOS	STAMPS
ENCOMENDAS [PACOTES]	PARCELS
VALES DE CORREIO	MONEY ORDERS

Telegrams *Telegramas*

In Portugal and Brazil telegrams are sent through the post office.

I want to send a telegram/telex.	Queria mandar um telegrama/telex.	kerreeer mahngdahr oong terlergrermer/tehlehks
May I have a form, please?	Pode dar-me um formulário?	podder dahr mer oong foormoolahryoo
How much is it per word?	Qual é a taxa por palavra?	kwahl eh er tahsher poor perlahvrer
How long will a cable to Boston take?	Quanto tempo leva um telegrama para chegar a Boston?	kwahngtoo tayngpoo lehver oong terlergrermer perrer shergahr er "Boston"
How much will this telex cost?	Quanto custará este telex?	kwahngtoo kooshterrah ayshter tehlehks

Telephoning *Telefones*

In Portugal, coin telephones are found in bars, restaurants and on the street. You can dial most of the world direct, however international calls can also be made through the clerk at any post office or at your hotel. In major cities you'll find English-speaking operators. But if you must say a number in Portuguese, give it in digits, e.g. 87912 = *oito, sete, nove, um, dois*. Dialling codes are listed in the directory.

In Brazil you must buy tokens, which are sold at most newsstands, in bars and small shops near public phones. Long-distance and overseas calls can be made from public telephone offices *(estação telefônica)* or your hotel.

Where's the telephone?	**Onde é o telefone?**	awngder eh oo terlerfonner
I'd like ... telephone tokens.	**Queria ... fichas (de telefone).**	kerreeer ... feesherss (der terlerfonner)
Where's the nearest telephone booth?	**Onde fica a cabine telefónica mais próxima?**	awngder feeker er kahbeener terlerfonnikker mighsh prossimmer
May I use your phone?	**Posso utilizar o seu telefone?**	possoo ootillizzahr oo sehoo terlerfonner
Do you have a telephone directory for Faro?	**Tem uma lista telefónica de Faro?**	tahng^y oomer leeshter terlerfonnikker der fahroo
What's the dialling (area) code for ...?	**Qual é o indicativo de ...?**	kwahl eh oo eengdikkerteevoo der
How do I get the international operator?	**Como posso obter o serviço internacional?**	koamoo possoo obtayr oo serrveessoo eengterrnerssyoonahl

Operator *Telefonista*

Good morning, I want São Paulo 23 45 67.	**Bom dia, quero ligar para o 23 45 67 em São Paulo.**	bawng deeer kehroo liggahr perrer oo 23 45 67 ahng^y sahng^w powloo
Can you help me get this number?	**Pode ajudar-me a ligar para este número?**	podder erzhoodahr mer er liggahr perrer ayshter noomerroo

I want to place a personal (person-to-person) call.	**Quero uma comunicação com pré-aviso.**	kehroo oomer koomoo-nikker**ssahng**w kawng preh erveezoo
I want to reverse the charges (call collect).	**Quero uma comunicação pagável no destino.**	kehroo oomer koomoo-nikker**ssahng**w pergahvehl noo dishteenoo

Telephone alphabet *Alfabeto telefónico*

A	**Aveiro**	ahvayroo		N	**Nazaré**	nerzerreh
B	**Braga**	brahger		O	**Ovar**	ovvahr
C	**Coimbra**	kweengbrer		P	**Porto**	poartoo
D	**Dafundo**	dahfoongdoo		Q	**Queluz**	kehloosh
E	**Évora**	ehvoorer		R	**Rossio**	roosseeoo
F	**Faro**	fahroo		S	**Setúbal**	sertooberl
G	**Guarda**	gwahrder		T	**Tavira**	terveerer
H	**Horta**	orrter		U	**Unidade**	ooniddahder
I	**Itália**	ittahlyer		V	**Vidago**	viddahgoo
J	**José**	zhoozeh		W	**Waldemar**	vahldermahr
K	**Kodak**	koddahk		X	**Xavier**	shervyehr
L	**Lisboa**	lizhboaer		Y	**York**	"york"
M	**Maria**	merreeer		Z	**Zulmira**	zoolmeerer

Speaking *Ao telefone*

Hello, this is … speaking.	**Está [Alô]? Aqui fala …**	ishtah [ahloa]. erkee fahler
I'd like to speak to …	**Queria falar com …**	kerreeer ferlahr kawng
I'd like extension …	**Queria o interno [ramal] …**	kerreeer oo eengtehrnoo [rahmahl]
Speak louder/more slowly, please.	**Pode falar mais alto/mais devagar?**	podder ferlahr mighsh ahltoo/mighsh dervergahr

Bad luck *Pouca sorte*

Would you try again later, please?	**Pode voltar a chamar um pouco mais tarde?**	podder voltahr er shermahr oong poakoo mighsh tahrder
Operator, you gave me the wrong number.	**A menina [senhorita] deu-me um número errado.**	er merneener [sinnyoareetah] dehoo mer oong noomerroo irrahdoo

| Operator, we were cut off. | **Cortaram-nos a ligação.** | koortahrahng^w noosh er liggerssahng^w |

Not there   *A pessoa não está*

When will he/she be back?	**Quando é que ele/ ela estará de volta?**	kwahngdoo eh ker ayler/ ehler ishterrah der vollter
Will you tell him/her I called? My name is …	**Pode dizer-lhe que eu telefonei? O meu nome é …**	podder dizzayr lyer ker ehoo terlerfoonay oo mehoo noamer eh
Would you ask him/her to call me?	**Pode pedir-lhe para me telefonar?**	podder perdeer lyer perrer mer terlerfoonahr
Would you take a message, please?	**Pode dar-lhe um recado?**	podder dahr lyer oong rerkahdoo

Charges   *Taxas*

| What was the cost of that call? | **Qual foi o preço da chamada?** | kwahl foy oo prayssoo der shermahder |
| I want to pay for the call. | **Quero pagar a chamada.** | kehroo pergahr er shermahder |

Há uma chamada para o senhor/a senhora.	There's a telephone call for you.
Que número deseja?	What number are you calling?
A linha está impedida [ocupada].	The line's engaged.
Ninguém atende.	There's no answer.
Enganou-se no número.	You've got the wrong number.
O telefone está avariado [com defeito].	The phone is out of order.
É só um momento.	Just a moment.
Não desligue, por favor.	Hold on, please.
Ele/Ela não está neste momento.	He's/She's out at the moment.

Doctor

Make sure your health insurance policy covers any illness or
accident while on holiday. If it doesn't, ask your insurance
representative, automobile association or travel agent for
details of special health insurance.

General *Generalidades*

Can you get me a doctor?	**Pode chamar-me um médico?**	podder shermahr mer oong mehdikkoo
Is there a doctor here?	**Há aqui um médico?**	ah erkee oong mehdikkoo
I need a doctor, quickly.	**Preciso de um médico, depressa.**	prersseezoo der oong mehdikkoo derprehsser
Where can I find a doctor who speaks English?	**Onde posso encontrar um médico que fale inglês?**	awngder possoo ayngkawngtrahr oong mehdikkoo ker fahler eengglaysh
Where's the surgery (doctor's office)?	**Onde é o consultório médico?**	awngder eh oo kawngsooltorryoo mehdikkoo
What are the surgery (office) hours?	**Qual é o horário das consultas?**	kwahl eh oo orrahryoo dersh kawngsooltersh
Could the doctor come to see me here?	**O médico pode vir consultar-me aqui?**	oo mehdikkoo podder veer kawngsooltahr mer erkee
What time can the doctor come?	**A que horas pode vir o médico?**	er ker orrersh podder veer oo mehdikkoo
Can you recommend a/an …?	**Pode recomendar-me …?**	podder rerkoomayngdahr mer
general practitioner	**um médico de clínica geral**	oong mehdikkoo der kleenikker zherrahl
children's doctor	**um pediatra**	oong perdyahtrer
eye specialist	**um oftalmologista**	oong ofterlmooloozheeshter
gynaecologist	**um ginecologista**	oong zhinnerkooloozheeshter
Can I have an appointment …?	**Posso ter uma consulta …?**	possoo tayr oomer kawngsoolter
right now	**agora**	ergorrer
tomorrow	**amanhã**	ahmernyahng
as soon as possible	**o mais depressa possível**	oo mighsh derprehsser poosseevehl

CHEMIST'S, see page 108

Parts of the body *Partes do corpo*

appendix	o apêndice	oo erpayngdisser
arm	o braço	oo brahssoo
back	as costas	ersh koshtersh
bladder	a bexiga	er bersheeger
bone	o osso	oo oassoo
bowel	o intestino	oo eengtershteenoo
breast	o seio	oo sayoo
chest	o peito	oo paytoo
ear	a orelha	er oaraylyer
eye	o olho	oo oalyoo
face	o rosto	oo roashtoo
finger	o dedo	oo daydoo
foot	o pé	oo peh
genitals	os órgãos genitais	oosh orrgahng^{w}sh zhernittighsh
gland	a glândula	er glahngdooler
hand	a mão	er mahng^w
head	a cabeça	er kerbaysser
heart	o coração	oo koorerssahng^w
jaw	a maxila	er mahkseeler
joint	a articulação	er errtikkoolerssahng^w
kidney	o rim	oo reeng
knee	o joelho	oo zhwaylyoo
leg	a perna	er pehrner
lip	o lábio	oo lahbyoo
liver	o fígado	oo feegerdoo
lung	o pulmão	oo poolmahng^w
mouth	a boca	er boaker
muscle	o músculo	oo mooshkooloo
neck	o pescoço	oo pishkoassoo
nerve	o nervo	oo nayrvoo
nervous system	o sistema nervoso	oo sishtaymer nerrvoazoo
nose	o nariz	oo nerreesh
rib	a costela	er kooshtehler
shoulder	o ombro	oo awngbroo
skin	a pele	er pehler
spine	a coluna vertebral	er koolooner verrterbrahl
stomach	o estômago	oo ishtoamergoo
tendon	o tendão	oo tayngdahng^w
thigh	a coxa	er koasher
throat	a garganta	er gerrgahngter
thumb	o polegar	oo poolergahr
toe	o dedo do pé	oo daydoo doo peh
tongue	a língua	er leenggwer
tonsils	as amígdalas	ersh ermeederlersh

Accident—Injury   *Acidentes—Ferimentos*

There has been an accident.	**Houve um acidente.**	oaver oong erssiddayngter
My son/daughter has had a fall.	**O meu filho/a minha filha deu uma queda.**	oo mehoo feelyoo/er meenyer feelyer dehoo oomer kehder
He/She has hurt his/her head.	**Ele/Ela feriu a cabeça.**	ayler/ehler ferreeoo er kerbaysser
He's/She's unconscious.	**Ele/Ela está sem sentidos.**	ayler/ehler ishtah sahng^y sayngteedoosh
He's/She's bleeding (heavily).	**Ele/Ela está a sangrar (muito).**	ayler/ehler ishtah er sahnggrahr (moong^ytoo)
He's/She's (seriously) injured.	**Ele/Ela está (gravemente) ferido(a).**	ayler/ehler ishtah (grahvermayngter) ferreedoo(er)
His/Her arm is broken.	**Ele/Ela tem o braço partido [quebrado].**	ayler/ehler tahng^y oo brahssoo perrteedoo [kaybrahdoa]
His/Her ankle is swollen.	**Ele/Ela tem o tornozelo inchado.**	ayler/ehler tahng^y oo toornoozayloo eengshahdoo
I've been stung.	**Fui picado.**	fooy pikkahdoo
I've got something in my eye.	**Tenho qualquer coisa no olho.**	taynyoo kwahlkehr koyzer noo oalyoo
I've got a/an ...	**Tenho ...**	taynyoo
blister	**uma bolha**	oomer boalyer
boil	**um furúnculo**	oong fooroongkooloo
bruise	**uma contusão**	oomer kawngtoozahng^w
burn	**uma queimadura**	oomer kaymerdoorer
cut	**um corte**	oong korrter
graze	**uma esfoladela**	oomer ishfoolerdehler
lump	**um galo/um alto**	oong gahloo/oong ahltoo
rash	**uma erupção**	oomer irroopsahng^w
sting	**uma picada**	oomer pikkahder
swelling	**um inchaço**	oong eengshahssoo
wound	**uma ferida**	oomer ferreeder
Could you have a look at it?	**Pode dar uma olhadela?**	podder dahr oomer ollyerdehler
I can't move my ...	**Não posso mexer o/a/os/as ...**	nahng^w possoo mershayr oo/er/oosh/ersh
It hurts.	**Dói-me.**	doy mer

Onde lhe dói?	Where does it hurt?
Que género de dor sente?	What kind of pain is it?
crónica/aguda	dull/sharp
lancinante/persistente	throbbing/constant
intermitente	on and off
Está ...	It's ...
partido [quebrado]/torcido	broken/sprained
deslocado/rasgado	dislocated/torn
É preciso fazer uma radiografia.	I want you to have an X-ray.
É preciso pôr gesso.	You'll get a plaster.
Está infectado.	It's infected.
Está vacinado contra o tétano?	Have you been vaccinated against tetanus?
Vou dar-lhe um anti-séptico/ um analgésico.	I'll give you an antiseptic/ a painkiller.

Illness *Doenças*

I'm not feeling well.	Não me sinto bem.	nahng^w mer seengtoo bahng^y
I'm ill.	Estou doente.	ishtoa dwayngter
I feel ...	Tenho ...	taynyoo
dizzy	vertigens	verrteezhahng^ysh
nauseous	náuseas	nowzyersh
shivery	calafrios	kerlerfreeoosh
I've got a fever.	Tenho febre.	taynyoo fehbrer
My temperature is 38 degrees.	Tenho 38 de febre.	taynyoo 38 der fehbrer
I've been vomiting.	Vomitei.	voomittay
I'm constipated.	Tenho prisão de ventre [Estou constipado(a)].	taynyoo prizzahng^w der vayngtrer [istoa kawngstippahdoa(ah)]
I've got diarrhoea.	Tenho diarreia.	taynyoo dyerrayer
My ... hurts.	Dói-me o/a ...	doy mer oo/er

I've got (a/an) ...	Tenho ...	taynyoo
backache	dor nas costas	doar nersh koshtersh
cold	uma constipação [um resfriado]	oomer kawngshtipper-ssahng**ʷ** [oong rays-fryahdoa]
cough	tosse	tosser
cramps	cãibras	kahng**ʸ**brersh
earache	dor de ouvidos	doar der oaveedoosh
hay fever	a febre dos fenos	er fehbrer doosh faynoosh
headache	dor de cabeça	doar der kerbaysser
indigestion	uma indigestão	oomer eengdizhershtahng**ʷ**
nosebleed	uma hemorragia nasal	oomer immoorrerzheeer nerzahl
palpitations	palpitações	pahlpitterssawng**ʸ**sh
rheumatism	reumatismo	rehoomerteezhmoo
sore throat	dor de garganta	doar der gerrgahngter
stiff neck	um torcicolo	oong toorsikkolloo
stomach ache	dor de estômago	doar der ishtoamergoo
I have difficulties breathing.	Tenho dificuldade em respirar.	taynyoo diffikkooldahder ahng**ʸ** rishpirrahr
I have a pain in my chest.	Sinto uma dor no peito.	seengtoo oomer doar noo paytoo
I had a heart attack ... years ago.	Tive um ataque car-díaco há ... anos.	teever oong ertahker kerr-deeerkoo ah ... ernoosh
My blood pressure is too high/too low.	Tenho uma tensão arterial muito alta/baixa.	taynyoo oomer tayngsahng**ʷ** errterryahl moong**ʸ**too ahlter/bighsher
I'm allergic to ...	Sou alérgico(a) a ...	soa erlehrzhikkoo(er) er
I'm diabetic.	Sou diabético(a).	soa dyerbehtikkoo(er)

Women's section *Sector da mulher*

I have period pains.	Tenho dores menstruais.	taynyoo doarersh mayngshtrwighsh
I have a vaginal infection.	Tenho uma infecção vaginal.	taynyoo oomer eeng-fehssahng**ʷ** verzhinnahl
I'm on the pill.	Tomo a pílula.	tommoo er peelooler
I haven't had my period for 2 months.	Há 2 meses que não tenho menstruação.	ah 2 mayzersh ker nahng**ʷ** taynyoo mayngshtrwers-sahng**ʷ**
I'm pregnant.	Estou grávida.	ishtoa grahvidder

Há quanto tempo se sente assim?	How long have you been feeling like this?
É a primeira vez que sente isso?	Is this the first time you've had this?
Vou tirar-lhe a temperatura/a tensão arterial.	I'll take your temperature/blood pressure.
Arregace a manga, por favor.	Roll up your sleeve, please.
Dispa-se (da cintura para cima), se faz favor.	Please undress (down to the waist).
Deite-se ali, se faz favor.	Please lie down over here.
Abra a boca.	Open your mouth.
Respire fundo.	Breathe deeply.
Tussa, por favor.	Cough, please.
Onde é que lhe dói?	Where does it hurt?
Tem ...	You've got (a/an) ...
uma apendicite	appendicitis
asma	asthma
uma cistite	cystitis
uma doença venérea	venereal disease
uma gastrite	gastritis
uma gripe	flu
uma icterícia	jaundice
uma inflamação de ...	inflammation of ...
uma insolação	sunstroke
uma intoxicação alimentar	food poisoning
uma pneumonia	pneumonia
sarampo	measles
(Não) é contagioso.	It's (not) contagious.
Vou dar-lhe uma injecção.	I'll give you an injection.
Quero uma amostra do seu sangue/das suas fezes/da sua urina.	I want a specimen of your blood/stools/urine.
Deve ficar na cama durante ... dias.	You must stay in bed for ... days.
Quero que consulte um especialista.	I want you to see a specialist.

Prescription—Treatment   *Receita—Tratamento*

This is my usual medicine.	**Este é o meu medicamento habitual.**	ayshter eh oo mehoo merdikkermayngtoo erbittwahl
Can you give me a prescription for this?	**Pode dar-me uma receita para isto?**	podder dahr mer oomer rerssayter perrer eeshtoo
Can you prescribe a/an/some ...?	**Pode receitar-me ...**	podder rerssaytahr mer
antidepressant	**um antidepressivo**	oong ahngtidderprer-sseevoo
sleeping pills	**um sonífero**	oong sooneeferroo
tranquillizer	**um calmante**	oong kahlmahngter
I'm allergic to antibiotics/penicillin.	**Sou alérgico(a) a antibióticos/ à penicilina.**	soa erlehrzhikkoo(er) er ahngtibbyottikkoosh/ ah pernissilleener
I don't want anything too strong.	**Não quero nada muito forte.**	nahng^w kehroo nahder moong^ytoo forrter
How many times a day should I take it?	**Quantas vezes devo tomá-lo por dia?**	kwahngtersh vayzersh dayvoo toomah loo poor deeer
Must I swallow them whole?	**Devo engoli-los inteiros?**	dayvoo aynggoolee loosh eengtayroosh

Que tratamento está a fazer?	What treatment are you having?
Que remédio está a tomar?	What medicine are you taking?
Em injecção ou por via oral?	By injection or orally?
Tome ... colheres de chá deste remédio ...	Take ... teaspoons of this medicine ...
Tome um comprimido com um copo de água ...	Take one pill with a glass of water ...
de 2 em 2 horas	every 2 hours
3 vezes por dia	3 times a day
antes/depois das refeições	before/after each meal
de manhã/à noite	in the morning/at night
se tiver dores	if there is any pain
durante 7 dias	for 7 days

CHEMIST'S, see p. 108

Fee *Honorários*

How much do I owe you?	**Quanto lhe devo?**	kwahngtoo lyer dayvoo
May I have a receipt for my health insurance?	**Pode passar-me um recibo para o meu seguro de doença?**	podder perssahr mer oong rersseeboo perrer oo mehoo sergooroo der dwayngser
Can I have a medical certificate?	**Pode passar-me um certificado médico?**	podder perssahr mer oong serrtiffikkahdoo mehdikkoo
Would you fill in this health insurance form, please?	**Pode preencher esta folha de seguro?**	podder pryayngshayr ehshter foalyer der sergooroo

Hospital *Hospital*

Please notify my family.	**Por favor, avise a minha família.**	poor fervoar erveezer er meenyer fermeelyer
What are the visiting hours?	**Quais são as horas de visita?**	kwighsh sahng ersh orrersh der vizzeeter
When can I get up?	**Quando posso levantar-me?**	kwahngdoo possoo lervahngtahr mer
When will the doctor come?	**Quando vem o médico?**	kwahngdoo vahng oo mehdikkoo
I'm in pain.	**Estou com dores.**	ishtoa kawng doarersh
I can't eat/sleep.	**Não posso comer/dormir.**	nahng possoo koomayr/doormeer
Where is the bell?	**Onde está a campainha?**	awngder ishtah er kahngpereenyer

nurse	**a enfermeira**	er ayngferrmayrer
patient	**o(a) paciente**	oo(er) perssyayngter
anaesthesia	**a anestesia**	er ernershterzeeer
blood transfusion	**a transfusão de sangue**	er trahngshfoozahng der sahngger
injection	**a injecção**	er eengzhehssahng
operation	**a operação**	er opperrerssahng
bed	**a cama**	er kermer
bedpan	**a bacia de cama**	er bersseeer der kermer
thermometer	**o termómetro**	oo terrmommertroo

Dentist *Dentista*

Can you recommend a good dentist?	**Pode recomendar-me um bom dentista?**	podder rerkoomayng**dahr** mer oong bawng dayng**tee**sh**ter**
Can I make an (urgent) appointment to see Dr. ...?	**Posso marcar uma consulta (urgente) com o Dr. ...?**	possoo merr**kahr** oomer kawng**soolter** (oorzhayng-ter) kawng oo doa**toar**
Couldn't you make it earlier than that?	**Não pode ser antes?**	nahng^w podder sayr **ahng**tish
I have a bad tooth.	**Tenho um dente furado.**	taynyoo oong **dayng**ter foorahdoo
I have a broken tooth.	**Parti [Quebrei] um dente.**	perr**tee** [kaybray] oong **dayng**ter
I have a toothache.	**Tenho dor de dentes.**	taynyoo doar der **dayng**tish
I have an abscess.	**Tenho um abcesso.**	taynyoo oong erb**ssehs**soo
This tooth hurts.	**Dói-me este dente.**	doy mer **aysh**ter **dayng**ter
at the top at the bottom in the front at the back	**em cima em baixo à frente atrás**	ahng^y **see**mer ahng^y **bigh**shoo ah frayng**ter** er**trahsh**
Can you fix it temporarily?	**Pode tratá-lo provisoriamente?**	podder trer**tah** loo proovizzorryer**mayng**ter
I don't want it taken out.	**Não quero arrancá-lo.**	nahng^w **keh**roo errahngkah loo
Could you give me an anaesthetic?	**Pode fazer-me uma anestesia?**	podder fer**zayr** mer oomer ernersh**ter**zeeer
I've lost a filling.	**Perdi um chumbo.**	perr**dee** oong **shoong**boo
The gum ...	**A gengiva ...**	er zhayng**zhee**ver
is very sore	**está muito inflamada**	ish**tah** moong^ytoo eeng**fler**mahder
is bleeding	**sangra**	**sahng**grer
I've broken this denture.	**Parti [Quebrei] a dentadura.**	perr**tee** [kaybray] er dayngter**door**er
Can you repair this denture?	**Pode consertar esta dentadura?**	podder kawngserr**tahr** **ehsh**ter dayngter**door**er
When will it be ready?	**Quando estará pronta?**	kwahng**doo** ish**terr**ah **prawng**ter

Reference section

Where do you come from? *Donde é?*

Africa	a África	er ahfrikker
Asia	a Ásia	er ahzyer
Australia	a Austrália	er owshtrahlyer
Europe	a Europa	er ehooropper
North America	a América do Norte	er ermehrikker doo norrter
South America	a América do Sul	er ermehrikker doo sool
Algeria	a Argélia	er errzhehlyer
Azores	os Açores	oosh erssoarersh
Bolivia	a Bolívia	er booleevyer
Brazil	o Brasil	oo brerzeel
Canada	o Canadá	oo kernerdah
China	a China	er sheener
Colombia	a Colômbia	er koolawngbyer
England	a Inglaterra	er eengglertehrrer
France	a França	er frahngser
Germany	a Alemanha	er erlermernyer
Great Britain	a Grã-Bretanha	er grahng brerternyer
Greece	a Grécia	er grehssyer
India	a Índia	er eengdyer
Ireland	a Irlanda	er irlahngder
Israel	Israel	izhrerehl
Italy	a Itália	er ittahlyer
Japan	o Japão	oo zherpahng^w
Madeira	a Madeira	er merdayrer
Morocco	Marrocos	merrokkoosh
New Zealand	a Nova Zelândia	er novver zerlahngdyer
Paraguay	o Paraguai	oo perrergwigh
Peru	o Peru	oo perroo
Portugal	Portugal	poortoogahl
Scotland	a Escócia	er ishkossyer
South Africa	a África do Sul	er ahfrikker doo sool
Soviet Union	a União Soviética	er oonyahng^w soovyehtikker
Spain	a Espanha	er ishpernyer
Switzerland	a Suíça	er sweesser
Tunisia	a Tunísia	er tooneezyer
United States	os Estados Unidos	oosh ishtahdoosh oonee-doosh
Uruguay	o Uruguai	oo ooroogwigh
Venezuela	a Venezuela	er vernerzwehler
Wales	o País de Gales	oo pereesh der gahlersh

Numbers *Números*

0	**zero**	zehroo
1	**um, uma**	oong oomer
2	**dois, duas**	doysh **dooersh**
3	**três**	traysh
4	**quatro**	kwahtroo
5	**cinco**	seengkoo
6	**seis**	saysh
7	**sete**	sehter
8	**oito**	oytoo
9	**nove**	novver
10	**dez**	dehsh
11	**onze**	awngzer
12	**doze**	doazer
13	**treze**	trayzer
14	**catorze**	kertoarzer
15	**quinze**	keengzer
16	**dezasseis**	derzerssaysh
17	**dezassete**	derzerssehter
18	**dezoito**	derzoytoo
19	**dezanove**	derzernovver
20	**vinte**	veengter
21	**vinte e um**	veengter ee oong
22	**vinte e dois**	veengter ee doysh
23	**vinte e três**	veengter ee traysh
24	**vinte e quatro**	veengter ee kwahtroo
25	**vinte e cinco**	veengter ee seengkoo
26	**vinte e seis**	veengter ee saysh
27	**vinte e sete**	veengter ee sehter
28	**vinte e oito**	veengter ee oytoo
29	**vinte e nove**	veengter ee novver
30	**trinta**	treengter
31	**trinta e um**	treengter ee oong
32	**trinta e dois**	treengter ee doysh
33	**trinta e três**	treengter ee traysh
40	**quarenta**	kwerrayngter
41	**quarenta e um**	kwerrayngter ee oong
42	**quarenta e dois**	kwerrayngter ee doysh
43	**quarenta e três**	kwerrayngter ee traysh
50	**cinquenta**	seengkwayngter
51	**cinquenta e um**	seengkwayngter ee oong
52	**cinquenta e dois**	seengkwayngter ee doysh
53	**cinquenta e três**	seengkwayngter ee traysh
60	**sessenta**	serssayngter
61	**sessenta e um**	serssayngter ee oong
62	**sessenta e dois**	serssayngter ee doysh

63	**sessenta e três**	serss**sayng**ter ee traysh
70	**setenta**	ser**tayng**ter
71	**setenta e um**	ser**tayng**ter ee oong
72	**setenta e dois**	ser**tayng**ter ee doysh
73	**setenta e três**	ser**tayng**ter ee traysh
80	**oitenta**	oy**tayng**ter
81	**oitenta e um**	oy**tayng**ter ee oong
82	**oitenta e dois**	oy**tayng**ter ee doysh
83	**oitenta e três**	oy**tayng**ter ee traysh
90	**noventa**	noo**vayng**ter
91	**noventa e um**	noo**vayng**ter ee oong
92	**noventa e dois**	noo**vayng**ter ee doysh
93	**noventa e três**	noo**vayng**ter ee traysh
100	**cem/cento***	sahng^y/**sahng**^{y}too
101	**cento e um**	**sayng**too ee oong
102	**cento e dois**	**sayng**too ee doysh
110	**cento e dez**	**sayng**too ee dehsh
120	**cento e vinte**	**sayng**too ee **veeng**ter
130	**cento e trinta**	**sayng**too ee **treeng**ter
140	**cento e quarenta**	**sayng**too ee kwer**rayng**ter
150	**cento e cinquenta**	**sayng**too ee seengk**wayng**ter
160	**cento e sessenta**	**sayng**too ee serss**sayng**ter
170	**cento e setenta**	**sayng**too ee ser**tayng**ter
180	**cento e oitenta**	**sayng**too ee oy**tayng**ter
190	**cento e noventa**	**sayng**too ee noo**vayng**ter
200	**duzentos**	doo**zayng**toosh
300	**trezentos**	trer**zayng**toosh
400	**quatrocentos**	kwahtroos**sayng**toosh
500	**quinhentos**	kinn**yayng**toosh
600	**seiscentos**	saysh**sayng**toosh
700	**setecentos**	sehterss**sayng**toosh
800	**oitocentos**	oytoos**sayng**toosh
900	**novecentos**	novverss**sayng**toosh
1000	**mil**	meel
1100	**mil e cem**	meel ee sahng^y
1200	**mil e duzentos**	meel ee doo**zayng**toosh
2000	**dois mil**	doysh meel
5000	**cinco mil**	**seengkoo** meel
10,000	**dez mil**	dehsh meel
50,000	**cinquenta mil**	seengk**wayng**ter meel
100,000	**cem mil**	sahng^y meel
1,000,000	**um milhão**	oong mill**yahng**^{w}
1,000,000,000	**um bilhão**	oong bill**yahng**^{w}

---

* *cem* is used before nouns and adjectives.

first	**primeiro**	primmayroo
second	**segundo**	sergoongdoo
third	**terceiro**	terrsayroo
fourth	**quarto**	kwahrtoo
fifth	**quinto**	keengtoo
sixth	**sexto**	sayshtoo
seventh	**sétimo**	sehtimmoo
eighth	**oitavo**	oytahvoo
ninth	**nono**	noanoo
tenth	**décimo**	dehssimmoo
once	**uma vez**	oomer vaysh
twice	**duas vezes**	dooersh vayzersh
three times	**três vezes**	traysh vayzersh
a half	**uma metade**	oomer mertahder
half a ...	**meio ...**	mayoo
half of ...	**metade de ...**	mertahder der
half (adj.)	**meio**	mayoo
a quarter/one third	**um quarto/um terço**	oong kwahrtoo/oong tayrsoo
a pair of	**um par de**	oong pahr der
a dozen	**uma dúzia**	oomer doozyer
one per cent	**um por cento**	oong poor sayngtoo
3.4%	**3,4%**	traysh veergooler kwahrtoo poor sayngtoo
1981	**mil novecentos e oitenta e um**	meel novverssayngtoosh ee oytayngter ee oong
1992	**mil novecentos e noventa e dois**	meel novverssayngtoosh ee noovayngter ee doysh
2003	**dois mil e três**	doysh meel ee traysh

Year and age *Ano e idade*

year	**o ano**	oo ernoo
leap year	**o ano bissexto**	oo ernoo bissayshtoo
decade	**a década**	er dehkerder
century	**o século**	oo sehkooloo
this year	**este ano**	ayshter ernoo
last year	**o ano passado**	oo ernoo perssahdoo
next year	**o próximo ano**	oo prossimmoo ernoo
each year	**cada ano**	kerder ernoo
2 years ago	**há 2 anos**	ah 2 ernoosh
in one year	**dentro de um ano**	dayngtroo der oong ernoo
in the eighties	**nos anos oitenta**	noosh ernoosh oytayngter
the 16th century	**o século dezasseis**	oo sehkooloo derzerssaysh
in the 20th century	**no século vinte**	noo sehkooloo veengter

How old are you?	Que idade tem?	ker **iddah**der tahng^y
I'm 30 years old.	Tenho trinta anos.	taynyoo **treeng**ter ernoosh
He/She was born in 1960.	Ele/Ela nasceu em mil novecentos e sessenta.	ayler/**ehler** nersh**seh**oo ahng^y meel novver**ssayng**toosh ee sers**sayng**ter
What is his/her age?	Que idade tem ele/ela?	ker **iddah**der tahng^y ayler/**ehler**
Children under 16 are not admitted.	Não se admitem crianças menores de dezasseis anos.	nahng^w ser erd**mee**tahng^y kryahng**sersh** mer**norr**ersh der derzer**ssaysh** ernoosh

Seasons *Estações do ano*

spring/summer	a Primavera/o Verão	er primmer**veh**rer/oo ver**rahng**^{w}
autumn/winter	o Outono/o Inverno	oo oa**toa**noo/oo eeng**vehr**noo
in spring	na Primavera	ner primmer**veh**rer
during the summer	durante o Verão	doo**rahng**ter oo ver**rahng**^{w}
in autumn	no Outono	noo oa**toa**noo
during the winter	durante o Inverno	doo**rahng**ter oo eeng**vehr**noo
high/low season	a época alta/baixa	er **ehpoo**ker **ahl**ter/**bigh**sher

Months *Meses*

January	Janeiro	zher**nay**roo
February	Fevereiro	ferver**ray**roo
March	Março	**mahr**soo
April	Abril	er**breel**
May	Maio	**migh**oo
June	Junho	**zhoon**yoo
July	Julho	**zhool**yoo
August	Agosto	er**goash**too
September	Setembro	ser**tayng**broo
October	Outubro	oa**too**broo
November	Novembro	noo**vayng**broo
December	Dezembro	der**zayng**broo
in September	em Setembro	ahng^y ser**tayng**broo
since October	desde Outubro	**dayzh**der oa**too**broo
the beginning of ...	o princípio de ...	oo preeng**seep**yoo der
the middle of ...	os meados de ...	oosh myah**doosh** der
the end of ...	o fim de ...	oo feeng der

Days and date   *Dias e data*

What day is it today?	**Que dia é hoje?**	ker **dee**er eh **oa**zher
Sunday	**domingo***	doomeenggoo
Monday	**segunda-feira**	sergoongder fayrer
Tuesday	**terça-feira**	tayrser fayrer
Wednesday	**quarta-feira**	kwahrter fayrer
Thursday	**quinta-feira**	keengter fayrer
Friday	**sexta-feira**	sayshter fayrer
Saturday	**sábado**	sahberdoo
It's ...	**Estamos ...**	ishtermoosh
July 1	**no dia 1 [no 1º] de Julho**	noo **dee**er oong [noo primmayroa] der **zhoo**lyoo
March 10	**no dia 10 de Março**	noo **dee**er dehsh der **mahr**soo
in the morning	**de manhã**	der mernyahng
during the day	**durante o dia**	doorahngter oo **dee**er
in the afternoon	**à tarde**	ah tahrder
in the evening	**à noite**	ah noyter
at night	**à noite**	ah noyter
the day before yesterday	**anteontem**	ahng**tyawng**tahng^y
yesterday	**ontem**	**awng**tahng^y
today	**hoje**	**oa**zher
tomorrow	**amanhã**	ahmernyahng
the day before	**a véspera**	er **vehsh**perrer
the next day	**o dia seguinte**	oo **dee**er ser**gheeng**ter
two days ago	**há dois dias**	ah doysh **dee**ersh
in three days' time	**daqui a três dias**	derkee er traysh **dee**ersh
last week	**a semana passada**	er sermerner per**ssah**der
next week	**a próxima semana**	er **pro**ssimmer sermerner
for a fortnight (two weeks)	**durante duas semanas**	doorahngter dooersh sermernersh
birthday	**o dia de anos**	oo **dee**er der **er**nosh
day off	**o dia de folga**	oo **dee**er der **foll**ger
holiday	**o feriado**	oo ferr**yah**doo
holidays/vacation	**as férias**	ersh **feh**ryersh
week	**a semana**	er sermerner
weekday	**o dia de semana**	oo **dee**er der sermerner
weekend	**o fim-de-semana**	oo feeng der sermerner
working day	**o dia útil**	oo **dee**er ootill

---

* The names of days aren't capitalized in Portuguese.

Public holidays   *Feriados*

Listed below are the main public holidays in Portugal (P) and Brazil (B), when banks, offices and shops are closed.

January 1	**Ano Novo**	New Year's Day	P	B
April 21	**Tiradentes**	Tiradentes' Day		B
April 25	**Dia de Portugal**	National Day	P	
May 1	**Dia do Trabalho**	Labour Day	P	B
June 10	**Dia de Camões**	Camoens' Day	P	
August 15	**Assunção**	Assumption	P	
September 7	**Independência**	Independence Day		B
October 5	**Dia da República**	Republic Day	P	
October 12	**Nossa Senhora de Aparecida**	Patron Saint's day		B
November 1	**Todos-os-Santos**	All Saints' Day	P	
November 2	**Finados**	All Souls' Day		B
November 15	**Proclamação da República**	Republic Day		B
December 1	**Restauração**	Restoration Day	P	
December 8	**Imaculada Conceição**	Immaculate Conception	P	B
December 25	**Natal**	Christmas Day	P	B
Movable dates:	**Terça-feira de Carnaval**	Shrove Tuesday	P	B
	Sexta-feira Santa	Good Friday	P	B
	Corpo de Deus	Corpus Christi	P	B

Merry Christmas!	**Feliz Natal!**	ferleesh nertahl
Happy New Year!	**Próspero Ano Novo!**	proshperroo ernoo noavoo
Happy Easter!	**Páscoa feliz!**	pahshkwer ferleesh
Happy birthday!	**Parabéns!/Feliz aniversário!**	perrerbahng^ysh/ferleesh ernivversahryoo
Best wishes!	**Felicidades!**	ferlissiddahdish
Congratulations!	**Parabéns!**	perrerbahng^ysh
Good luck/ All the best!	**Boa sorte!**	boaer sorrter
Have a good trip!	**Boa viagem!**	boaer vyahzhahng^y
Have a good holiday!	**Boas férias!**	boaersh fehryersh
Best regards from ...	**Cumprimentos de ...**	koongprimmayngtoosh der ...
My regards to ...	**Cumprimentos a ...**	koongprimmayngtoosh er ...

What time is it? *Que horas são?*

Excuse me. Can you tell me the time?	Desculpe. Pode dizer-me as horas?	dishkoolper. podder diz-zayr mer ersh orrersh
It's one o'clock.	É uma hora*.	eh oomer orrer
It's two o'clock.	São duas horas.	sahng^w dooersh orrersh
five past ...	... e cinco	... ee seengkoo
ten past ...	... e dez	... ee dehsh
a quarter past ...	... e um quarto	... ee oong kwahrtoo
twenty past ...	... e vinte	... ee veengter
twenty-five past ...	... e vinte e cinco	... ee veengter ee seengkoo
half past ...	... e meia	... ee mayer
twenty-five to ...	vinte e cinco para as ...	veengter ee seengkoo perrer ersh ...
twenty to ...	vinte para as ...	veengter perrer ersh
a quarter to ...	um quarto para as ...	oong kwahrtoo perrer ersh
ten to ...	dez para as ...	dehsh perrer ersh ...
five to ...	cinco para as ...	seengkoo perrer ersh ...
in the morning/ afternoon/evening	da manhã/da tarde/da noite	der mernyahng/der tahrder/der noyter
noon/midnight	meio-dia/meia-noite	mayoo deeer/mayer noyter
The train leaves at ...	O comboio [trem] parte às ...	oo kawngboyoo [trahng^y] pahrter ahsh
13.04 (1.04 p.m.)	treze horas e quatro minutos	trayzer orrersh ee kwahtroo minnootoosh
0.40 (0.40 a.m.)	zero horas e quarenta minutos	zehroo orrersh ee kwer-rayngter minnootoosh
in five minutes	daqui a cinco minutos	derkee er seengkoo minnootoosh
in a quarter of an hour	daqui a um quarto de hora	derkee er oong kwahrtoo der orrer
half an hour ago	há meia-hora	ah mayer orrer
about two hours	cerca de duas horas	sayrker der dooersh orrersh
more than 10 minutes	mais de dez minutos	mighsh de dehsh minnootoosh
less than 30 seconds	menos de trinta segundos	maynoosh der treengter sergoongdoosh
The clock is fast/ slow.	O relógio está adiantado/atrasado.	oo rerlozhyoo ishtah er-dyahngtahdoo/ertrerzahdoo

---

* In ordinary conversation, time is expressed as shown here. However, in official time the 24-hour clock is used, which means that after noon hours are counted from 13 to 24.

NUMBERS, see page 147

REFERENCE SECTION

Informações diversas

Common abbreviations *Abreviaturas usuais*

(a)	assinado	signed
a/c	ao cuidado de	c/o
A.C.B.	Automóvel Clube do Brasil	Brazilian Automobile Association
A.C.P.	Automóvel Clube de Portugal	Portuguese Automobile Association
apart., ap.	apartamento	flat (apartment)
Calç.	calçada	paved street
c/c	conta corrente	current account
c/v	cave	basement; cellar
Cia., C.ia	companhia	company
CEE	Comunidade Económica Europeia	EEC, Common Market
CP	Caminhos de Ferro Portugueses	Portuguese Railways
D.	Dona	Mrs. (title of courtesy)
d., dto.	direito	on the right (in addresses)
e., esq.	esquerdo	on the left (in addresses)
ENATUR	Empresa Nacional de Turismo	Portuguese National Tourist Office
E.U.A.	Estados Unidos da América	U.S.A.
Exma., Ex.ma	Excelentíssima	title of courtesy
Exmo., Ex.mo	Excelentíssimo	(followed by Mrs. or Mr.)
G.N.R.	Guarda Nacional Republicana	National Republican Guard (police)
h	hora	o'clock
IVA	Imposto sobre o Valor Acrescentado	VAT, value-added tax
L., L.o	Largo	square
Lx.a	Lisboa	Lisbon
Men.a	Menina	Miss (Portugal)
P.	Praça	square
r/c	rés-do-chão	ground floor
Rem., Rem.te	remetente	sender
R.N.	Rodoviária Nacional	Portuguese Transport Company
R.P.	Rádio-Patrulha	Police Patrol
RTP	Rádio e Televisão Portuguesa	Portuguese Broadcasting Company
R.	rua	street
s.f.f.	se faz favor	please
Sr., Sra., Srta.	Senhor, Senhora Senhorita	Mr., Mrs., Miss (Brazil)

Signs and notices *Sinais e letreiros*

Aberto	Open
Alfândega	Customs
Aluga-se	For hire/To let (for rent)
Atenção	Caution
Avariado	Out of order
Aviso	Notice
Caixa	Cash desk
Cavalheiros	Gentlemen
Completo	Full/No vacancies
Correio	Post office
Cuidado com o cão	Beware of the dog
É favor não incomodar	Do not disturb
É favor não mexer	Do not touch
Elevador	Lift (elevator)
Empurre	Push
Encerrado	Closed
Entrada	Entrance
Entrada livre	Free entrance
Entre (sem bater)	Enter (without knocking)
Espere, s.f.f.	Please wait
Fechado	Closed
Frio	Cold
Fumadores	Smoking allowed
Homens	Gentlemen
Informações	Information
Leilão	Auction
Livre	Vacant/Free
Lotação esgotada	Sold out (Theatre)
Ocupado	Occupied
Perigo (de morte)	Danger (of death)
Pintado de fresco	Wet paint
Privado	Private
Proibido ...	... forbidden
Proibido a cães	Dogs not allowed
Proibido fumar	No smoking
Puxe	Pull
Quente	Hot
Reservado	Reserved
Saída	Exit
Saída de emergência	Emergency exit
Saldos	Sale
Senhoras	Ladies
Toque à campainha, s.f.f.	Please ring
Vende-se	For sale
Veneno	Poison

Emergency   *Urgências*

Call the police	Chame a polícia	shermer er pooleessyer
Consulate	Consulado	kawngsoolahdoo
DANGER	PERIGO	perreegoo
Embassy	Embaixada	ayngbighshahder
FIRE	FOGO	foagoo
Gas	Gás	gash
Get a doctor	Chame um médico	shermer oong mehdikkoo
Go away	Vá-se embora	vah ser ayngborrer
HELP	SOCORRO	sookoarroo
Get help	Vá buscar ajuda	vah booshkahr erzhooder
I'm ill	Estou doente	ishtoa dwayngter
I'm lost	Perdi-me	perrdee mer
Leave me alone	Deixe-me em paz	daysher mer ahng^w pash
LOOK OUT	ATENÇÃO	ertayngsahng^w
POLICE	POLÍCIA	pooleessyer
Quick	Depressa	derprehsser
STOP	ALTO	ahltoo
Stop that man/ woman	Prenda aquele homem/aquela mulher	prayngder erkayler ommahng^y/erkehler moolyehr
STOP THIEF	AGARRA QUE É LADRÃO	ergahrrer ker eh lerdrahng^w

Lost property—Theft   *Perda—Roubo*

Where's the ...?	Onde é ...?	awngder eh
lost property (lost and found) office	a secção dos perdidos e achados	er sehksahng^w doosh perrdeedoosh ee ershahdoosh
police station	o posto da polícia	oo poashtoo der pooleessyer
I want to report a theft.	Quero dar parte de um roubo.	kehroo dahr pahrter der oong roaboo
My ... has been stolen.	Roubaram-me ...	roabahrahng^w mer
handbag	a mala de mão [bolsa]	er mahler der mahng^w [boalsah]
passport	o passaporte	o persserporrter
I've lost my ...	Perdi ...	perrdee
ticket	o meu bilhete	oo mehoo billyayter
wallet	a minha carteira	er meenyer kerrtayrer
I lost it in ...	Perdi-o(a) em ...	perrdee oo(er) ahng^y

CAR ACCIDENTS, see page 78

Conversion tables

Centimetres and inches

To change centimetres into inches, multiply by .39.

To change inches into centimetres, multiply by 2.54.

	in.	feet	yards
1 mm.	0.039	0.003	0.001
1 cm.	0.39	0.03	0.01
1 dm.	3.94	0.32	0.10
1 m.	39.40	3.28	1.09

	mm.	cm.	m.
1 in.	25.4	2.54	0.025
1 ft.	304.8	30.48	0.305
1 yd.	914.4	91.44	0.914

(32 metres = 35 yards)

Temperature

To convert centigrade into degrees Fahrenheit, multiply centigrade by 1.8 and add 32.

To convert degrees Fahrenheit into centigrade, subtract 32 from Fahrenheit and divide by 1.8.

C°
100
40
36,9
35
30
25
20
15
10
5
0
−5
−10
−15
−20

F°
212
105
98,6
90
80
70
60
50
40
32
30
20
10
0

inches
1
2
3
4

cm. 1
2
3
4
5
6
7
8
9
10
11
12

REFERENCE SECTION

Kilometres into miles												
1 kilometre (km.) = 0.62 miles												
km.	10	20	30	40	50	60	70	80	90	100	110	120	130
miles	6	12	19	25	31	37	44	50	56	62	68	75	81

Miles into kilometres										
1 mile = 1.609 kilometres (km.)										
miles	10	20	30	40	50	60	70	80	90	100
km.	16	32	48	64	80	97	113	129	145	161

Fluid measures										
1 litre (l.) = 0.88 imp. quart or 1.06 U.S. quart										
1 imp. quart = 1.14 l. 1 U.S. quart = 0.95 l.										
1 imp. gallon = 4.55 l. 1 U.S. gallon = 3.8 l.										
litres	5	10	15	20	25	30	35	40	45	50
imp. gal.	1.1	2.2	3.3	4.4	5.5	6.6	7.7	8.8	9.9	11.0
U.S. gal.	1.3	2.6	3.9	5.2	6.5	7.8	9.1	10.4	11.7	13.0

Weights and measures
1 kilogram or kilo (kg.) = 1000 grams (g.)

100 g. = 3.5 oz.	½ kg. = 1.1 lb.
200 g. = 7.0 oz.	1 kg. = 2.2 lb.
1 oz. = 28.35 g.	
1 lb. = 453.60 g.	

CLOTHING SIZES, see page 115/YARDS AND INCHES, see page 112

Informações diversas

Basic Grammar

Here's the briefest possible outline of some essential features of Portuguese grammar.

Articles

Articles agree with the noun in gender and number.

Definite article (the):

	masculine	feminine
singular	**o**	**a**
plural	**os**	**as**

Indefinite article (a/an):

	masculine	feminine
singular	**um**	**uma**
plural	**uns**	**umas**

Note: The plural corresponds to the English "some" or "a few".

To show possession, the preposition **de** (of) + the article is contracted to **do, da, dos** or **das.**

o princípio do mês	the beginning of the month
o fim da semana	the end of the week

Nouns

All nouns in Portuguese are either masculine or feminine. Normally, those ending in **o** are masculine and those ending in **a** are feminine. Generally, nouns which end in a vowel add **-s** to form the plural:

a menina	the little girl
as meninas	the little girls
o pato	the duck
os patos	the ducks

Words ending in **r, s** or **z** form the plural by adding **-es:**

a mulher	the woman
as mulheres	the women
o país	the country
os países	the countries
a luz	the light
as luzes	the lights

Words ending in a nasal sound (**em, im, om, um**) change their endings to **ens, ins, ons, uns** in the plural.

Adjectives

These agree with the nouns they modify in gender and number.

o belo livro	the nice book
a bela estátua	the fine statue
os homens altos	the tall men
as mulheres altas	the tall women

From these examples you can see that adjectives can come before or after the noun. This is a matter of sound and idiom.

Demonstrative adjectives

this	**este** (masc.)/**esta** (fem.)
that	**esse, aquele** (masc.)/ **essa, aquela** (fem.)
these	**estes** (masc.)/**estas** (fem.)
those	**esses, aqueles** (masc.)/ **essas, aquelas** (fem.)

The difference between the three forms is that **este** means within reach, **esse** a bit farther and **aquele** means out of reach. There are also three invariable demonstrative adjectives in Portuguese: **isto, isso** and **aquilo.**

Tome isto.	Take this.
Deixe isso, por favor.	Leave that, please.
Dê-me aquilo, ali.	Give me that, over there.

Possessive adjectives

These agree in number and gender with the noun they modify, i.e., with the thing possessed and not the possessor.

	masculine	feminine
my	meu	minha
your	teu	tua
his/her/its	seu	sua
our	nosso	nossa
your	vosso	vossa
their	seu	sua

All these forms add an **s** to form the plural.

Note: The form of the third person can be used instead of the second, as a form of politeness:

Meu amigo, o seu livro deixou-me óptima impressão.	My friend, your book made a very good impression on me.

Personal pronouns

	subject	direct object	indirect object
I	eu	me	mim
you	tu	te	ti
he/it	ele	o	lhe
she/it	ela	a	lhe
we	nós	nos	nos
you	vós	vos	vos
they (masc.)	eles	os	lhes
they (fem.)	elas	as	lhes

There are two forms for "you" (singular) in Portuguese: the intimate **tu** when talking to relatives, friends and children and **você,** which is used in all other cases between people who don't know each other very well. But when addressing someone you normally use the third person of the singular or of the plural (this is the polite form used throughout this book):

Como está (estão)?	How are you?

Verbs

There are four auxiliary verbs in Portuguese:

ter/haver	to have
ser/estar	to be

Ter indicates possession or a condition:

Tenho uma casa.	I have a house.
Tenho febre.	I have a fever.

Haver in the meaning of "to exist" is only used in the third person of the singular (there is/there are):

Há muitas pessoas aqui.	There are too many people here.

Ser indicates a permanent state:

Sou inglês.	I am English.

Estar indicates movement or a non-permanent state:

Estou a passear [Estou passeando].	I am walking.
Está doente.	He is ill.

	ter (to have)	ser (to be)	estar (to be)
eu	tenho	sou	estou
tu	tens	és	estás
ele/ela	tem	é	está
nós	temos	somos	estamos
vós	tendes	sois	estais
eles	têm	são	estão

Normally, the Portuguese do not use personal pronouns since the form of the verb and the sense of the phrase indicate the person:

Tens sede?	Are you thirsty?
Do que está a falar?	What is he/she talking about?

The three conjugations for regular verbs are distinguished by the ending of the infinitive.

	falar (to speak)	viver (to live)	partir (to leave)
eu	falo	vivo	parto
tu	falas	vives	partes
ele/ela	fala	vive	parte
nós	falamos	vivemos	partimos
vós	falais	viveis	partis
eles	falam	vivem	partem

As in all languages, the irregular verbs have to be learned. Here are four you'll find useful:

	poder (to be able)	dizer (to say)	ir (to go)	pedir (to ask)
eu	posso	digo	vou	peço
tu	podes	dizes	vais	pedes
ele/ela	pode	diz	vai	pede
nós	podemos	dizemos	vamos	pedimos
vós	podeis	dizeis	ides	pedis
eles	podem	dizem	vão	pedem

The **negative** is formed by placing **não** before the verb.

Falo português.	I speak Portuguese.
Não falo português.	I don't speak Portuguese.

In Portuguese, **questions** are often formed by changing the intonation of your voice. Very often the personal pronoun is left out both in affirmative sentences and in questions.

Está bem.	It's all right.
Está bem?	Is it all right?
Falo inglês.	I speak English.
Fala inglês?	Do you speak English?

Dictionary
and alphabetical index

English–Portuguese

f feminine	*m* masculine	*pl* plural

Brazilian alternatives are given in brackets [ ].

a um,uma 159
abbreviation abreviatura *f* 154
able, to be poder 163
about *(approximately)* cerca de 153
above acima (de) 16; por cima 63
abscess abcesso *m* 145
absorbent cotton algodão hidrófilo *m* 109
accept, to aceitar 62, 102
accessories acessórios *m/pl* 116, 125
accident acidente *m* 78, 139
accommodation alojamento *m* 22
account conta *f* 131
ache dor *f* 141
adaptor adaptador *m* 119
address endereço *m* 21, 31, 76, 79, 102
address book livrinho de endereços *m* 104
adhesive autocolante 105
admission entrada *f* 82
admission charge entrada *f* [ingresso *m*] 90
admit, to admitir 150
Africa África *f* 146
after depois (de) 16, 77
afternoon tarde *f* 151, 153
after-shave lotion loção para depois da barba *f* 110
against contra 140
age idade *f* 149, 150
ago há 149, 151
air conditioner ar condicionado *m* 23, 28
airmail por avião 133
airplane avião *m* 65
airport aeroporto *m* 17, 21, 65
alarm clock despertador *m* 121
alcohol álcool *m* 107; bebidas alcoólicas *f/pl* 37

alcoholic alcoólico(a) 58
all tudo 103
allergic alérgico(a) 141, 143
allow, to permitir 79
almond amêndoa *f* 52
alphabet alfabeto *m* 10, 135
also também 16
alter, to *(garment)* modificar 115
amazing espantoso(a) 84
amber âmbar *m* 122
ambulance ambulância *f* 79
American americano(a) 93, 105, 126
American plan pensão completa *f* 24
amethyst ametista *f* 122
amount importância *f* 62, 131
amplifier amplificador *m* 119
anaesthesia anestesia *f* 144, 145
analgesic analgésico *m* 109
anchovy anchova *f* 41
and e 16
animal animal *m* 85
aniseed erva-doce *f* 51
ankle tornozelo *m* 139
another outro(a) 55, 58, 123
answer, to *(phone)* atender 136
antibiotic antibiótico *m* 143
antidepressant antidepressivo *m* 143
antiques antiguidades *f/pl* 83
antique shop antiquário *m* 98
antiseptic anti-séptico(a) 109
antiseptic anti-séptico *m* 140
anyone alguém 13
anything alguma coisa 18, 25, 113
apartment *(flat)* apartamento *m* 22
aperitif aperitivo *m* 55
appendicitis apendicite *f* 142
appendix apêndice *m* 138
appetizer acepipe [salgadinho] *m* 41
apple maçã *f* 52, 64

appliance aparelho m 119
appointment marcação f 30; encontro marcado m 131; *(doctor)* consulta f 137, 145
apricot alperce [damasco] m 52
April Abril m 150
aquarium aquário m 81
archaeology arqueologia f 83
architect arquitecto m 83
area code indicativo m 134
arm braço m 138, 139
arrival chegada f 17, 65
arrive, to chegar 65, 68, 130
art arte f 83
art gallery galeria de arte f 81, 98
artichoke alcachofra f 49
article artigo m 101, 159
artificial artificial 37, 124
artist artista m/f 81,83
ashtray cinzeiro m 27, 36
Asia Ásia f 146
ask, to perguntar 76; *(for)* pedir 25, 61, 136, 163
asparagus espargo [aspargo] m 41, 42, 49
aspirin aspirina f 109
assistance assistência f 78
assorted variado(a) 41
asthma asma f 142
at a, em 16
at least pelo menos 24
at once já 31
aubergine berinjela f 49
August Agosto m 150
aunt tia f 93
Australia Austrália f 146
automatic automático(a) 20, 122, 124
autumn Outono m 150
awful horroroso(a) 84; horrível 94
Azores Açores m/pl 146

B

baby bebé [nenê] m 24, 111
baby food comida para bebé [nenê] f 111
babysitter babysitter f 27
back atrás 30, 87, 145
back *(body)* costas f/pl 138
backache dor nas costas f 141
backpack mochila f 106
bacon toucinho m 38, 46
bad mau, má 15, 95
bag saco m 18, 103
baggage bagagem f 18, 26, 31, 71

baggage cart carrinho da bagagem m 18, 71
baggage check depósito da bagagem m 67, 71
baked no forno 45, 47
baker's padaria f 98
balance *(account)* balanço m 131
balcony varanda f 23
ball *(inflated)* bola f 128
ballet ballet m 88
ball-point pen esferográfica f 104
banana banana f 52, 64
bandage ligadura [atadura] f 109
Band-Aid penso rápido [bandaid] m 109
bangle bracelete m 121
bangs franja f 30
bank *(finance)* banco m 98, 129, 130
banknote nota f 130
barber's barbeiro m 30, 98
basilica basílica f 81
basketball basquetebol m 90
bath *(hotel)* banho m 23, 25
bathing cap touca de banho f 116
bathing hut barraca de praia) f 91
bathing suit fato [maiô] de banho m 116
bathroom casa de banho f [banheiro m] 27
bath towel toalha de banho f 27
battery pilha f 119, 121, 125; *(car)* bateria f 75, 76
bay baía f 74
bay leaf louro m 51
be, to ser, estar 162; ficar 12
beach praia f 91
beach ball balão m 128
bean feijão m 49
beard barba f 31
beautiful lindo(a) 15, 84
beauty salon instituto de beleza m 30, 98
bed cama f 24, 144
bed and breakfast dormida e pequeno almoço [pernoite e café da manhã] f 24
bedpan bacia de cama f 144
beef carne de vaca f 46
beer cerveja f 55, 64
beet(root) beterraba f 49
before *(place)* em frente (de) 16; *(time)* antes (de) 16
begin, to começar 80, 87, 88
beginning princípio m 150

behind atrás (de) 16, 77
bell (electric) campainha f 144
bellboy paquete, groom [boy de ho-
tel] m 26
below abaixo (de) 16; por baixo 63
belt cinto m 117
bend (road) f 79
berth beliche m 69, 70, 71
better melhor 15, 25, 101, 113
between entre 16
beverage bebida f 60
bicycle bicicleta f 74
big grande 15, 101
bill conta f 31, 62, 102; (banknote)
nota f 130
billion (Am.) bilhão m 148
binoculars binóculos m/pl 123
bird pássaro m 85
birth nascimento m 25
birthday dia de anos m 151; aniver-
sário m 152
biscuit (Br.) bolacha f 64
bitter amargo(a) 61
black preto(a) 113
bladder bexiga f 138
blade lâmina f 111
blanket cobertor m 27
bleach descoloração f 30
bleed, to sangrar 139, 145
blind (window) estore m 29
blister bexiga f 139
block, to entupir 28
blood sangue m 142
blood pressure tensão arterial f 141
blood transfusion transfusão de sangue f 144
blouse blusa f 116
blow-dry brushing m 30
blue azul 113
boarding house pensão f 22
boat barco m 74
bobby pin gancho [grampo] de cabelo
m 111
body corpo m 138
boil furúnculo m 139
boiled cozido(a) 47
boiled egg ovo cozido m 38
bond obrigação f 131
bone osso m 138
book livro m 13, 104
booking office marcação de lugares
f 19, 67
booklet (of tickets) caderneta f 72
bookshop livraria f 98, 104
boot bota f 118

born, to be nascer 150
botanical gardens jardim botânico m
81
botany botânica f 83
bottle garrafa f 17, 55, 58
bottle-opener abre-garrafas [abridor
de garrafas] m 106
bottom baixo m 145
bowel intestino m 138
box caixa f 120
boxing boxe m 90
boy menino m 112, 128
boyfriend namorado m 93
bra soutien m 116
bracelet pulseira f 121
braces (suspenders) suspensórios
m/pl 116
brake travão [freio] m 78
brake fluid líquido dos travões
[freios] m 75
brandy aguardente velha f 59
Brazil Brasil m 146
Brazilian brasileiro(a) 114, 127
bread pão m 36, 38, 64
break, to partir [quebrar] 123, 139,
145
break down, to avariar-se 78
breakdown avaria f 78
breakdown van pronto-socorro m 78
breakfast pequeno almoço [café da
manhã] m 24, 34, 38
breast seio m 138
breathe, to respirar 141, 142
bricks (toy) jogo de construções m
128
bridge ponte f 85
briefs calças [calcinhas] f/pl 116
bring, to trazer 14
British britânico(a) 93
broiled grelhado(a) 45, 47
broken partido(a) [quebrado(a)] 29,
140
brooch broche m 121
brother irmão m 93
brown castanho(a) [marrom] 113
bruise contusão f 139
brush escova f 111
bubble bath banho de espuma m
110
bucket balde m 128
buckle fivela f 117
build, to construir 83
building edifício m 81, 83
building blocks jogo de construções
m 128

bulb lâmpada f 28,75, 119
bullfight tourada f 89
bullring praça de touros f 81
burn queimadura f 139
burn out, to (bulb) fundir 28
bus autocarro [ônibus] m 18, 19, 65, 72, 73
business negócios m/pl 17
business district centro de negócios m 81
business trip viagem de negócios f 93
bus stop paragem do autocarro [parada de ônibus] f 72, 73
busy, to be ter que fazer 96
but mas 16
butane gas gás butano m 32, 106
butcher's talho [açougue] m 98
butter manteiga f 36, 38, 64
button botão m 29, 117
buy, to comprar 68, 82, 104

C

cabana barraca (de praia) f 91
cabbage couve f 49
cabin (ship) cabine f 74
cable telegrama f 133
cable car teleférico m 74
cable release disparador m 125
cake bolo m 54, 64
cake shop pastelaria f 98
calculator calculadora f 105
calendar calendário m 104
call (phone) comunicação f 135; chamada f 136
call, to (give name) chamar 12; (summon) 78, 79, 156; (phone) telefonar 136
calm calmo(a) 91
cambric cambraia f 114
camel-hair pêlo de camelo m 114
camera máquina fotográfica f 124, 125
camera case capa de máquina fotográfica f 125
camera shop loja de artigos fotográficos f 98
camp, to acampar 32
campbed cama de campismo f 106
camping campismo m 32
camping equipment equipamento de campismo m 106
camp site parque de campismo m 32
can (of peaches) lata f 120
can (to be able) poder 13, 163

Canada Canadá m 146
Canadian canadiano(a) 93
cancel, to anular 65
candle vela f
candy rebuçado m [bala f] 126
can opener abre-latas [abridor de latas] m 106
cap boné m
caper alcaparra f 50
capital (finance) capital m 131
car automóvel m, carro m 19, 20, 75, 76, 78
carafe jarro m 58
carat quilate m 121
caravan rulote f 32
caraway cominho m 51
carbonated com gás 59
carburettor carburdor m 78
card carta f 93; cartão m 131
card game baralho de cartas m 128
cardigan casaco de malha m 116
car hire aluguer de automóveis m 20
car park parque de automóveis m 77
car racing corridas de automóveis f/pl 90
car rental aluguer de automóveis m 20
carrot cenoura f 49
carry, to levar 21
cart carrinho m 18
carton (of cigarettes) pacote (de cigarros) m 17, 126
cartridge (camera) chargeur m 124
case (glasses) caixa f 123; (camera) capa f 125
cash, to levantar 130, 133
cash desk caixa f 103, 155
cassette cassete f 119, 127
castle castelo m 81
catalogue catálogo m 82
cathedral sé f, catedral f 81
Catholic católico(a) 84
cauliflower couve-flor f 49
caution cuidado m 79; atenção f 155
celery aipo m 49
cellophane tape fita adesiva f 104
cemetery cemitério m 81
centimetre centímetro m 112
centre centro m 19, 21, 76, 81
century século m 149
ceramics cerâmica f 83
cereal cereais m/pl 38
certificate certificado m 144
chain (jewellery) corrente f 121

chain bracelet corrente de pulso *f* 121

chair cadeira *f* 106

change *(money)* troco *m* 62; dinheiro trocado *m* 77, 130

change, to mudar 65, 68, 69, 73, 75, 123; *(money)* trocar 18, 19, 130

chapel capela *f* 81

charcoal carvão de lenha *m* 106

charge preço *m* 20, 32, 77, 89; taxa *f* 136

charge, to *(commission)* cobrar 130

charm *(trinket)* berloque *m* 121

charm bracelet pulseira de berloques *f* 121

cheap barato(a) 15, 24, 25, 101

check cheque *m* 130; *(restaurant)* conta *f* 62

check, to verificar 75; *(luggage)* despachar 71

check book livro de cheques *m* 131

check in, to *(airport)* apresentar-se 65

check out, to partir 31

cheese queijo *m* 51, 64

chemist's farmácia *f* 98, 108

cheque cheque *m* 130

cheque book livro de cheques *m* 131

cherry cereja *f* 52

chess xadrez *m* 93

chess set jogo de xadrez *m* 128

chest peito *m* 138, 141

chestnut castanha *f* 52

chewing gum pastilha elástica [chiclete] *f* 126

chewing tobacco tabaco [fumo] de mascar *m* 126

chicken frango *m* 48, 63; galinha *f* 48

chiffon chiffon *m* 114

child criança *f* 24, 61, 82, 150

children filhos *m/pl* 93

children's doctor pediatra *m/f* 137

china porcelana *f* 127

China China *f* 146

chips *(Br.)* batatas fritas *f/pl* 51, 63; *(Am.)* batatas fritas *f/pl* 64

chocolate chocolate *m* 120, 126; *(hot)* chocolate quente *m* 38, 60

chocolate bar tablete de chocolate *f* 64

choice escolha *f* 40

chop costeleta *f* 46

Christmas Natal *m* 152

chromium cromo *m* 122

church igreja *f* 81, 84

cigar charuto *m* 126

cigarette cigarro *m* 17, 95, 126

cigarette case cigarreira *f* 121, 126

cigarette holder boquilha [piteira] *f* 126

cigarette lighter isqueiro *m* 121

cine camera máquina de filmar *f* 124

cinema cinema *m* 86, 96

cinnamon canela *f* 50

circle *(theatre)* balcão *m* 87

city cidade *f* 81

clam amêijoa *f* 41, 44

classical clássico(a) 128

clean limpo(a) 61

clean, to limpar 29, 76

cleansing cream creme de limpeza *m* 110

cliff falésia *f* 85

clip broche de mola *m* 121

cloakroom vestiário *m* 87

clock relógio *m* 121, 153

clock-radio rádio-despertador *m* 119

close, to fechar 11, 82, 108, 132

closed fechado(a), encerrado(a) 155

cloth tela *f* 118

clothes roupa *f* 29, 116

clothes peg mola da roupa *f* 106

clothing vestuário *m* 112

cloud nuvem *f* 94

clove cravinho *m* 50

coach *(bus)* camioneta *f* [ônibus *m*] 72

coast costa *f* 85

coat casaco comprido *m* 116

coconut coco *m* 52, 54, 59, 60

cod bacalhau *m* 44, 45

coffee café *m* 38, 60, 64

cognac conhaque *m* 58

coin moeda *f* 130

cold frio(a) 15, 25, 38, 61, 94

cold *(illness)* constipação *f* [resfriado *m*] 108, 141

collect call comunicação pagável no destino *f* 135

colour cor *f* 103, 112, 124, 125

colour chart mostruário de cores *m* 30

colourfast de cor fixa 113

colour rinse rinsage *f* 30

colour slide slide *m* 124

comb pente *m* 111

come, to vir 35, 94, 95, 137,

comedy comédia f 86
commission comissão f 130
common (frequent) usual 154
compact disc disco compacto m 127
compartment compartimento m 70
compass bússola f 106
complaint reclamação f 61
concert concerto m 88
confirm, to confirmar 65
confirmation confirmação f 23
congratulation parabéns m/pl 152
connection (train) correspondência [conexão] f 65, 68
constipated com prisão de ventre [constipado(a)] 140
consulate consulado m 156
contact lens lente de contacto f 123
contain, to conter 37
contraceptive contraceptivo m 109
contract contrato m 131
control controle m 17
conversion conversão f 157
cookie bolacha f 64
cool box mala frigorífica f 106
copper cobre m 122
corduroy bombazina f 114
cork rolha f 61
corkscrew saca-rolhas m 106
corn (Am.) milho m 49; (foot) calo m 109
corner canto m 36; (street) esquina f 21, 77
corn plaster penso para os calos m 109
cosmetic cosmético m 110
cost custo m 131; preço m 136
cost, to custar 12, 80, 133
cotton algodão m 113, 114
cotton wool algodão hidrófilo m 109
cough tosse f 108, 141
cough, to tossir 142
cough drops pastilhas para a tosse f/pl 109
counter guiché m 133
country país m 92
countryside campo m 85
court house palácio de justiça m 81
cousin primo(a) m/f 93
crab caranguejo m 44
cramp cãibra f 141
crayon lápis de cor m 104
cream nata f 54; (toiletry) creme m 110; (pharmaceutical) pomada f 109

credit crédito m 130
credit card cartão de crédito m 20, 31, 62, 102, 130
crisps batatas fritas f/pl 64
crockery louça f 107
crossroads cruzamento m 77
cruise cruzeiro m 74
crystal cristal m 122
cucumber pepino m 49
cuff link botão de punho m [abotoadura f] 121
cup chávena [xícara] f 36, 60, 107
currency moeda corrente f 129
currency exchange office agência de câmbio f, câmbio m 18, 67, 129
current corrente f 91
curtain cortinado m 28
curve (road) curva f 79
customs alfândega f 16, 102
cut (wound) corte m 139
cut, to cortar 30, 136
cuticle remover produto para tirar as cutículas m 110
cutlery talheres m/pl 107, 121
cutlet costeleta f 46
cycling ciclismo m 89
cystitis cistite f 142

D

dairy leitaria f 98
dance, to dançar 88, 96
danger perigo m 155, 156
dangerous perigoso(a) 90
dark escuro(a) 25, 101, 112, 113
date (day) data f 25, 151; (fruit) tâmara f 52; (appointment) encontro m 95
daughter filha f 93
day dia m 16, 20, 24, 32, 80, 151
daylight luz do dia m 124
day off dia de folga m 124
death morte f 155
decade década f 149
decaffeinated sem cafeína 38, 60
December Dezembro m 150
decision decisão f 25, 102
deck (ship) convés m 74
deck chair cadeira de encosto f 91, 106
declare, to declarar 17, 18
deep fundo(a) 142
define, to descrever 101
delay atraso m 69
delicatessen salsicharia f 98
delicious delicioso(a) 62

deliver, to entregar 102
delivery entrega f 102
denim sarja f 114
dentist dentista m/f 98, 145
denture dentadura f 145
deodorant desodorizante [desodo-
rante] m 110
department secção f 83, 100
department store grande armazém
m 98
departure partida f 65, 80
deposit (car hire) sinal m 20; (bank)
depósito m 130
deposit, to (bank) depositar 131
dessert sobremesa f 37, 53
detour (traffic) desvio m 79
develop, to revelar 124
diabetic diabético(a) 141
diabetic diabético(a) m/f 37
dialling code indicativo m 134
diamond diamante m 122
diaper fralda f 111
diarrhoea diarreia f 140
dictionary dicionário m 104
diesel gasóleo m 75
diet dieta f 37
difficult difícil 15
difficulty dificuldade f 28, 102, 141
digital digital 122
dine, to jantar 94
dining car carruagem-restaurante f
71
dining room sala de jantar f 27
dinner jantar m 34, 94
direct directo(a) 65
direct, to indicar a direcção 14
direction direcção f 76
director (theatre) realizador m 86
directory (phone) lista telefónica f
134
disabled deficiente físico(a) m/f 82
disc disco m 127
discotheque discoteca f 88, 89, 96
discount desconto m 131
disease doença f 142
dish prato m 36, 40
dishwashing detergent detergente
para a louça m 106
disinfectant desinfectante m 109
dislocate, to deslocar 140
display case banca f 100
dissatisfied insatisfeito(a) 103
disturb, to incomodar 155
diversion (traffic) desvio m 79
dizziness vertigem f 140

doctor médico(a) m/f 79, 137, 144,
156; doutor(a) m/f 145
doctor's office consultório m 137
dog cão m 155
doll boneca f 128
dollar dólar m 18, 130
door porta f 28
double duplo(a) 58, 60
double bed cama de casal f 23
double room quarto duplo m 19, 23
down para baixo 16
downstairs em baixo 16
downtown centro da cidade m
dozen dúzia f 149
drawing paper papel de desenho m
104
drawing pin pionés m [tacha f] 104
dress vestido m 116
drink bebida f 58, 59, 61, 94, 95
drink, to beber 35, 36, 37
drinking water água potável f 32
drip, to (tap) verter 28
drive, to conduzir 21
driving licence carta de condução
[carteira de motorista] f 20, 79
drop (liquid) gota f 109
drugstore farmácia f 98, 108
dry seco(a) 30, 58, 111
dry cleaner's lavandaria a seco f 29,
98
duck pato m 48
dummy chupeta f 111
during durante 16, 150, 151
duty (customs) direitos m/pl 18
duty-free shop free shop f 19
dye pintura do cabelo f 30

E

each cada 149
ear orelha f 138
earache dor de ouvidos f 141
early cedo 15
earring brinco m 121
east (l)este m 77
Easter Páscoa f 152
easy fácil 15
eat, to comer 36, 37, 144
eel enguia f 44
egg ovo m 38, 42, 64
eggplant berinjela f 49
eight oito 147
eighteen dezoito 147
eighth oitavo(a) 149
eighty oitenta 148
elastic elástico(a) 109

elastic bandage ligadura [atadura] elástica f 109
Elastoplast pensos rápidos [bandaids] m/pl 109
electric(al) eléctrico(a) 119
electrical appliance aparelho eléctrico m 119
electrician electricista m 98
electricity electricidade f 32
electronic electrónico(a) 125, 128
elevator elevador m 27, 74, 100
eleven onze 147
embarkation embarque m 74
embassy embaixada f 156
embroidery bordados m/pl 127
emerald esmeralda f 122
emergency urgência f 156
emergency exit saída de emergência f 27, 99, 155
emery board lima [lixa] de unhas f 110
empty vazio(a) 15
end fim m 150
engagement ring anel de noivado m 122
engine (car) motor m 78
England Inglaterra f 146
English inglês(esa) 13, 80, 82, 84, 104, 126
enjoy, to gostar 62, 92
enjoyable agradável 31
enjoy oneself, to divertir-se 96
enlarge, to ampliar 125
enough bastante 15
enquiry informação f 68
entrance entrada f 67, 99, 155
entrance fee entrada f [ingresso m] 82
envelope envelope m 27, 104
equipment equipamento m 91, 106
eraser borracha f 104
escalator escada rolante f 100
estimate estimação f 131
Europe Europa f 146
evening noite f 87, 94, 95, 96, 151, 153
evening dress traje de noite m 88; (woman) vestido de noite m 116
everything tudo 31
exchange, to trocar 103
exchange rate câmbio m 19, 130
excursion excursão f 80
excuse, to desculpar 12, 78, 153
exercise book caderno m 104
exhaust pipe tubo de escape m 78

exhibition exposição f 81
exit saída f 67, 79, 99, 155
expect, to estar à espera 130
expenses despesas f/pl 131
expensive caro(a) 15, 19, 24, 101
exposure counter contador m 125
express por expresso 133
expression expressão f 11
expressway auto-estrada f 76
extension cord/lead extensão f 119
external externo(a) 109
extra mais 24, 27
eye olho m 138, 139
eyebrow pencil lápis para os olhos m 110
eye drops gotas para os olhos f/pl 109
eye shadow sombra para os olhos f 110
eyesight vista f 123
eye specialist oftalmologista m/f 137

F

fabric (cloth) tecido m 113
face rosto m 138
face-pack máscara de beleza f 30
face powder pó de arroz m 110
factory fábrica f 81
fair feira f 81
fall queda f 139; (autumn) Outono m 150
family família f 93
fan ventoinha f 28
fan belt correia da ventoinha f 75
far longe 14, 100
fare preço m 21, 68, 73
farm quinta [fazenda] f 85
fat (meat) gordura f 37
father pai m 93
faucet torneira f 28
February Fevereiro m 150
fee (doctor) honorários m/pl 144
feeding bottle biberon m 111
feel, to (physical state) sentir-se 140, 142
felt feltro m 114
felt-tip pen caneta feltro f 104
ferry ferry-boat m 74
fever febre f 140
few poucos(as) 15; (a) alguns, algumas 15
field campo m 85
fifteen quinze 147
fifth quinto(a) 149

fifty cinquenta 147
fig figo *m* 52
file *(tool)* lima [lixa] *f* 110
fill in, to preencher 26, 144
filling *(tooth)* chumbo *m* 145
filling station estação de serviço *f* 75
film filme *m* 86; *(photography)* rolo [filme] *m* 124, 125
film winder botão de bobinagem *m* 125
filter filtro *m* 125
filter-tipped com filtro 126
find, to encontrar 12, 100, 137
fine *(OK)* (está) bem 12, 25
fine arts belas-artes *f/pl* 83
finger dedo *m* 138
finish, to acabar 87
fire fogo *m* 156
first primeiro(a) 68, 73, 149
first-aid kit estojo de primeiros-socorros *m* 106
first class primeira classe *f* 69
first course primeiro prato *m* 40
first name nome próprio [nome] *m* 25
fish peixe *m* 44
fish, to pescar 90
fishing tackle apetrechos de pesca *m/pl* 106
fishmonger's peixaria *f* 98
fit, to ficar bem 115
fitting room cabine de provas *f* 114
five cinco 147
fix, to consertar 75
fizzy *(mineral water)* com gás 59
flannel flanela *f* 114
flash *(photography)* flash *m* 125
flash attachment encaixe do flash *m* 125
flashlight lanterna de bolso *f* 106
flat raso(a) 118
flat *(apartment)* apartamento *m* 22
flat tyre furo *m* 75; pneu vazio *m* 78
flea market feira da ladra *f* 81
flight voo *m* 65
flippers barbatanas *f/pl* 128
floor andar *m* 27
florist's florista *m/f* 98
flour farinha *f* 37
flower flor *f* 85
flu gripe *f* 142
fluid líquido *m* 75, 123
fog nevoeiro *m* 94
folding chair cadeira de fechar *f* 106
folding table mesa de fechar *f* 107

folk dancing dança folclórica *f* 89
folk music música folclórica *f* 128
follow, to seguir 77
food alimentos *m/pl* 37; comida *f* 61, 111
food box caixa para alimentos *f* 106
food poisoning intoxicação alimentar *f* 142
foot pé *m* 138
football futebol *m* 89, 90
foot cream creme para os pés *m* 110
footpath caminho pedestre *m* 85
for por, para 16; durante 143, 151
forbid, to proibir 155
forecast previsão *f* 94
forest floresta *f* 85
forget, to esquecer-se 61
fork garfo *m* 36, 61, 107
form *(document)* formulário *m* 133; ficha *f* 25, 26
fortnight duas semanas *f/pl* 151
fortress fortaleza *f* 81
forty quarenta 147
foundation cream creme de base *m* 110
fountain fonte *f* 81
fountain pen caneta de tinta permanente [caneta-tinteiro] *f* 104
four quatro 147
fourteen catorze 147
fourth quarto(a) 149
frame *(glasses)* armação *f* 123
France França *f* 146
free livre 15, 70, 95, 155
french fries batatas fritas *f/pl* 50, 63
fresh fresco(a) 52, 61
Friday sexta-feira *f* 151
fried frito(a) 45, 47
fried egg ovo estrelado *m* 38, 42
friend amigo(a) *m/f* 95
fringe franja *f* 30
from de 16
front frente *f* 23, 75
fruit fruta *f* 52
fruit juice sumo [suco] de fruta *m* 37, 38, 59
frying-pan frigideira *f* 106
full cheio(a) 15; inteiro(a) 80; completo(a) 155
full board pensão completa *f* 24
full insurance seguro contra todos os riscos *m* 20
funicular elevador *m* 74
furniture mobiliário *m* 83
furrier's casa de peles *f* 98

G

gabardine gabardine f 114
gallery galeria f 81
game jogo m 128; *(food)* caça f 48
garage garagem f 26, 78
garden jardim m 81, 85
garlic alho m 50
gas gás m 156
gasoline gasolina f 75, 78
gastritis gastrite f 142
gauze gaze f 109
gem pedra preciosa f 121
general geral 27, 100
general delivery posta restante f 133
general practitioner médico(a) de clínica geral m/f 137
genitals órgãos genitais m/pl 138
gentleman cavalheiro m 155
genuine autêntico(a) 118
geology geologia f 83
Germany Alemanha f 146
get, to *(find)* arranjar [arrumar] 12, 32, 90; *(take)* apanhar [pegar] 19, 21, 69; *(call)* chamar 21, 31, 137, 156; *(obtain)* obter 134; *(go)* ir 76, 100
get off, to descer 73
get to, to ir para 19; chegar a 70
get up, to levantar-se 144
gherkin pepino de conserva m 49
gift presente m 127
gin gim m 60
gin and tonic gim tónico m 60
ginger gengibre m 51
girdle cinta f 116
girl menina f 112, 128
girlfriend namorada f 93; amiga f 95
give, to dar 14, 123, 135
gland glândula f 138
glass vidro m 122; *(drinking)* copo m 36, 55, 58, 61, 143
glasses óculos m/pl 123
gloomy lúgubre 84
glove luva f 116
glue cola f 104
go, to ir 96, 163
gold ouro m 121, 122
golden dourado(a) 113
gold-plated banhado a ouro 122
golf golfe m 90
golf club clube de golfe m 90
golf course campo de golfe m 90
good bom, boa 15, 101
good-bye adeus 10
Good Friday Sexta-feira Santa f 152

goods artigos m/pl 17
goose ganso m 48
go out, to sair 95
gram grama f 120
grammar book gramática f 104
grandfather avô m 93
grandmother avó f 93
grape uva f 52, 64
grapefruit toranja f 52
grapefruit juice sumo [suco] de toranja m 38
gray cinzento(a) 113
graze esfoladela f 139
greasy oleoso(a) 30, 111
great *(excellent)* óptimo(a) 95
Great Britain Grã-Bretanha f 146
Greece Grécia f 146
green verde 113
green bean feijão verde m [vagem f] 49
greengrocer's lugar de frutas e legumes m [quitanda f] 98
green salad salada de alface f 42
greeting saudação f 11
grey cinzento(a) 113
grilled grelhado(a) 45, 47
grocery mercearia f 98, 120
groundsheet tapete m 106
group grupo m 82
guide guia m/f 80
guidebook guia turístico m 82, 105
gum *(teeth)* gengiva f 145
gynaecologist ginecologista m/f 137

H

hair cabelo m 30, 111
hairbrush escova de cabelo f 111
haircut corte de cabelo m 30
hairdresser's cabeleireiro(a) m/f 27, 30, 98
hair dryer secador de cabelo m 119
hairgrip gancho [grampo] de cabelo m 111
hair lotion loção capilar f 111
hair slide travessão [clipe] m 111
hairspray laca [laquê] f 30, 111
half meio(a) 149
half metade f 149
half an hour meia-hora f 153
half board meia-pensão f 24
half price *(ticket)* meio-bilhete m 69
hall *(large room)* sala f 81, 88
hall porter porteiro m 26
ham presunto m 38, 41, 46; fiambre m 63, 64

hammer martelo *m* 106
hammock cama de rede [rede] *f* 106
hand mão *f* 138
handbag mala de mão [bolsa] *f* 116, 156
hand cream creme para as mãos *m* 110
handicrafts artesanato *m* 83
handkerchief lenço de bolso *m* 127
handmade feito(a) à mão 113
hanger cabide *m* 27
happy feliz 152
harbour porto *m* 81
hardware shop loja de ferragens *f* 98
hare lebre *f* 48
hat chapéu *m* 116
have, to ter 162
hayfever febre dos fenos *f* 108
hazelnut avelã *f* 52
he ele 161
head cabeça *f* 138, 139
headache dor de cabeça *f* 141
headphone auscultador [fone] *m* 119
headscarf lenço de pescoço *m* 127
head waiter chefe de mesa *m* 61
health saúde *f* 55
health food shop loja de produtos dietéticos *f* 98
health insurance seguro de doença *m* 144
health insurance form folha de seguro *f* 144
heart coração *m* 138
heart attack ataque cardíaco *m* 141
heat, to aquecer 91
heating aquecimento *m* 23, 28
heavy pesado(a) 14, 101
heel salto *m* 118
helicopter helicóptero *m* 74
hello! *(phone)* está [alô]? 135
help ajuda *f* 156
help! socorro! 156
help, to ajudar 13, 14, 21, 71, 100, 134; *(oneself)* servir-se 120
her seu, sua 161
here aqui 14
high alto(a) 91, 141
high season época alta *f* 150
high tide maré alta *f* 91
hill colina *f* 85
hire aluguer *m* 20
hire, to alugar 19, 20, 90, 91, 155
his seu, sua 161
history história *f* 83

hitchhike, to pedir boleia [carona] 74
hold on! *(phone)* não desligue! 136
hole buraco *m* 29
holiday feriado *m* 151
holidays férias *f/pl* 17, 151
home address morada *f* 25, 31
home-made caseiro(a) 40
honey mel *m* 38
hope, to esperar 96
horseback riding equitação *f* 90
horse racing corridas de cavalos *f/pl* 90
hospital hospital *m* 98, 144
hot quente 15, 25, 38, 61
hotel hotel *m* 19, 21, 22, 80
hot dog cachorro (quente) *m* 63
hotel guide guia de hotéis *m* 19
hotel reservation reserva de hotel *f* 19
hot water água quente *f* 23, 28
hot-water bottle saco de água quente *m* 27
hour hora *f* 153
house casa *f* 83, 85
hovercraft hovercraft *m* 74
how como 12
how far a que distância 12, 76, 85
how long quanto tempo 12, 24
how many quantos(as) 12
how much quanto 12, 24
hundred cem, cento 148
hungry, to be ter fome 14, 35
hunt, to caçar 90
hurry *(to be in a)* estar com pressa 21
hurt, to doer 139, 145; *(oneself)* ferir-se 139
husband marido *m* 93
hydrofoil hidroplano [aerobarco] *m* 74

I
I eu 161
ice gelo *m* 94
ice-cream gelado [sorvete] *m* 53, 64
ice cube cubo de gelo *m* 27
ice pack placa frigorífica *f* 106
ill doente 140, 156
illness doença *f* 140
important importante 14
imported importado(a) 113
impressive impressionante 84
in em 16
include, to incluir 24

DICTIONARY

included incluído(a) 20, 31, 32, 62, 80
indigestion indigestão f 141
indoor *(swimming pool)* coberto(a) 91
inexpensive barato(a) 35, 124
infect, to infectar 140
infection infecção f 141
inflammation inflamação f 142
inflation inflação f 131
inflation rate índice de inflação m 131
influenza gripe f 142
information informação f 67, 155
injection injecção f 142, 144
injure, to ferir 139
injured ferido(a) 79, 139
injury ferimento m 139
ink tinta f 105
inn pousada f 22, 33; estalagem f 22, 23
inquiry informação f 68
insect bite picada de insecto f 108
insect repellent produto insectífugo m 109
insect spray spray insecticida m 109
inside dentro 16
instead of em vez de 37
insurance seguro m 20, 79, 144
insurance company companhia de seguros f 79
interest interesse m 80; *(bank)* juro m 131
interested, to be estar interessado(a) 83, 96
interesting interessante 84
international internacional 133, 134
interpreter intérprete m/f 131
intersection cruzamento m 77
introduce, to apresentar 92
introduction apresentação f 92, 130
investment investimento m 131
invitation convite m 94
invite, to convidar 94
invoice factura f 131
iodine tintura de iodo f 109
Ireland Irlanda f 146
Irish irlandês(esa) 93
iron *(laundry)* ferro de engomar m 119
iron, to passar a ferro 29
ironmonger's loja de ferragens f 98
Italy Itália f 146
its seu, sua 161
ivory marfim m 122

J

jacket casaco m 116
jade jade m 122
jam doce de fruta m [geléia f] 38, 63
jam, to empenar 28; encravar 125
January Janeiro m 150
Japan Japão m 146
jar frasco m 120
jaundice icterícia f 142
jaw maxila f 138
jeans jeans m/pl 116
jewel jóia f 121
jewel box cofre de jóias m 121
jeweller's ourivesaria f 99, 121
joint articulação f 138
journey viagem f 72, 152
juice sumo [suco] m 38, 59, 60
July Julho m 150
June Junho m 150
just *(only)* só 37, 100

K

keep, to guardar 62
kerosene petróleo m 106
key chave f 27
kidney rim m 46, 138
kilo(gram) quilo(grama) m 120
kilometre quilómetro m 20
kind amável 95
kind *(type)* espécie f 44; género m 140
knee joelho m 138
knife faca f 36, 61, 107
knock, to bater 155
know, to saber 16, 24; conhecer 96, 114

L

label etiqueta f 105
lace renda f 114, 127
lady senhora f 155
lake lago m 85
lamb borrego m 46
lamp candeeiro [abajur] m 29, 119
landmark ponto de referência m 85
landscape paisagem f 92
lantern lanterna f 106
large grande 20, 101, 118
last último(a) 15, 68, 73; passado(a) 149, 151
last name apelido [sobrenome] m 25
late tarde 15
later mais tarde 135
laugh, to rir 95

Dicionário

launderette lavandaria automática *f* 99

laundry *(place)* lavandaria *f* 29, 99; *(clothes)* roupa *f* 29

laundry service serviço de lavandaria *m* 23

laxative laxativo *m* 109

lead *(metal)* chumbo *m* 75

leap year ano bissexto *m* 149

leather cabedal [couro] *m* 114, 118

leatherwork artigos de couro *m/pl* 127

leave, to partir 31, 68, 163; sair 69, 74; deixar 26, 96, 156

leek alho porro *m*

left esquerda 21, 63, 69, 77

left-luggage office depósito da bagagem *m* 67, 71

leg perna *f* 48, 138

lemon limão *m* 36, 38, 52, 60, 64

lemonade gasosa *f* 59

lens *(glasses)* lente *f* 123; *(camera)* objectiva *f* 125

lens cap tampa para a objectiva *f* 125

lentil lentilha *f* 49

less menos 15

let, to *(hire out)* alugar 155

letter carta *f* 132

letter box caixa do correio *f* 132

letter of credit carta de crédito *f* 132

lettuce alface *f* 49

level crossing passagem de nível *f* 79

library biblioteca *f* 81, 99

lie down, to deitar-se 142

life belt cinto de salvação *m* 74

life boat bote salva-vidas *m* 74

lifeguard banheiro [salva-vidas] *m* 74

lift elevador *m* 27, 74, 100

light leve 15, 53, 101; ligeiro(a) 128; *(colour)* claro(a) 101, 112, 113

light luz *f* 28, 124; *(cigarette)* lume *m* 95

lighter isqueiro *m* 126

lighter fluid gasolina para isqueiro *f* 126

lighter gas gás para isqueiro *m* 126

light meter fotómetro *m* 125

lightning relâmpago *m* 94

like, to gostar 25, 92, 102, 112; *(want, wish)* querer 14, 23, 103; desejar 35, 103

line linha *f* 73, 136

linen *(cloth)* linho *m* 114

lip lábio *m* 138

lipsalve bâton para o cieiro *m* 110

lipstick bâton *m* 110

liqueur licor *m* 58

listen, to ouvir 128

litre litro *m* 58, 75, 120

little *(a)* um pouco 15

live, to viver 83, 163

liver fígado *m* 46, 138

lobster lavagante *m* 44

London Londres *f* 130

long comprido(a) 15, 115, 116

long-sighted presbita 123

look, to ver 100, 123

look for, to procurar 14

look out! atenção! 156

loose *(clothes)* largo(a) 115

lorry camião [caminhão] *m* 79

lose, to perder 123, 156; *(one's way)* perder-se 14, 156

loss perda *f* 131

lost and found office secção dos perdidos e achados *f* 67, 156

lost property office secção dos perdidos e achados *f* 67, 156

lot *(a)* muito 15

lotion loção *f* 110

loud *(voice)* alto(a) 135

lovely lindo(a) 94

low baixo(a) 91, 141

lower inferior 69, 71

low season época baixa *f* 150

low tide maré baixa *f* 91

luck sorte *f* 135, 152

luggage bagagem *f* 26, 31, 71

luggage locker depósito da bagagem automático *m* 18, 67, 71

luggage trolley carrinho da bagagem *m* 18, 71

lump *(bump)* galo, alto *m* 139

lunch almoço *m* 34, 80

lunch, to almoçar 94

lung pulmão *m* 138

M

machine máquina *f* 113

mackerel cavala *f* 44

Madeira wine vinho da Madeira *m* 55, 58

magazine revista *f* 105

magnificent magnífico(a) 84

maid criada de quarto [arrumadeira] *f* 26

mail, to pôr no correio 28
mail correio *m* 28, 133
mailbox caixa do correio *f* 132
main principal 40
make, to fazer 131
make-up remover pad disco de algodão *m* 110
man homem *m* 115, 155
manager gerente *m* 26
manicure manicura *f* 30
many muitos(as) 15
map mapa *m* 76, 105; planta *f* 105
March Março *m* 150
marinated marinado(a) 45
market mercado *m* 81, 99
marmalade doce *m* [geléia *f*] de laranja 38
married casado(a) 93
mass *(church)* missa *f* 84
match fósforo *m* 106, 126; *(sport)* jogo *m* 89; combate *m* 90
match, to *(colour)* condizer 112
matinée matinée *f* 87
mattress colchão *m* 106
mauve lilás 113
May Maio *m* 150
may *(can)* poder 13, 162
meadow prado *m* 85
meal refeição *f* 24, 62, 143
mean, to querer dizer 11, 25
means meio *m* 74
measles sarampo *m* 142
measure, to tirar as medidas 114
meat carne *m* 46, 61
mechanic mecânico *m* 78
mechanical pencil lapiseira *f* 105
medical médico(a) 144
medical certificate certificado médico *m* 144
medicine medicina *f* 83; *(drug)* medicamento, remédio *m* 143
medium *(meat)* meio passado(a) 47
medium-sized de tamanho médio 20
meet, to encontrar 96
melon melão *m* 41, 52
memorial monumento comemorativo *m* 81
mend, to consertar 75; *(clothes)* arranjar [consertar] 29
menthol *(cigarettes)* mentolado(a) 126
menu ementa *f* [cardápio *m*] 36, 37, 39, 40
message recado *m* 28, 136

methylated spirits álcool desnaturado *m* 106
metre metro *m* 112
mezzanine *(theatre)* balcão *m* 87
middle meio *m* 69, 87
midnight meia-noite *f* 153
mild suave 126
mileage quilometragem *f* 20
milk leite *m* 38, 60, 64
milkshake batido [milkshake] *m* 59, 60
milliard bilhão *m* 148
million milhão *m* 148
mineral water água mineral *f* 59
minister *(religion)* pastor *m* 84
mint hortelã *f* 51
minute minuto *m* 153
mirror espelho *m* 114, 123
Miss Menina [Senhorita] *f* 11
miss, to faltar 18, 29, 61
mistake engano *m* 61; *(to make a mistake)* enganar-se 31, 62, 102
mixed salad salada mista *f* 42
modified American plan meia-pensão *f* 24
moisturizing cream creme hidratante *m* 110
moment momento *m* 136
monastery mosteiro *m* 81
Monday segunda-feira *f* 151
money dinheiro *m* 129, 130
money order vale de correio *m* 133
month mês *m* 16, 150
monument monumento *m* 81
moon lua *f* 94
moped bicicleta motorizada *f* 74
more mais 16
morning manhã *f* 151, 153
Morocco Marrocos *m* 146
mortgage hipoteca *f* 131
mosque mesquita *f* 84
mosquito net mosquiteiro *m* 106
mother mãe *f* 93
motorbike motocicleta *f* 74
motorboat barco a motor *m* 91
motorway auto-estrada *f* 76
mountain montanha *f* 85
mountain range serra *f* 85
moustache bigode *m* 31
mouth boca *f* 138
mouthwash gargarejo *m* 109
move, to mexer 139
movie filme *m* 86
movie camera máquina de filmar *f* 124

movies cinema f 86, 96
Mr. Senhor m 11
Mrs. Senhora f 11
much muito 15
mug caneca f 55, 107
muscle músculo m 138
museum museu m 81
mushroom cogumelo m 49
music música f 83, 128
musical comédia musical f 86
mussel mexilhão m 44
must, to ter de 23, 31; dever 37, 61
mustard mostarda f 36, 51, 64
mutton carneiro m 46
my meu, minha 161

N

nail (human) unha f 110
nail brush escova de unhas f 110
nail clippers corta-unhas m 110
nail file lima [lixa] de unhas f 110
nail polish verniz [esmalte] de unhas m 110
nail polish remover dissolvente de verniz [esmalte] m 110
nail scissors tesoura de unhas f 110
name nome m 23, 25, 79, 85
napkin guardanapo m 36, 105, 107
nappy fralda f 111
narrow apertado(a) 118
nationality nacionalidade f 25, 92
natural natural 83
natural history ciências naturais f/pl 83
nausea náusea f 140
near perto (de) 15, 16
nearby aqui perto 77, 84
nearest mais próximo(a) 78, 98
neat (drink) puro(a) 56
neck pescoço m 138; (nape) nuca f 30
necklace colar m 121
need, to precisar 29, 118, 137
needle agulha f 27
negative negativo m 124, 125
nephew sobrinho m 93
nerve nervo m 138
nervous nervoso(a) 138
nervous system sistema nervoso m 138
never nunca 16
new novo(a) 15
newspaper jornal m 104, 105
newsstand quiosque m [banca f] de jornais 19, 67, 99, 104

New Year Ano Novo m 152
New York Nova Iorque f 130
New Zealand Nova Zelândia f 146
next próximo(a) 15, 65, 68, 73, 76, 149, 151; seguinte 151
next to ao lado de 16, 77
niece sobrinha f 93
night noite f 24, 151
nightclub boîte f 88
night cream creme de noite m 110
nightdress camisa de dormir [camisola] f 116
nine nove 147
nineteen dezanove 147
ninety noventa 148
ninth nono(a) 149
no não 11
noisy barulhento(a) 25
nonalcoholic não alcoólico(a) 59
none nenhum(a) 16
nonsmoker não-fumador m 36, 70
noon meio-dia m 31, 153
normal normal 30
north norte m 77
North America América do Norte f 146
nose nariz m 138
nosebleed hemorragia nasal f 141
nose drops gotas para o nariz f/pl 109
not não 16, 163
note (banknote) nota f 130
notebook bloco de apontamentos m 105
note paper papel de carta m 105
nothing nada 16, 17
notice (sign) letreiro m 155
notify, to avisar 144
November Novembro m 150
now agora 16
number número m 25, 26, 65, 135, 136, 147
nurse enfermeira f 144
nutmeg noz-moscada f 51

O

occupied ocupado(a) 14, 155
o'clock hora(s) 153
October Outubro m 150
octopus polvo m 44
offer, to oferecer 95
office secção f 67, 156; estação f 99, 132; agência f 129
oil óleo m 75, 111
oily (greasy) oleoso(a) 111

old velho(a), idoso(a) 15
old town cidade velha f 81
olive azeitona f 41
olive oil azeite m 36, 50
omelet omelete f 42
on sobre 16
on and off intermitente 140
once uma vez 149
one um, uma 147
one-way *(ticket)* ida 65, 69; *(street)* de sentido único 77
onion cebola f 49
only só 16, 24, 80
onyx ónix m 122
open aberto(a) 15, 82, 155
open, to abrir 12, 18, 108, 130, 132, 142
open-air ao ar livre 91
opening hours horas de abertura f/pl 82
opera ópera f 88
opera house teatro da ópera m 81, 88
operation operação f 144
operator telefonista m/f 134
operetta opereta f 88
opposite en frente (de) 77
optician oculista m/f 99, 123
or ou 16
orange cor-de-laranja 113
orange laranja f 52, 64
orange juice sumo [suco] de laranja m 38, 59
orangeade laranjada f 59
orchestra orquestra f 88; *(seats)* plateia f 87
order *(goods, meal)* encomenda f 40, 102
order, to *(goods, meal)* encomendar 61, 102, 103
oregano orégão m 51
ornithology ornitologia f 83
other outro(a) 58
our nosso(a) 161
out of order avariado(a) 155
out of stock esgotado(a) 103
outlet *(electric)* tomada f 27
outside (lá) fora 16, 36
oval oval 101
overdone passado(a) demais 61
overheat, to *(engine)* aquecer demais 78
overnight *(stay)* por uma noite 24
owe, to dever 144
oyster ostra f 41, 44

P
pacifier chupeta f 111
packet pacote m 120; *(cigarettes)* maço m 126
page *(hotel)* paquete, groom [boy de hotel] m 26
pail balde m 128
pain dor f 140, 141, 144
painkiller analgésico m 140
paint, to pintar 83
paintbox caixa de tintas f 105
painter pintor m 83
painting pintura f 83
pair par m 116, 118, 149
pajamas pijama m 117
palace palácio m 81
palpitation palpitação f 141
pancake crepe m [panqueca f] 63
panties calças [calcinhas] f/pl 116
pants *(trousers)* calças compridas f/pl 116
panty girdle cinta-calça f 116
panty hose collant m 116
paper papel m 105
paperback livro de bolso m 105
paperclip clipe m 105
paper napkin guardanapo de papel m 105
paraffin *(fuel)* petróleo m 107
parcel encomenda f [pacote m] 132
pardon? como disse? 12
parents pais m/pl 93
park parque m 81
park, to estacionar 26, 77
parking estacionamento m 77, 79
parking meter parcómetro m 77
parliament assembleia nacional f 81
parsley salsa f 51
part parte f 138
partridge perdiz f 48
party *(social gathering)* festa f 94
passport passaporte m 17, 18, 25, 26, 156
passport photo fotografia de passaporte f 124
pass through, to estar de passagem 17
paste *(glue)* cola f 105
pastry bolo m 64
pastry shop pastelaria f 99
patch, to *(clothes)* remendar 29
path caminho m 85
patient paciente m/f 144
pattern padrão m 112
pay, to pagar 31, 62, 68, 102

DICTIONARY

Dicionário

payment pagamento *m* 102, 131
pea ervilha *f* 49
peach pêssego *m* 54
peak pico *m*, cume *m* 85
peanut amendoim *m* 55
pear pêra *f* 52
pearl pérola *f* 122
pedestrian peão [pedestre] *m* 79
pen caneta *f* 105
pencil lápis *m* 105
pencil sharpener apara-lápis [apontador] *m* 105
pendant pingente *m* 121
penicilline penicilina *f* 143
penknife canivete *m* 107
pensioner reformado(a) [aposentado(a)] *m/f* 82
people pessoas *f/pl* 93
pepper pimenta *f* 36, 51, 64
per cent por cento 149
percentage percentagem *f* 131
per day por dia 20, 32, 90
perform, to *(theatre)* representar 86
perfume perfume *m* 110
perfume shop perfumaria *f* 108
perhaps talvez 16
per hour à hora 77
period *(monthly)* menstruação *f* 141
period pains dores menstruais *f/pl* 141
permanent wave permanente *f* 30
permit licença *f* 90
per night por noite 24
person pessoa *f* 32
personal pessoal 17
personal/person-to-person call comunicação com pré-aviso *f* 135
per week por semana 20, 24
petrol gasolina *f* 75, 78
pewter estanho *m* 122
pheasant faisão *m* 48
photo fotografia *f* 124
photocopy fotocópia *f* 131
photograph, to tirar fotografias 82
photographer fotógrafo *m/f* 99
photography fotografia *f* 124
phrase expressão *f* 13
pick up, to *(person)* buscar 80, 96
picnic piquenique *m* 63
picnic basket cesto de piquenique *m* 107
picture quadro *m* 83; *(photo)* fotografia *f* 82
piece pedaço *m* 120
pigeon pombo *m* 48

pill comprimido *m* 143; *(contraceptive)* pílula *f* 141
pillow almofada *f* [travesseiro *m*] 27
pimiento piri-piri *m* 51
pin alfinete *m* 111, 121; *(hair)* gancho [grampo] *m* 111
pineapple ananás [abacaxi] *m* 52, 59
pink cor-de-rosa 113
pipe cachimbo *m* 126
pipe cleaner limpa-cachimbos *m* 126
pipe tobacco tabaco [fumo] para cachimbo *m* 126
pipe tool esgaravatador de cachimbos *m* 126
place lugar *m* 25, 76
place of birth lugar de nascimento *m* 25
plane avião *m* 65
planetarium planetário *m* 81
plaster *(cast)* gesso *m* 140
plastic plástico *m* 107
plastic bag saco de plástico *m* 107
plate prato *m* 36, 61, 107
platform *(station)* cais *m* [plataforma *f*] 67, 68, 69, 70
platinum platina *f* 122
play *(theatre)* peça *f* 86
play, to *(theatre)* desempenhar 86; *(music)* tocar 88; *(game)* jogar 89, 93
playground campo de jogos *m* 32
playing card carta de jogar *f* 105
please por favor, se faz favor 11
plimsolls ténis *m/pl* 118
plug *(electric)* ficha *f* 29, 119
plum ameixa *f* 52
pneumonia pneumonia *f* 142
poached escaldado(a) 45; *(eggs)* escalfado(a) 42
pocket bolso *m* 117
pocket calculator calculadora de bolso *f* 105
pocket watch relógio de bolso *m* 121
point, to *(show)* mostrar 13
poison veneno *m* 109, 155
poisoning intoxicação *f* 142
police polícia *f* 78, 156
police station posto da polícia *m* 99, 156
polish *(nails)* verniz [esmalte] *m* 110
pop music música pop *f* 128
poplin popelina *f* 114
porcelain porcelana *f* 127

pork porco *m* 46
port porto *m* 74; *(wine)* vinho do Porto *m* 58
portable portátil 119
porter carregador *m* 18, 71; *(hotel)* bagageiro *m* 26
portion bocado *m* 37, 53; dose *f* 61
Portugal Portugal *m* 146
Portuguese português(esa) 12, 13, 104, 114, 127
possible possível 137
post *(letters)* correio *m* 28, 133
post, to pôr no correio 28
postage franquia *f* 132
postage stamp selo *m* 28, 126, 132
postcard bilhete postal *m* 105, 126, 132
poste restante posta restante *f* 133
post office estação de correios *f* 99, 132
potato batata *f* 49, 50
pottery olaria *f* 83; loiça de barro *f* 127
poultry criação *f* 48
pound *(money)* libra *f* 18, 130
powder pó *m* 110
powder compact caixinha de pó de arroz *f* 121
prawn gamba *f* [camarão grande *m*] 44
preference preferência *f* 101
pregnant grávida 141
premium *(gasoline)* super *f* 75
prescribe, to receitar 143
prescription receita (médica) *f* 108, 143
press, to *(iron)* passar a ferro ao vapor 29
press stud botão de mola [de pressão] *m* 117
pressure pressão *f* 75
pretty bonito(a) 84
price preço *m* 24
priest padre *m* 84
print *(photo)* cópia *f* 125
private particular 23, 80; privado(a) 80, 91, 155
processing *(photo)* revelação *f* 124
profession profissão *f* 25
profit lucro *m* 131
programme programa *m* 87
prohibit, to proibir 79
pronunciation pronúncia *f* 6, 10, 95
propelling pencil lapiseira *f* 105
Protestant protestante 84

provide, to arranjar [arrumar] 131
prune ameixa seca *f* 52
public holiday feriado *m* 152
pull, to puxar 155
pullover camisola de malha *f* [pulôver *m*] 116
pumpkin abóbora *f* 49
puncture furo *m* 75
purchase compra *f* 131
pure puro(a) 113
purple roxo(a) 113
push, to empurrar 155
put, to pôr 24
pyjamas pijama *m* 116

Q

quality qualidade *f* 103, 113
quantity quantidade *f* 15, 103
quarter quarto *m* 149; *(part of town)* bairro *m* 81
quarter of an hour quarto de hora *m* 153
quartz quartzo *m* 122
question pergunta *f* 12
quick rápido(a) 15
quickly depressa 137, 156
quiet tranquilo(a) 23; sossegado(a) 25

R

rabbi rabino *m* 84
rabbit coelho *m* 48
race course/track hipódromo *m* 90
racket *(sport)* raquete *f* 90
radiator radiador *m* 78
radio *(set)* rádio *m* 23, 28, 119
radish rabanete *m* 49
railroad crossing passagem de nível *f* 79
railway caminho de ferro *m* [estrada de ferro *f*] 66, 154
railway station estação (dos caminhos de ferro) [estação (ferroviária)] *f* 21, 66, 67, 70
rain chuva *f* 94
rain, to chover 94
raincoat capa da chuva *f* 117
rain forest selva *f* 85
raisin passa (de uva) *f* 52
rangefinder telémetro *m* 125
rare *(meat)* mal passado(a) 47, 61
rash erupção *f* 139
raspberry framboesa *f* 52
rate tarifa *f* 20; *(inflation)* índice *m* 131

razor gilete f [barbeador m] 110
razor blade lâmina de barbear f 111
read, to ler 40
reading lamp candeeiro [abajur] m 27
ready pronto(a) 29, 118, 123, 125, 145
rear atrás 75
receipt recibo m 103, 144
reception recepção f 23
receptionist recepcionista m/f 26
recommend, to recomendar 22, 35, 36, 80, 86, 88, 137, 145
record (disc) disco m 127, 128
record player gira-discos [toca-discos] m 119
rectangular rectangular 101
red vermelho(a) 113; (wine) tinto 59
reduction desconto m 24, 82
refill carga f 105
refund reembolso m 103
regards cumprimentos m/pl 152
region região f 92
register, to (luggage) despachar 71
registered mail registado(a) 133
registration registo m 25
registration form ficha f 25, 26
regular (petrol) normal f 75
religion religião f 83
religious service serviço religioso m, culto m 84
rent, to alugar 20, 90, 91, 155
rental aluguer m 20
repair conserto m 25
repair, to consertar 29, 118, 119, 121, 123, 125, 145
repeat, to repetir 13
report, to (a theft) dar parte de 156
reservation reserva f 19, 23; (seat) marcação de lugares f 65, 69
reservations office marcação de lugares 19, 67
reserve, to reservar 19, 23, 35, 87; (seat) marcar 69
restaurant restaurante m 19, 32, 34, 35, 67
return (ticket) ida e volta 65, 69
return, to (give back) devolver 103
reverse the charges, to fazer uma comunicação pagável no destino 135
rheumatism reumatismo m 141
rib costela f 138
ribbon fita f 105
rice arroz m 50

right direita 21, 63, 69, 77, 79; (correct) certo(a) 15
ring (on finger) anel m 122
ring, to tocar 155; telefonar 134
river rio m 85
road estrada f 76, 77, 85
road assistance assistência na estrada f 78
road map mapa das estradas m 105
road sign sinal de trânsito m 79
roasted assado(a) 47
roll (bread) papo-seco [pãozinho] m 38, 64
roller skate patim de rodas m 128
roll film rolo (de fotografias) m 124
roll-neck de gola alta 116
room quarto m 19, 23, 24, 25, 28; (space) lugar m 32
room number número do quarto m 26
room service serviço de quartos m 23
rope corda f 107
rosary rosário m 122
rosé rosé 57, 58
rosemary rosmaninho m 51
round redondo(a) 101
round (golf) volta m 90
round-neck de decote redondo 116
roundtrip (ticket) ida e volta 65, 69
route itinerário m 85
rowing boat barco a remos m 91
rubber borracha f 105, 118
ruby rubi m 122
rucksack mochila f 107
rug tapete m 127
ruin ruína f 81
ruler (for measuring) régua f 105
rum rum m 58
running water água corrente f 23

S

safe (not dangerous) sem perigo 91
safe cofre m 26
safety pin alfinete-de-ama m 111
saffron açafrão m 50
sailing boat barco à vela m 91
salad salada f 42
sale venda f 131; (bargains) saldos m/pl 100, 155
sales tax IVA m 24, 102, 154
salmon salmão m 44
salt sal m 37, 51, 64
salty salgado(a) 61
same mesmo(a) 118

sand areia f 91
sandal sandália f 118
sandwich sanduíche f [m] 63
sanitary towel/napkin penso higiénico [toalha higiénica f] 109
sapphire safira f 122
sardine sardinha f 41, 44
satin cetim m 114
Saturday sábado m 151
saucepan tacho m 107
saucer pires m 107
sausage salsicha m 46, 64
say, to dizer 163
scarf lenço de pescoço m 117
scarlet escarlate 113
scissors tesoura f 110
scooter scooter f 74
Scotland Escócia f 146
scrambled egg ovo mexido m 38, 42
sculptor escultor m 83
sculpture escultura f 83
sea mar m 23, 85, 91
sea bass robalo m 44
seafood mariscos m/pl 44
season época f 40, 150; estação do ano f 150
seasoning condimentos m/pl 51
seat lugar m 69, 70, 87
seat belt cinto de segurança m 75
second segundo(a) 149
second segundo m 153
second class segunda classe f 69
second hand ponteiro de segundos m 122
second-hand em segunda mão 104
second-hand shop loja de velharias f 99
secretary secretário(a) m/f 27
section sector m 141
see, to ver 89, 90
sell, to vender 100
send, to mandar 78, 102, 133; enviar 103, 133
sentence frase f 13
separately separadamente 62
September Setembro m 150
service serviço m 24, 62, 98, 100; (religion) culto m 84
serviette guardanapo m 36
set (hair) mise f 30
set menu refeição a preço fixo f 36
setting lotion fixador m 30, 111
seven sete 147
seventeen dezassete 147
seventh sétimo(a) 149

seventy setenta 148
sew, to (button) pregar 29
shade (colour) tom m 112
shampoo shampoo [xampu] m 30, 111
shape forma f 103
share (finance) acção f 131
sharp (pain) agudo(a) 140
shave, to fazer a barba 31
shaver máquina de barbear f [barbeador eléctrico m] 27, 119
shaving cream creme da barba m 111
she ela 161
shelf prateleira f 120
shellfish crustáceos m/pl 40
sherry Xerez m 58
ship navio m 74
shirt camisa f 117
shivers calafrios m/pl 140
shoe sapato m 118
shoelace atacador [cordão] de sapatos m 118
shoemaker's sapateiro m 99
shoe polish graxa f 118
shoe shop sapataria f 99
shop loja f 98
shopping compras f/pl 97
shopping area zona comercial f 82, 100
shopping centre centro comercial m 99
shop window vitrine f 100, 112
short curto(a) 15, 30, 115, 116
shorts calções m/pl 117
short-sighted míope 123
shoulder ombro m 138
shovel pá f 128
show espectáculo m 86, 87
show, to mostrar 13, 14, 76, 100, 101, 103, 119, 124
shower duche m 23, 32
shrimp camarão m 41, 44
shrink, to encolher 113
shut fechado(a) 15
shutter (window) janela de madeira f 29; (camera) obturador m 125
sick (ill) doente 140, 156
sickness (illness) doença f 140
side lado m 30
sideboards/burns suíças [costeletas] f/pl 31
sightseeing visita turística f 80
sightseeing tour circuito turístico m 80

sign *(notice)* letreiro *m* 155; *(road)* sinal *m* 79
sign, to assinar 26, 130
signature assinatura *f* 25
signet ring anel de sinete *m* 122
silence silêncio *m* 79
silk seda *f* 114
silver *(colour)* prateado(a) 113
silver prata *f* 121, 122
silver-plated banhado(a) a prata 122
silverware pratas *f/pl* 122
simple simples 124
since desde 15, 150
sing, to cantar 88
single *(not married)* solteiro(a) 93; *(ticket)* ida 65, 69
single room quarto individual *m* 19, 23
sister irmã *f* 93
sit down, to sentar-se 95
six seis 147
sixteen dezasseis 147
sixth sexto(a) 149
sixty sessenta 147
size tamanho *m* 124; *(clothes)* medida *f* 114, 115; *(shoes)* número *m* 118
ski esqui *m* 91
skin pele *f* 138
skin-diving pesca submarina *f* 91
skirt saia *f* 117
sky céu *m* 94
sleep, to dormir 144
sleeping bag saco-cama *m* 107
sleeping car carruagem-camas *f* [vagão-leitos *m*] 69, 70
sleeping pill sonífero *m* 143
sleeve manga *f* 116
slice *(ham)* fatia *f* 120
slide *(photo)* slide *m* 124
slip saia de baixo *f* 117
slipper chinelo *m* 118
slow lento(a) 15
slow down, to afrouxar 79
slowly devagar 13, 21, 135
small pequeno(a) 15, 20, 25, 101, 118
smoke, to fumar 95
smoked fumado(a) [defumado(a)] 45
smoker fumador *m* 70
snack refeição leve *f* 63
snack bar snack-bar *m* [lanchonete *f*] 33, 67
snail caracol *m* 41

snap fastener botão de mola [de pressão] *m* 117
sneakers ténis *m/pl* 118
snuff rapé *m* 126
soap sabonete *m* 27, 111
soccer futebol *m* 89, 90
sock peúga [meia curta] *f* 117
socket *(outlet)* tomada *f* 27
soft drink refrigerante *m* 40, 64
sold out *(theatre)* lotação esgotada 87, 155
sole sola *f* 118; *(fish)* linguado *m* 44
soloist solista *m/f* 68
someone alguém 95
something qualquer coisa 29, 108, 112, 113, 139
somewhere em qualquer lado 87
son filho *m* 93
song canção *f* 128
soon em breve 16
sore throat dor de garganta *f* 141
sorry desculpe, perdão 12; *(to be)* lamentar 87
sort *(kind)* género *m* 86, 120
soup sopa *f* 43
south sul *m* 77
South Africa África do Sul *f* 146
South America América do Sul *f* 146
souvenir lembrança *f* 127
souvenir shop loja de lembranças *f* 99
Soviet Union União Soviética *f* 146
spade pá *f* 128
Spain Espanha *f* 146
spare tyre pneu sobresselente *m* 75
sparking plug vela *f* 76
sparkling *(wine)* espumante 57, 58
spark plug vela *f* 76
speak, to falar 12, 135, 163
speaker *(loudspeaker)* alto-falante *m* 119
special especial 20, 37
special delivery por expresso 133
specialist especialista *m/f* 142
speciality especialidade *f* 40
specimen amostra *f* 142
spectacle case caixa de óculos *f* 123
spell, to soletrar 13
spend, to gastar 101
spinach espinafre *m* 49
spine coluna vertebral *f* 138
spiny lobster lagosta *f* 44
sponge esponja *f* 111
spoon colher *f* 36, 61, 107
sport desporto [esporte] *m* 89

sporting goods shop loja de artigos desportivos [esportivos] f 99
sprain, to torcer 140
spring *(season)* Primavera f 150; *(water)* nascente f 85
square quadrado(a) 101
square praça f 82; largo m 154
stadium estádio m 82
staff pessoal m 26
stain nódoa [mancha] f 29
stainless steel aço inoxidável m 107, 122
stalls *(theatre)* plateia f 87
stamp *(postage)* selo m 28, 126, 132
staple agrafo [grampo] m 105
star estrela f 94
start, to começar 80, 87; *(car)* pegar 78
starter *(appetizer)* acepipe [salgadinho] m 41
station *(railway)* estação f 21, 67, 70, 73
stationer's papelaria f 99, 104
statue estátua f 82
stay estadia f 31
stay, to ficar 17, 24, 26; *(reside)* estar hospedado(a) 93
steak bife [filé] m
steal, to roubar 156
steamed cozido(a) ao vapor 45
steamer vapor m 74
steering wheel volante m 78
stewed guisado(a) 47
stiff neck torcicolo m 141
still *(mineral water)* sem gás 59
sting picada f 139
sting, to picar 139
stitch, to coser [costurar] 29, 118
stock exchange bolsa f 82
stocking meia f 117
stomach estômago m 138
stomach ache dor de estômago f 141
stools fezes f/pl 142
stop *(bus)* paragem [parada] f 72, 73
stop! alto! 156
stop, to parar 21, 68, 72
stop thief! agarra que é ladrão! 156
store *(shop)* loja f 98
straight ahead sempre em frente 21, 77
strange estranho(a) 84
strawberry morango m 52
street rua f 25

streetcar eléctrico [bonde] m 72
street map planta da cidade f 19
string cordel [barbante] m 105
strong forte 126, 143
student estudante m/f 82, 93
study, to estudar 93
stuffed recheado(a) 41, 42, 47
sturdy resistente 101
subway *(railway)* metro(politano) m 73
suede camurça f 114, 118
sugar açúcar m 37, 63, 64
suit *(man)* fato [terno] m 117; *(woman)* fato [terno] de saia e casaco m 117
suitcase mala f 18
summer Verão m 150
sun sol m 94
sunburn queimadura do sol f 108
Sunday domingo m 151
sunglasses óculos de sol m/pl 123
sunshade *(beach)* chapéu de sol m 91
sunstroke insolação f 141
sun-tan cream creme para bronzear m 111
sun-tan oil óleo para bronzear m 111
super *(petrol)* super f 75
superb estupendo(a) 84
supermarket supermercado m 99
suppository supositório m 109
surcharge suplemento m 68, 69
surfboard prancha de surf f 91
surgery *(consulting room)* consultório m 137
surname apelido [sobrenome] m 25
suspenders *(Am.)* suspensórios m/pl 117
swallow, to engolir 143
sweatshirt camisola f [suéter m] de algodão 117
sweet doce 59, 61
sweet *(candy)* rebuçado m [bala f] 126
sweet corn milho m 49
sweetener edulcorante m 37
swell, to inchar 139
swelling inchaço m 139
swim, to nadar, tomar banho 91
swimming natação f 90
swimming pool piscina f 32, 90
swimming trunks fato [maiô] de banho m 117
swimsuit fato [maiô] de banho m 117

switch interruptor *m* 29
switchboard operator telefonista *m/f* 26
Switzerland Suíça *f* 146
swollen inchado(a) 139
swordfish espadarte *m* 44
synagogue sinagoga *f* 84
synthetic sintético(a) 113
system sistema *m* 138

T

table mesa *f* 35, 36, 107; *(list)* tábua *f* 157
tablet comprimido *m* 109
take, to levar 18, 21, 63, 73
talcum powder pó de talco *m* 111
tampon tampão higiénico *m* 109
tangerine tangerina *f* 52
tap *(water)* torneira *f* 28
tape recorder gravador *m* 119
tart tarte *f* 54
tax taxa *f* 32; IVA *m* 24, 102
taxi táxi *m* 19, 21, 31
tea chá *m* 38, 60, 64
team equipa *f* 89
tear, to rasgar 140
tearoom salão de chá *m* 34
teaspoon colher de chá *f* 107, 143
telegram telegrama *m* 133
telegraph office estação telegráfica *f* 99
telephone telefone *m* 28, 79, 134
telephone, to telefonar 134
telephone booth cabine telefónica *f* 134
telephone call comunicação *f* 135; chamada *f* 136
telephone directory lista telefónica *f* 134
telephone number número de telefone *m* 134, 135
telephoto lens teleobjectiva *f* 125
television *(set)* televisão *f* 23, 28, 119
telex telex *m* 133
telex, to mandar um telex 130
tell, to dizer 13, 76, 136; indicar 76
temperature temperatura *f* 91, 142; *(fever)* febre *f* 140
temporary provisório(a) 145
ten dez 147
tendon tendão *m* 138
tennis ténis *m* 90
tennis court campo de ténis *m* 90
tennis racket raquete de ténis *f* 90

tent tenda *f* 32, 107
tenth décimo(a) 149
tent peg estaca de tenda *f* 107
tent pole mastro de tenda *m* 107
term *(word)* termo *m* 131
terminal *(transport)* terminal *m* 72
terrace esplanada *f* 36
terrifying pavoroso(a) 84
terrycloth pano turco [tecido felpudo] *m* 114
tetanus tétano *m* 140
than (do) que 16
thank you obrigado(a) 11
that esse(a), aquele(a) 160; isso, aquilo 11, 100
the o, a 159
theatre teatro *m* 82, 86
theft roubo *m* 156
their seu, sua 161
then então 16
there aí 14, 15
thermometer termómetro *m* 109, 144
these estes(as) 160
they eles(as) 161
thief ladrão *m* 156
thigh coxa *f* 138
thin fino(a) 113
think, to *(believe)* crer 31, 62
third terceiro(a) 149
third terço *m* 149
thirsty, to be ter sede 13, 35
thirteen treze 147
thirty trinta 147
this este(a) 160; isto 12, 100
those esses(as), aqueles(as) 160
thousand mil 148
thread linha *f* 27
three três 147
throat garganta *f* 138, 141
throat lozenge pastilha para a garganta *f* 109
through através (de) 16
through train comboio [trem] directo *m* 68, 69
thumb polegar *m* 138
thumbtack pionés *m* [tacha *f*] 105
thunder trovão *m* 94
thunderstorm trovoada *f* 94
Thursday quinta-feira *f* 151
thyme tomilho *m* 51
ticket bilhete *m* 65, 69, 72, 87, 89, 156
ticket office bilheteira [bilheteria] *f* 67

tide maré f 91
tie gravata f 117
tie clip mola de gravata f 122
tie pin alfinete de gravata m 122
tight *(clothes)* apertado(a) 115
tights collant m 117
time tempo m 80; *(clock)* hora f 80, 137, 153; *(occasion)* vez f 143
timetable horário m 68
tin *(can)* lata f 120
tinfoil papel de alumínio m 107
tin opener abre-latas [abridor de latas] m 107
tint produto colorante m 111
tinted de cor 123
tire pneu m 75, 76
tired cansado(a) 14
tissue *(handkerchief)* lenço de papel m 111
to a 16
toast torrada f 38, 63
tobacco tabaco [fumo] m 126
tobacconist's tabacaria f 99, 126
today hoje 29, 151
toe dedo do pé m 138
toilet casa de banho f [banheiro m] 32, 37, 67
toilet paper papel higiénico m 111
toiletry produtos de higiene e cosméticos m/pl 110
toilet water água-de-colónia f 111
token *(phone)* ficha f 134
toll portagem f [pedágio m] 75, 79
tomato tomate m 49
tomb túmulo m 82
tomorrow amanhã 29, 151
tongue língua f 46, 138
tonic water água tónica f 59
tonight hoje à noite 86, 87, 88, 95
tonsil amígdala f 138
too demasiado(a) 15; demais 24; *(also)* também 16
tooth dente m 145
toothache dor de dentes f 145
toothbrush escova de dentes f 111, 119
toothpaste pasta de dentes f 111
top cima f 30, 145
topaz topázio m 122
torch *(flashlight)* lanterna de bolso f 107
touch, to mexer 155
tough *(meat)* duro(a) 61
tour circuito m 80
tourist office turismo m 22, 80

tourist tax taxa de turismo f 32
towards para, cerca de 16
towel toalha f 27, 111
tower torre f 82
town cidade f 19, 21, 76, 105
town hall câmara municipal f 82
tow truck pronto-socorro m 78
toy brinquedo m 128
toy shop loja de brinquedos f 99
track *(station)* linha f 68, 69; *(race course)* hipódromo m 90
tracksuit fato de treino [training] m 117
traffic trânsito m 76
traffic light semáforo m 77, 79
trailer rulote f 32
train comboio [trem] m 66, 67, 68, 69, 70
tram eléctrico [bonde] m 72
tranquillizer calmante m 143
transfer *(bank)* transferência f 131
transformer transformador m 119
translate, to traduzir 13
transport transporte m 74
travel, to viajar 93
travel agency agência de viagens f 99
travel guide guia turístico m 105
traveller's cheque cheque de viagem m 18, 62, 102, 130
travel sickness enjoo (da viagem) m 108
treatment tratamento m 143
tree árvore f 85
tremendous tremendo(a) 84
trim, to *(beard)* aparar 31
trip viagem f 72, 93, 152
trolley carrinho m 18, 71
trousers calças compridas f/pl 117
trout truta f 45
truck camião [caminhão] m 79
try, to provar 58, 114
T-shirt camiseta f 117
tube tubo m 120
Tuesday terça-feira f 151
tumbler copo m 107
tuna atum m 44
tunny atum m 44
turkey peru m 48
turn, to *(change direction)* virar 21, 77
turnip nabo m 49
turquoise azul-turquesa 113
turquoise turquesa f 122
turtleneck de gola alta 116

tweezers pinça para depilar f 111
twelve doze 147
twenty vinte 147
twice duas vezes 149
twin beds duas camas f/pl 23
two dois, duas 147
typewriter máquina de escrever f 27, 105
typewriter ribbon fita para máquina de escrever f 105
typical típico(a) 127
typing paper papel para máquina de escrever m 105
tyre pneu m 75, 76

U

ugly feio(a) 15, 84
umbrella guarda-chuva m 117; (beach) chapéu de sol m 91
uncle tio m 93
unconscious sem sentidos 139
under debaixo (de) 16
underdone (meat) mal passado(a) 47, 61
underground (railway) metro(politano) m 73
underpants cuecas f/pl 117
undershirt camisola interior [camiseta] f 117
understand, to compreender [entender] 13
undress, to despir(-se) 142
United States Estados Unidos m/pl 146
university universidade f 82
unleaded sem chumbo 75
until até 16
up para cima 16
upper superior(a) 69, 71
upset stomach indigestão f 108
upstairs em cima 16
urgent urgente 14, 145
urine urina f 142
use uso m 17, 109
use, to utilizar 134
useful útil 16
usual habitual 143

V

vacancy quarto vago m 23
vacant livre 14,155
vacation férias f/pl 151
vaccinate, to vacinar 140
vacuum flask termo m [garrafa térmica f] 107

vaginal vaginal 141
vaginal infection infecção vaginal f 141
valley vale m 85
value valor m 131
value-added tax IVA m 24, 102, 154
vanilla baunilha f 50
VAT (sales tax) IVA m 24, 102, 154
veal vitela f 46
vegetable legume m 49
vegetable store lugar de frutas e legumes m [quitanda f] 99
vegetarian vegetariano(a) 37
velvet veludo m 114
velveteen veludo de algodão m 114
venereal disease doença venérea f 142
venison veado m 48
vermouth vermute m 55,58
very muito 16
vest camisola interior [camiseta] f 117; (Am.) colete m 117
veterinarian veterinário(a) m/f 99
video cassette videocassete f 119, 124, 127
video recorder gravador vídeo m 119
view vista f 23, 25
village aldeia f 85; povoação f 76
vinegar vinagre m 37, 51
vineyard vinha f 85
visit, to visitar 84
visiting hours horas de visita f/pl 144
vitamin pills vitaminas f/pl 144
V-neck de decote em bico 116
volleyball voleibol m 90
voltage voltagem f 27, 119
vomit, to vomitar 140

W

waistcoat colete m 117
wait, to esperar 21, 108
waiter criado de mesa [garçom] m 26
waiting room sala de espera f 67
waitress criada de mesa [garçonete] f 26
wake, to acordar 27, 71
Wales País de Gales m 146
walk, to andar a pé 74; ir a pé 85
wall muro m 85
wallet carteira f 156
walnut noz f 52

want, to *(wish)* querer, desejar 14
wash, to lavar 29, 113
wash basin lavatório *m* [pia *f*] 28
washing powder detergente para a
  roupa *m* 107
watch relógio *m* 121, 122
watchband correia de relógio *f* 122
watchmaker's relojoaria *f* 99, 121
watchstrap correia de relógio *f* 122
water água *f* 23, 28, 32, 38, 75, 91
waterfall cascada *f* 85
water flask cantil *m* 107
watermelon melancia *f* 52
waterproof à prova de água 122
water-ski esqui aquático *m* 91
wave onda *f* 91
way caminho *m* 76
we nós 161
weather tempo *m* 94
weather forecast previsões do
  tempo *f/pl* 94
wedding ring aliança *f* 122
Wednesday quarta-feira *f* 151
week semana *f* 17, 20, 24, 80, 151
weekday dia de semana *m* 151
weekend fim-de-semana *m* 20, 151
well *(healthy)* bem 11, 140
well-done *(meat)* bem passado(a) 47
west oeste *m* 77
what o quê 12; o que 12, 14;
  que 151, 153; qual 20, 21; como
  12
wheel roda *f* 78
when quando 12
where onde 12
which qual 12
whisky uísque *m* 58
white branco(a) 58, 113
whiting pescada *f* 44
who quem 12
why porquê 12
wick torcida *f* 126
wickerware artigos de verga *m/pl*
  127
wide largo(a) 118
wide-angle lens objectiva grande
  angular *f* 125
wife mulher *f* 93
wig peruca *f* 111
wind vento *m* 94
windmill moinho *m* 85
window janela *f* 28, 36, 69; *(shop)*
  vitrine *f* 100, 112
windscreen/shield pára-brisas *m* 76
windsurfer prancha à vela *f* 91

wine vinho *m* 56, 58, 61
wine list lista dos vinhos *f* 58
wine merchant's comerciante de
  vinhos *m* 99
winter Inverno *m* 150
wiper limpa-vidros *m* 76
with com 16
withdraw, to *(bank)* levantar 130
without sem 16
woman mulher *f* 141; senhora *f* 115
wonderful maravilhoso(a) 96
wood madeira *f* 127; *(forest)* mata *f*
  85
wood alcohol álcool desnaturado *m*
  107
woodwork artigos de madeira *m/pl*
  127
wool lã *f* 113, 114
word palavra *f* 13, 16, 133
work, to *(function)* funcionar 28,
  119
working day dia útil *m* 151
worse pior 15
worsted lã cardada *f* 114
wound ferida *f* 139
wrap, to embrulhar 103
wristwatch relógio de pulso *m* 122
write, to escrever 13, 101
writing pad bloco de papel *m* 105
writing paper papel de carta *m* 27
wrong errado(a) 15, 135

X
X-ray *(photo)* radiografia *f* 140

Y
year ano *m* 149
yellow amarelo(a) 113
yes sim 11
yesterday ontem 151
yet ainda 16
yoghurt iogurte *m* 64
you tu, você 161
young jovem 15
your teu, tua, seu, sua, vosso(a)
  161
youth hostel pousada de juventude *f*
  22, 32

Z
zero zero *m* 147
zip(per) fecho éclair *m* 117
zoo jardim zoológico *m* 82
zoology zoologia *f* 83

Índice português

Say BERLITZ®

... and most people think of outstanding language schools. But Berlitz has also become the world's leading publisher of books for travellers – Travel Guides, Phrase Books, Dictionaries – plus Cassettes and Self-teaching courses.

Informative, accurate, up-to-date, Books from Berlitz are written with freshness and style. They also slip easily into pocket or purse – no need for bulky, old-fashioned volumes.

Join the millions who know how to travel. Whether for fun or business, put Berlitz in your pocket.

BERLITZ®

Leader in
Books and Cassettes
for Travellers

A division of Macmillan, Inc.

BERLITZ® Books for travellers

TRAVEL GUIDES

They fit your pocket in both size and price. Modern, up-to-date, Berlitz gets all the information you need into 128 lively pages with colour maps and photos throughout. What to see and do, where to shop, what to eat and drink, how to save.

ASIA, MIDDLE EAST	China (256 pages)
	Hong Kong
	India (256 pages)
	Japan (256 pages)
	Singapore
	Sri Lanka
	Thailand
	Egypt
	Jerusalem and the Holy Land
	Saudi Arabia
AUSTRAL-ASIA	Australia (256 pages)*
	New Zealand
BRITISH ISLES	Channel Islands
	London
	Ireland
	Oxford and Stratford
	Scotland
BELGIUM	Brussels

AFRICA	Kenya
	Morocco
	South Africa
	Tunisia

*in preparation

PHRASE BOOKS

World's bestselling phrase books feature all the expressions and vocabulary you'll need, and pronunciation throughout. 192 pages, 2 colours.

Arabic	Hebrew	Serbo-Croatian
Chinese	Hungarian	Spanish (Castilian)
Danish	Italian	Spanish (Lat. Am.)
Dutch	Japanese	Swahili
Finnish	Norwegian	Swedish
French	Polish	Turkish
German	Portuguese	European Phrase Book
Greek	Russian	European Menu Reader

FRANCE	Brittany		Costa Blanca
	France (256 pages)		Costa Brava
	French Riviera		Costa del Sol and Andalusia
	Loire Valley		Ibiza and Formentera
	Normandy*		Madrid
	Paris		Majorca and Minorca
GERMANY	Berlin	EASTERN EUROPE	Budapest
	Munich		Dubrovnik and Southern Dalmatia
	The Rhine Valley		Hungary (192 pages)
AUSTRIA and SWITZER-LAND	Tyrol		Istria and Croatian Coast
	Vienna		Moscow & Leningrad
	Switzerland (192 pages)		Split and Dalmatia
GREECE, CYPRUS & TURKEY	Athens	NORTH AMERICA	U.S.A. (256 pages)
	Corfu		California
	Crete		Florida
	Rhodes		Hawaii
	Greek Islands of the Aegean		New York
	Peloponnese		Toronto
	Salonica and Northern Greece		Montreal
	Cyprus	CARIBBEAN, LATIN AMERICA	Puerto Rico
	Istanbul/Aegean Coast		Virgin Islands
ITALY and MALTA	Florence		Bahamas
	Italian Adriatic		Bermuda
	Italian Riviera		French West Indies
	Italy (256 pages)*		Jamaica
	Rome		Southern Caribbean
	Sicily		Mexico City
	Venice		Rio de Janeiro
	Malta	EUROPE	Business Travel Guide – Europe (368 pages)
NETHER-LANDS and SCANDI-NAVIA	Amsterdam		Pocket guide to Europe (480 pages)
	Copenhagen		Cities of Europe (504 pages)
	Helsinki	CRUISE GUIDES	Caribbean cruise guide (368 pages)
	Oslo and Bergen		Alaska cruise guide (168 pages)
	Stockholm		Handbook to Cruising (240 pages)
PORTUGAL	Algarve		
	Lisbon		
	Madeira		
SPAIN	Barcelona and Costa Dorada		
	Canary Islands		

*in preparation

Most titles with British and U.S. destinations are available in French, German, Spanish and as many as 7 other languages.

DICTIONARIES

Bilingual with 12,500 concepts each way. Highly practical for travellers, with pronunciation shown plus menu reader, basic expressions and useful information. Over 330 pages.

Danish	Finnish	German	Norwegian	Spanish
Dutch	French	Italian	Portuguese	Swedish

Berlitz Books, a world of information in your pocket!
At all leading bookshops and airport newsstands.

Finally... a fast, fun, and affordable way to learn a foreign language...

INTRODUCING THE BERLITZ EXPRESS PROGRAMS
Self-study programs for beginners

Available in:
- Spanish
- French
- German
- Italian

Imagine, in a short time from now, being able to speak an entirely new language. French, perhaps. Or Spanish. German. Or Italian.

Berlitz, the world-renowned language instruction institution, has developed these self-study programs *expressly* for those people who want to learn to speak a foreign language *fast.* And without going through the tedious, repetitive drills and grammar rule memorization that are featured in other courses.

Instead, with the Berlitz Express programs, you learn to speak *naturally,* by listening to—and then joining in on—"real-life" dialogue on cassette tapes. This helps you *absorb* correct grammar and vocabulary almost unconsciously. And because the tapes use *sound effects* to convey meaning, you can learn your new language while you're driving, biking, walking, or doing just about anything.

Each Express Program Contains:

- TWO CASSETTES TOTALLING 100 minutes of instruction and using lively *sound effects* to identify objects, actions, and situations in your new language.

- LESSON TEXT explains new words and grammar variations as you encounter them.

- BERLITZ ROTARY VERB FINDER. How do you change the expression "I go" to "I will go" or "I went" in the language you're learning? Just spin the dial and you'll have your answer for a wide variety of common verbs.

- CONVENIENT STORAGE ALBUM protects tapes, book, and Verb Finder from damage.

Dial (no charge, USA)
24 hours, 7 days a week.

In the U.S.A.
1-800-431-9003

In Great Britain
0323-638221

Refer to Dept. No: 11604. Why not give us a ring – right now!

Treat yourself to an hour with BERLITZ®

Just listen and repeat

It's fun, not work. And you'll surprise your friends and yourself: it's so easy to pick up some basic expressions in the foreign language of your choice. These cassettes are recorded in hi-fi with four voices. Bringing native speakers into your home, they permit you to improve your accent and learn the basic phrases before you depart.

With each cassette is a helpful 32-page script, containing pronunciation tips, plus complete text of the dual-language recording.

An ideal companion for your Berlitz phrase book, pocket dictionary or travel guide. Order now!

$9.95/£5.95 (incl. VAT)
use convenient envelope attached.